Carleton Beals

MEXICAN
MAZE

With Illustrations by
DIEGO RIVERA

▼

▼ ▼

J. B. Lippincott Company
Philadelphia & London

MEXICAN
MAZE

Carleton Beals

MEXICO: AN INTERPRETATION
ROME OR DEATH: THE STORY OF FASCISM

BRIMSTONE AND CHILI
DESTROYING VICTOR
ETC.

Contents

I

THE MAZE
page 9

II

NEW IDOLS
page 31

III

GUADALUPE HIDALGO:
RELIGIOUS CAPITAL
page 55

IV

TLAXCALA: ANCIENT
REPUBLIC
page 70

V

AMECAMECA: TOWN OF
DOOM
page 94

VI

MILPA ALTA: GRAY
PEACE
page 107

VII

TEPOZTLAN: THE LIFE
AND LEGEND OF A
PUEBLO
page 121

VIII

VALERIO TRUJANO:
BLACK JOY
page 139

IX

MEXICO: OLD AND NEW
page 151

X

MULETEERS
page 164

XI

THE YAQUIS
page 176

XII

THE NEW INDIAN
page 190

XIII

DON MELCHOR: FLESH
OF THE REVOLUTION
page 205

XIV

THE UNBURIED
PATRIOT
page 214

XV

CARICATURE
page 232

5

CONTENTS

XVI
STREET THEATRES: *Las Carpas*
page 248

XVII
THE NOISEMAKERS: *Los Estridentistas*
page 259

XVIII
CHURCH AND STATE
page 284

XIX
BLACK GOLD
page 333

XX
MEXICO AND THE MACHINE AGE
page 352

6

MEXICAN MAZE

THE MAZE

1

THE SHADOW OF THE MAYAS

Moon-drenched figures, figures in snowy garb, walk the white, white road to Totuta between rows of white-trunk palms. The slight breeze slides over the hot limestone, which crops out in gray masses from the thin soil of the Yucatán peninsula. The balmy wind is sirupy, saturated with the incense of papaya, rotting bananas, bitter oranges, humid smells of writhing gourd-vines. It rustles the sail-like banana leaves and the tall crests of the cocoanuts leaning against the moon-plated sky. Through the corn milpas it passes, whispering legends of this land of the pheasant and the deer. We heed its mystery as we walk the white palm road to Totuta. A little rise, and beyond is the limitless jungle sea of silver.

From the distance comes a regular booming, like drums of doom, in a still white world. The sound gathers up into itself the deep-bosomed uncanniness, the potent strangeness of this setting, becomes ominous. We reach the town and discover that the mysterious primitive thud has been produced by a modern Delco light plant.

The oval, white-plastered, thatched houses cluster close together. Such a house is the hotel. At the entrance is a weeping throng—the eighth day of mourning for a lost child. The mourners are drinking *atole*, ground corn in milk and water, flavored with cinnamon. The atole water has been made holy and efficacious by boiling in it the finger- and toe-nails of the deceased.

Two women extract themselves from the keening group and usher me into a plain, white-walled room. In spite of the evening breeze, the hotel is sultry. Though the doors and windows are left wide open, all night I toss restlessly in my hammock. Strange world! For long unreal hours, I listen to the wails of the mourners, the incessant zzzz of a bell at the entrance to a movie house across the street. The zzzz alternates with the screech of one phonograph record played over and over—"I want to go where you go"—and that relentless balance-wheel of sound—dark like some fungus of death—the hard drumming thud of the electric light plant.

Morning breaks glaring hot. And the people, all in spotless white, melt into wall and shadow unobtrusively, quietly. Their speech, too, melts—soft Chinese-sounding Maya. But they walk erect, proud. The hair of the women is sleeked back from slanting curved foreheads, massed in divided rolls at the back of the neck, just as it appears on the ancient Maya stone carvings. Their white one-piece dresses, cut square over buxom brown breasts, arms bare, are embroidered at every hem in rich red patterns of orchids and roses, of deer and herons. This dress falls to the knees; below is the full petticoat of exquisite lace, rustling about slim bare ankles—

10

the dress of ancient times, seen also in the carvings, save that now occasionally the embroideries stitched on are German machine-made importations, cleverly imitating designs that were evolved long before the time when the Saxons crouched in skins and ate raw meat by the gloomy shores of the North Sea.

I seek shade by massive scalloped walls, painted and re-painted a dozen delicate tints, now peeling so that all colors are inextricably blended like a series of phantom rainbows, a palimpsest of fairy azures and amethysts and pinks. Over these walls are draped the flaming orange-red blossoms of leafless *flamboyón* trees. I come to the vast deserted castle, built centuries ago by the Spaniards to save the pride of the last of the great Maya chiefs, a price for rendition. Now a huge *zopilote* crouches, with black outstretched wings and raw-red head, upon the cupola above the crumbling facade.

The market. Clean white-washed walls rise above a floor, made of a native cement, laboriously ground by hand, a floor identical with those that once graced the great ancient stone temples of Uxmal and Chichén Itzá, when we Anglo-Saxons were still living in miserable huts. Potatoes for sale, each carefully washed, lie in neat piles on clean white canvas.

Such is a picture of the Maya peoples of Southeast Mexico—Yucatán, Tabasco, Quintana Roo, Campeche. And on beyond are their brethren, the Quichés and Lacandóns, a tide of busy brown people overflowing the highlands of Guatemala and the Petén and Alta Vera Paz.

Near Mérida, the capital of Yucatán.

I stand beside the tomb of martyred Felipe Carrillo Puerto, a great race chief of our times, who freed his people from the serfdom of the henequen fincas. Dead now, but I hear his voice, talking in that fine tone of his, night after night, as we walk through the soft tropic dark. He tells me of his hopes and plans for the people of his race. I see him standing

11

in the heavy shadow of the great temple of Chichén Itzá. Its white columns glisten in the moonlight, rise in white glory out of the black expanse of jungle. "We must restore the old monuments, that my people may have pride in their race and build again as they builded of old.

"We must tell them of their brethren in slavery—the dark peoples of Africa, of Asia, of India, all struggling toward the light. Some day, perhaps not far distant, we shall make a league of all the mute peoples of the earth, that they know their ways are righteous as those of the powerful."

I see him, back in Diaz' days, a mere boy, striking the lash from the hand of a brutal overseer, and being dragged off to jail.

I see him reading the Mexican constitution to the Mayas in their own tongue, that they may know their rights, and being dragged off to jail again.

I see him sweltering in tropic prisons for seven long years, waiting, hoping, spirit unbroken, striding forth more confident than ever.

The hour is struck. He is ruler of Yucatán.

"We have used force, now let us use love," are his words to the white-clad throngs that flock everywhere to hear him, to see him, to touch the hem of his garments.

"In the name of Jesus, you have been betrayed," he declared at a ceremony transforming a church into a community center. "In the name of Jesus, you have been driven under the lash. In the name of your ancient gods, I declare you free."

For such words the "generals" assassinated him.

With such words, the bureaucrats betrayed his followers.

He was the Ghandi of the Mayas. He is dead. But every year the white clad folk, bring flowers to his tomb, like a tide of new hope.

12

2

THE LITTLE PATRIA

Tehuantepec drowses among its rolling hills by the silver river where nude brown bodies flash in the sun. Women with white kerchiefs about their heads wash clothes on the golden sands. Red tasseled burros pass, loaded with water from wells dug in the river bank.

It is fiesta time. A solemn yet happy crowd gathers under a thatched ramada fully fifty feet long and thirty feet wide and decorated with colored tissue paper, hung on strings in the fashion of prehistoric religious celebration. A few dagger thrusts of sun cut sharp through the wattle walls, striking the pinks and greens and reds of silk shirts and embroidered blouses, yellow on red; upon heavy necklaces of clinking coins—fire on gold—which hang from dusky necks, over brown skin more velvety smooth than the white woman knows. Huge, fan-shaped lace headdresses quiver above black eyes. Every movement, every hint of mirth, is translated into quiver of lace. And from beneath the long ruffles of pure expensive laciness, fully a foot wide, peek bare feet, faultlessly clean, nails carefully manicured.

At the head of the hall sit the Principales, headmen from seven of the *barrios* or wards of the town, all in starched white, their shirt-tails hanging out Chinese fashion. The stranger is greeted with grave words of formal courtesy from unsmiling faces. He must drink a copita of *mescal*, take lukewarm chocolate, thick and cinnamon-flavored, drink the curled corn-meal atole, and partake of native pastry. If he wishes, he may then with good grace contribute a modest fee toward the expense of the fiesta. After this ceremony he becomes part of the assemblage, free to dance with whom he pleases—provided the girl is willing and has no *novio*, scowling in the offing, hand on his knife.

It is early yet. The older folk have their chance, tracing out the steps of the venerable *zandunga*, the historic dance of Tehuantepec—a slow weaving motion to slow moaning unmelodious music.

As the day advances, jazz pushes the zandunga aside. The young folk will one-step and fox-trot and waltz. After their own fashion—for some of these dances will not be exactly as we know them; it is difficult to glide on dirt floors with bare feet; the one-step is a hopping whirl—rapid, exhilarating, energetic, sensuous.

A visiting woman from an Oaxacan hill-village is eyeing you speculatively. Perhaps she will offer you her virgin daughter to be taken up to the double baths—for fifty pesos; or mayhap for nothing, if she is pleased with you. Not prostitution, but venerable custom. In her branch of the Zapoteca, a virgin is not marriageable. Until a girl has slept with a man she cannot win a husband. And so the parents look after the preliminary nuptials with zealous care, and are not averse to turning the transaction to financial advantage, provided they can find an *extranjero* (Mexican or otherwise), who values virginity higher than their own native men-folk.

The regular Tehuantepec courtship has its formalities. A youth, wishing to marry a girl, flirts with her until he sees that she is amenable to his advances. Thereupon, he will choose the best of his loved possessions—the best cow, or if he has no cow the best sheep, or the best pig, or the best turkey, or the best chicken, and leave it at the door of his prospective father-in-law. If the offering is accepted, he is then an established suitor. He may follow the first offering with a load of wood. Negotiations are begun. The nearest relative of the youth calls upon the father of the girl; and, after various formalities, the matter is finally arranged. But among the poorer people, the woman often takes the initiative in picking a mate; her methods are always much more direct.

14

Yet not two villages of Zapotecs and Mixtecs, the races to whom the Tehuanos belong, are quite alike in their ways. Some are more "civilized"; others, closer to their original customs. Between many of them exists extreme rivalry. In some villages the women are considered very immoral, in others very chaste. But all of them, to the outsider, seem grave and formal on set occasions; delightfully jolly and honest in more casual relationships. These people extend from Chiapas up through Oaxaca and Vera Cruz, and strive to maintain their own language and customs. They are loyal to their *patria chica*—their little fatherland.

An old lady in the market winked at me, asking for a cigarette. "The young lady to whom you are talking (a quite beautiful Tehuana) is your sweetheart, is she not?"

"I would be enchanted if that were the case," I replied, "but I fear the young lady would not have me."

"Oh, yes, I would," retorted the Tehuana, "but for one difficulty: you would want to take me away from Tehuantepec, and a true Tehuana never leaves her *tierra*."

3

THE CROSS

A slanting tile-roof village nestles into the Oaxaca foothills. In the little shrine tucked against the valley wall, the people have long worshipped a Saint John the Baptist, carved from the stone of an ancient idol. In the same interior are other saints, clasping thin holy hands on incense blackened canvases in dim niches, but the flowers and fruit are laid at the feet of humble Saint John. The priest long wished to replace this stone image, which smacks of idolatry. One day he hired a local painter to make a canvas of a gaunt, dark-skinned saint, who would appeal to his flock. An elaborate ceremony replaced the old saint with the new. But the people no longer brought their humble offerings to Saint John.

Six months later, during the De la Huerta revolt, the neighboring Serranos rose in the rear of the rebels, on the side of the Government. They galloped into the village in wild circles, carbines in hand. Spurring their horses into the church, they shot the new canvas to pieces.

Came the war between Church and State. The priest abandoned the little church. The villagers kept it clean and fresh with flowers. The stone Saint John reappeared, doubly decked with garlands.

"What do you do for confession, now that there is no priest?" I asked an aged worshipper. "Don't you miss the little father?"

"We miss him, yes; because he is a good man. But for confession—now we tell our sins to an aged oak. When it has heard enough sins, it will wither up and die."

One twilight in the Durango sierras, when I was pushing on anxiously to a village in order not to have to sleep in the open, I came upon a place where the rock walls of the ravine made a natural chapel. In a niche of rock stood a black cross bearing a white Christ, bent head crowned with a gilt chaplet of thorns, skin stained with long, bloody streaks. Before it knelt a lone Indian, arms outstretched, body inclined, face suffused with appeal and hope.

I finally broke his trance. "Where, pray tell, is the village? . . . Do you belong to the village?"

He crossed his bony hands respectfully over his white blouse. "Sí, señor."

"Why, then, are you out here so late where the wild beasts may harm you? Is there no Christ in your village? Why don't you pray to him?"

"Ah, señor, the Christ in the village is always busy. He has so much to do. Everybody asks him to do things. And who am I? Nobody, nobody." A lugubrious shake of the head. "Do you think the Christ in the village would remember what I ask? But this Christ is lonely. Few people pay any attention to him. He is humble like myself. He has more time to listen to me, to do what I ask."

4

GENERALS

One of the great chiefs of the land, a general in gold braid, sits in the Don Quixote ball-room of the Regis Hotel in Mexico City. Two mestizan prostitutes, in frowsy evening dresses, fondle his fat brown jowls and sip champagne. Suddenly, with bleary eyes, he rises from the table, draws his revolver, and shouts, "Somebody's laughing at me. If anybody cracks a smile, I'll shoot him dead." The jazz slithers to a blank. Stillness clamps down upon the gay dance hall. Not a

17

glass clinks. The white-bosomed pelican waiters sink into the corners.

The Great Chief turns and blazes away at one of the panels of expensive Don Quixote tiles that line the establishment. They tumble down, crashing in a cloud of plaster.

A heavy-set, big paunched man in a Veracruz cinema hammers the floor with his gold-headed cane, and shouts, "Music, give us music."

A runty policeman slides down the aisle and requests the *caballero* to cease disturbing public order, then returns to his post.

The heavy-set man stops his noise, but even in the dark, his creased fat neck glows angrily. Presently he rises, strides to the rear of the theater.

"Pam, pam." The runty policeman falls in a pool of blood. The heavy-set man is a GENERAL. No one shall reprimand *him*.

Meet General "Aspirin" and his aide.

"I have a headache, my general."

"Here is some aspirin," says the general, and blows his aide's brains out.

It is a good joke. Everyone laughs heartily.

General X enters Uruápam and falls in love with the daughter of a French drygoods man. She repulses him. He arrests her brother. The virtue of the girl is the price of liberation. In this way he seduces not only her, but her younger sister. Then he shoots the brother anyway. The father protests to higher authorities. The general burns his store.

The tables turn. The general becomes a rebel. He is captured and taken toward the cemetery to be shot. On the way, debonairly he tosses his silver-braided sombrero to a passing girl.

18

Romance knots her heart. She rallies other girls of the town; they rush into the cemetery and interpose themselves before the firing squad. She is the daughter of the leading personage of the community. The federals do not fire. The general is saved. He marries her—his fourth wife.

General Y leads his triumphant troops into Tampico. As his first "gesture," he organizes an orgiastic dance for his soldiers and the town prostitutes in the cathedral—"to show his contempt for the Church."

General Z and the wealthy *hacendado* Irigoyen sit over a banquet in the manor house. The table is littered with expensive china and wine-glasses.

The hacendado toasts the general with champagne. "Benítez, the agrarian leader, is stirring up the peasants to ask the Agrarian Commission for my lands."

"Leave it to me," boasts General Z.

Ten thousand pesos in bills change hands.

The next day Benítez is loaded into a cattle car of a passing train and threatened with death if he ever shows up again in the district controlled by General Z.

Los Altos in Jalisco is declared a combat zone. All the inhabitants are ordered to migrate into concentration centers under penalty of being considered rebels.

"Let me leave ten men on my hacienda to harvest the crop," pleads the owner of the Hacienda Estrella to General F, an officer who has risen with the ideals of the revolution but now owns an entire block of the most fashionable residence in Guadalajara.

"If a man is there after May first, he'll be shot," announces General F. "Unless, of course ——"

"What would be the consideration?" demands the owner.

"You might contribute fifteen thousand pesos to the Social

19

Defense Fund," announces General F, "in cash, delivered to me personally."

"I have no ready cash."

"Too bad," declares General F. As the owner leaves the office, he dictates:

Colonel M. Sixth Regiment—
Send captain and twenty-five men to harvest crop Hacienda Estrella, same to be delivered as promptly as possible ready for shipment at Station Ocotlan.

General F.

A man in an embroidered leather jacket, tall gray-braided sombrero, and skin-tight trousers, and an officer sit over *tequila* in the private "Pullman" of a Guadalajara cantina.

Says the officer with a leer, "Next Tuesday, two thousand rounds of cartridges, five machine guns, and two hundred rifles will arrive in Actopan. The federal garrison will then be reduced to fifteen men."

"In that case, the 'Hail, Christ the King' rebels will very likely attack the town," chuckles the other. "They can well use such supplies."

Twenty-five thousand in bills change hands.

The officer visits the nearest jewelry store, buys his newest

20

sweetheart a two-thousand peso ring, and telegraphs two hundred pesos to his wife and five children in Mexico City.

Down from Guadalajara to Colima, all day under the hot sun, the train-guard rides in an open steel car, sides slit for rifle holes. In the morning, the soldiers build fires on the steel bottom, toast tortillas, and boil coffee, into which they drop a lump of sweet *pinoche*. All day they ride, stretching red sarapes for shade, playing with Spanish cards for cartridges, thrumming guitars, telling yarns.

With them, as mascot, goes an eleven-year-old boy, cartridge belt criss-crossed over his chest, rifle in his hand, straw sombrero tilted cockily over one ear, his black, touseled hair hanging into his perky eyes.

The train swings through a rocky pass. "Man the rifle holes!" cries the captain.

A withering fire whips down from behind a cropping of rock. The mascot gives a cry. His sombrero flies into the air. His teeth smash smash against the sprawling feet of a machine gun.

The train rolls on without being stopped.

"Where do the sonnabiches get their ammunition?" com-

21

plains the captain, handing his smoking rifle to a soldier to be cleaned and reoiled.

Two other soldiers dump the boy's body over the edge into the abyss. "We aren't supposed to have his kind along. It would look bad," declares the captain.

A pock-faced soldier puckers up his thick-lipped mouth, rips a flower from the cord of his visor and tosses it after the body.

5

LAND AND LIBERTY

We sit on a platform draped with red bunting in the church-yard at Cuatla: the governor of the state, high dignitaries faultlessly clad, peasant leaders in high-crown sombreros. Below us is the white marble tomb of Emiliano Zapata, the black moustached whirlwind of the agrarian revolution in south Mexico. Incongruously, his tomb is surmounted by a sentimental angel, holding an unrolled scroll. About her pedestal are great masses of flowers, and huge purple funeral wreaths, sent from all the villages around. The church-yard is choked with peasants, wearing *guaraches* on their feet, clad in white "pyjamas" and enormous broad-brimmed som-

22

breros. Here and there gleams a scarlet sarape flung gracefully over stalwart shoulders. The throng crowds under the
languid palm trees, in every nook and corner; brown-faced
men are perched like white birds along the high surrounding
walls.

Later, from the governor's palace, we look down upon ten
thousand mounted agrarians, riding by in formation on their
wiry cayuses. Huge silver-embroidered felt and straw sombreros bob to the slow gait of the horses. The riders carry
their guns, butt against the knee, or strapped to their pom-
mels. Many of them wear white, pleated blouses, shirt-tails
out; others are in gray flannel.

The revolution is over now. But once these same men
thundered out of the rocky fastness of Morelos, dashing with
quirt and spur and cry of liberty down upon this same town,
upon Cuernavaca, upon Yautepec. "Land and Water!" "Land
and Schools!" "Land and Liberty!" were their cries.

Zapata in his day ruled an empire, coined money, gave
away lands with the omnipotence of an oriental sultan. Today
he is a legend. When the sky grows dark and it thunders,
people run to the doors of their thatched cabins to see Zapata
galloping across the heavens. His figure is outlined in the
clouds; his voice echoes in the winds.

6

HEALERS

Mexico is a land of witchcraft. It is a land of miracles. People
are bewitched and unbewitched. Love is gained and held by
potions and charms. Evil spirits and dark fate still rule the
destinies of millions.

"Yesterday María Ivanova was arrested in Mexico City by
the police for selling María Morales Olvera two love reliques
for sixty pesos that she might have success with her lover.
To other people María Ivanova for sixty pesos and an egg

23

offered to rid them of bewitchment and restore health and peace of mind."

"María Inés Fernández, witch-doctor, was arrested, accused of having caused J. Felix Vargas to go insane because of love potions which she had placed in the hands of his sweetheart, Rutilia Ramirez.

"Felix Vargas was interned in the insane asylum of Castañeda, according to his father, because the love potions drove him crazy. Felix Vargas had extended relations with Rutilia Ramírez till she had a child. Then he abandoned her. She went to the witch doctor and secured a potion to recover his love. Shortly, he began to lose his mind and was finally interned in Castañeda. María Inés Fernández has been arrested and thrust into Belém prison, charged with witchcraft. Rutilia Ramírez has been arrested as the intellectual author of the supposed crime."

Scarcely a month goes past without arrests of this sort in Mexico City. Out in the rural regions, where there are no legal physicians, the witchdoctors ply a trade even more lucrative and undisturbed.

In Mexico City, witchdoctors, herb-doctors, sooth-sayers, and medicine men abound in the poor quarters of the town. Fringed about the center of the Mexican capital (which is rather more Spanish, French, and American than Mexican) lie tenement districts crowded with a dislocated Indian population, living in great squalor. These poor folk have never truly been incorporated to civilized ways or thought. They ride on street-cars and autos, work in factories, but the twentieth century mind has never struck them. They live in dark, damp *viviendas*, with little or no furniture, usually sleeping on mats spread on the brick floors. They know nothing of hygiene and for the most part are unable to read or write. Such people still cling to their old superstitions, and are afraid to go to legitimate doctors. Among them the *curanderos*, or witch-doctors, occupy a favored position.

These pseudo-doctors are descendents of the pre-conquest

medicine-men who cured people and performed many mysterious services mixing scientific and reliable herb lore with a play on gross superstition. Many of the herbs they used, such as quinine, sarsaparilla, malva, and so forth, have passed into the modern use. But with the rise of true medicine, the *curanderos*, stripped of what little honest lore they possessed, practiced their profession on a base superstition, resorting to all sorts of uncanny black magic. Magic still cures the larger part of the rural population of Mexico. For though there are far too many doctors in the capital, the country districts often lack any at all.

Police records, even in the capital, reveal many arrests of such *curanderos* on charges of bewitchment, giving herbs which drive to insanity, the improper use of love potions, and other such ministrations to superstition. The witchdoctor, for a proper fee, not only cures, drives out evil spirits, but perpetrates injuries on enemies, causes people through his black art to wither and die. The *curandero* recovers the love of erring husbands, changes bad luck, overcomes the pending tragedy when an owl hoots over the rooftrees, and wards off death. Given a piece of clothing of the intended victim, and the *curandero* can perpetrate any injury or bewitch any person against whom a grudge is entertained. I once had a servant who always carefully counted my clothing after guests had been in the house to see that nothing was missing. Had anything been missing, I suppose I would immediately have had to seek a witch doctor to exorcise possible evil.

Bits of clothing, toe-nails, human hair, and other such tokens, are also sufficient for diagnosis of a malady, even though the sick person be leagues away; and these things when brewed together with herbs and the proper mumbo jumbo can effect complete cures of the most dangerous illnesses.

Swollen places, inflamed spots, ulcers, places where pain exists are often cured by sucking. The *curandera* applies her mouth to the inflammation or sore and sucks. When she finishes, she extracts from her mouth a toad or some other small animal, which she announces was living in the infection and was indeed the cause of it. Thanks to nature, the victim often recovers and the *curandera's* fame spreads.

Eggs are often sucked out of the body in the same way. Throughout Mexico, the egg has mysterious properties. An egg broken into a glass of water will often take on strange shapes, a likeness of some animal or reptile. The disease is diagnosed according to the animal formed by the white of the egg, each animal representing a specific ailment. In the case of fever, the patient may be disrobed and his body rubbed all over carefully with an egg. He is then given hot herb drinks and sent to bathe in a *temascal*, or native adobe steam bath house. The temascal is a conical shaped structure with a low door and a fire box. Water thrown against the heated walls fills the room with steam, and the patient sweats.

The most common cause of disease is "being hit by the air." Witch doctors sell little round stones to be hung around the neck to ward off being "hit by the air." These wind-stones to protect against sickness are sold in all the public markets throughout Mexico, but have more potent effect when properly charmed and sold by *curanderos*. Such wind-stones have been found in the oldest archaeological ruins.

Petrified deer-eyes also ward off evil spirits.

On one occasion when I was riding horseback in the Oaxaca Sierras, my horse tumbled from a steep embankment. The Mazotecan Indians accompanying us refused to go any further until a witch-doctor had been brought from a ranchería six miles back. Copal, an incense in use before the coming of the Spaniards, was burnt to dispel further bad luck. All accidents are ascribed to evil spirits, and when a man knows that spirits are trying "to get him," he is a plain fool if he refuses to take proper precautions. . . . After the copal was burned, an egg was buried on the spot of the tumble, all with due ceremony, and much palaver in Mazotecan. The Indians then ate of a fungus-like plant, which set them in a

26

sort of religious ecstasy. Like practices are found all over the Mexican Republic.

Naturally the Catholic Church does not recognize or countenance these practices, but the *curanderos* often couple their own magic with that of the supposed magic of the Church; on other occasions native magic is tied up with the religions which existed before the conquest. In Taxco, Guerrero, I found a *curandera* who had in her possession an image of the Virgin, which was reputed to work miraculous cures; and she received fabulous donations, even from the rich people of the place. All the silver, of course, went into her own pocket.

In Tepoztlán, I witnessed a religious procession with ancient teponastle drums, made at the suggestion of a *curandera*, Doña Rosa from the nearby pueblo of Santiago. This procession, in which Doña Rosa participated, went up to the prehistoric pyramid to beg the old god Tepoztecatl for rain. The rain came—proof enough for any sane man.

In the north appears a prophet and healer. His name is Niño Fidencio, the Child Fidencio. A new laying on of hands —and the maimed, the halt and the blind go their ways cured, or so report spreads. His fame grows, and tens of thousands, with chronic diseases, flood into the little village where he lives in a thatched hut. For miles over the mountains, they come: some on crutches, some dragging their paralyzed limbs. The poor, the tatterdemalion, the lepers, and the have-nots, struggle across the blazing desert; the rich, the elegantly gowned, drive to the place in their limousines.

It is a fantastic scene. Water is inadequate; there is no sanitation; a great stench strikes to heaven for miles around. The people fling up shacks and lean-tos; they sleep on mother earth, under their blankets, in long compact rows, like mummeys in a morgue, body warming body, disease touching disease. Before them glow their cooking fires; slow curls of smoke rise night and day into the dry transparent sky. Many of these people will have to wait months before reaching the healer.

Niño Fidencio puts a dumb man into a swing and sets him in motion. When the patient is swinging high, Fidencio hits him a terrific blow in the small of the back. The man lets out an animal-like cry, "Ugh!"

The mob yells, "He speaks! He speaks!" News of another cure runs like a wind through the impromptu camp, shaking the miserable hopefuls like tasseled corn. The camp sways and ebbs. "Another cure!" . . . "When will my turn come? Glory be to God, soon I shall walk again!"

A female mountain of flesh pulls out her cancered breast before all beholders, and throws her head back to heaven in a wail of grieving happiness.

The frantic press becomes too great to be controlled. The State sends its soldiers, hundreds of them, to keep the throng in order. But the passion to be cured becomes so frenzied, that the mob sweeps over the soldiers. Consumptives, paralyzed, paralitics, lame, blind, lepers, syphilitics, the ulcered, the itchy, the club-footed, the hunch-backed, swirl in mad struggle for place in the queue. Suddenly a cry is raised; "Niño Fidencio!"

The festering mob falls back before his even tread. He is a lean Indian, dressed like an Indian, wearing simple *guaraches*. His black hair falls over his ascetic shoulders in long locks. His eyes blaze with fanatic cunning fire.

The throng watches him in breathless silence. Hope in a hundred breasts. Perhaps he will choose someone at random from the cringing crowd.

But he goes straight to the captain of the guard. In a loud voice he tells him, "A thread is more powerful than all your bayonets. Put up your guns."

And unrolling a thread, he lays it along the ground; he makes a long wide lane. "Let no man step over this thread, for no man who does so, will be cured."

28

And a tiny thread proves more potent than the guns of the state.

7

OIL

Come the seekers for oil, sniffing along the "golden lane" of Tamaulipas for hidden black treasure. On that lane lived an humble family, Señor Ignacio Ramírez and his sweet young bride. Dark of skin, she wears beautiful red and gold embroidered *huipiles* and flowers in her black hair. Their cornfield whispers song at the caress of the breeze from the Gulf; their orchards shed blossoms in the early spring. They are happy, little knowing that under their feet flows the black tide of power, which turns turbines and flings battleships across far seas.

The oil seekers try to buy Ramárez' property. He is happy as he is; he refuses. So they try to lease merely the oil rights. Ramírez ponders. Money after all is good. Why should he give over his wealth cheaply. He has heard tales: Cerro Azul, making hundreds of millions; wells that gush tens of thousands of barrels of the precious black liquid in a day.

He demands a million dollars for his property.

Two nights later he is murdered. The culprits are arrested by the police, but the military commandant snatches them away to the island prison fortress of San Juan de Ulua. Later they are poisoned.

Sadly Concha walks through the whispering cornfield; its songs are different now.

Some days later, she notices a foreigner in a wide Texan hat, riding past her gate. He is young and handsome, probably an American. Every day he rides by. One morning he asks her for a drink of water. They talk.

He claims to be a rancher, further up in the Sierra. He is

29

very nice and courteous; and he seems to like her. She looks after him a bit wistfully.

She does not know that he is a lawyer for one of the most powerful foreign petroleum companies, that he is a southern gentleman with violent color prejudices.

Now he stops at her gate every day. He makes love to her and ere long she responds to his simulated passion. There are long walks under the swollen tropic moon; junkets by the rippling shore. At first she was afraid, thinking he wished merely to possess her. But he offers marriage. The day is set. Her former husband is a remote dream now.

One day, he suggests a marriage contract should be signed. Such a course is always customary among his people. This seems foolish to Concha, but she acquiesces. He is a sun god to her; anything he says must be wholly right.

They journey to an elegant office in Tampico. There are numbers of men, some Mexican, some foreigners. They have hard wolfish faces, or soft cunning feline faces—but simple Concha does not perceive this. There is champagne and congratulations; and then papers. Long typewritten sheets. She is to sign here.

She takes up the pen, hesitates a moment.

Breathless suspense. Is she going to refuse to sign? No, she is merely looking for the proper line. She affixes her signature.

She has signed away all of her oil rights. She is dispossessed. The blond foreigner rides by no longer.

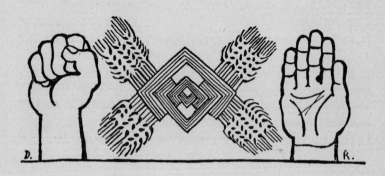

II   NEW IDOLS

1

I<small>N</small> <small>THE</small> very center of the
vast bowl of the Valley of Anáhuac, on Tepeyac Hill, a
few miles north of Mexico City, rises the church of the
Virgin of Guadalupe, the patroness of Mexico's independence.
Steep walled-in lanes and zig-zagged stone steps lead up to the
pink horse-shoe facade and high-flung nave, constructed on
the very site of the ancient holy *cu* of the native Goddess of
Maize, Tonantzín, long ago beloved by the Totonoqui Indians. According to local legends Tonantzín was also a virgin.
And in the vivid, semi-picaresque novel, *The Bandits of Cold
River*, by Manuel Payno, occurs a lively description of how
the indigenes, identifying Tonantzín with Guadalupe, still
perform the ancient rites. Like her brown-skin predecessor,
the more recent Christian Guadalupe "is not happy unless she
has received her due meed of innocent blood."

Similar confusions are encountered everywhere in the
Mexican land. Guadalupe is not the only holy image, Tonantzín not the only surviving idol, still demanding "due meed of
innocent blood." Villegas remarks in his *Mexican Sociology*:
"The saint of stone sculptured with such intimate care and

31

great love by the native is not a Christian saint but an idol."
Behind the most venerated altars are frequently found pre-
Cortez images; popular saints have been carved out of the
volcanic stone of older gods; here a pacifist Saint Francis,
there a meek Saint John, has been mutilated into more holy
grotesqueness better to thrill the native heart; and the Indians still bring their old-time offerings—fruit, wigged with
cornfloss, shells, beads, wind-stones, "deer-eyes," herbs, miniature animals—to the feet of their favorite saints. In that great
novel, *Periquillo Sarniento*, is related how the Indians of
Tuxtla, in the ancient fashion brought offerings of fruit,
tamales, atole, mole and other native foods to the temple and
threw pieces of fruit over the sepulchres. The priest did not
remonstrate.

Many churches still harbor aboriginal dances to the tune of
armadillo guitars and *teponastles*; the gods of the Deer, the
Harvest, the Moon are still at home in many church-yards.
This ceremonial hodge-podge, this Pagan-Christian pantheon,
is a projection of the psychological and religious confusion of
the mass of the Mexican people—Christianity, paganism,
totemism, etiologism, magic, superstition, and idolatry, curiously, beautifully jumbled, rarely blended.

These contradictions in Mexican religious life are indicative
of the unruly, unsynthesized character of all Mexican life.
Dubious religious idols have their analogue in grotesque
political idols. Practices of today are often merely the thinly
disguised mechanism of the Moctezumas and their tribal
caciques, or political headsmen, whom the Spaniards absorbed
into their system of colonial control four centuries ago. The
laws of things kosher change but slowly. Thus recent political
tags, the "ground-roaring words": "Effective Suffrage,"
"Revolution," "Rights of Labor," "Land and Liberty," "class-
struggle," are second-hand names of the moment for age-
long strivings. Just as the mangled Christs remind the native
delicately of the original human sacrifices to Huitzilopochtli,
God of War, so these revolutionary slogans are, in turn, often

merely new poisoned tips of old arrows of rebellion. Or, ironically, quite often, sharper thorns on the gilt thorn of a suffering people that has know too much humility. Noisy catch words of the day are but the distorted echoes of a deeper struggle of races and cultures of which the varied political upheavals are but volcanic ash and smoke. Thus behind the "revolutionary" demagogues of the moment are the demoniacal shadows of the barbaric crop-raiders and princes who lorded it over the Aztec Empire. The past in Mexico is curiously persistent, curiously protean, albeit grotesquely masked, insistent upon its "due meed of innocent blood." Ancient instincts, motives, and habits are interwoven with modern theories of revolution and progress into a most tangled skein.

Few Mexican leaders have any vital conception of the ethnological and sociological pattern of their country and its ultimate implications. But three recent leaders have shown real evidence of such knowledge: Felipe Carrillo, race-chief of Yucatán (assassinated); Manuel Gamio, the sociological anthropologist (ousted from the Calles government); and Diego Rivera, the neo-Aztec painter (despised by the political hangers-on). To understand the real Mexico, the basic Mexico, from which the political pyramid rises, to understand all this flux of races and creeds and tendencies, one must burrow down into the root motives of men and societies, to the first axioms of human association and from these work up to a political, social, economic, and psychological superstructure, startlingly alien to Western Europe—and far more complex.

Underneath the involved functioning of the Mexican Mind is the stolid, fantastic, brooding temperament of the native races, a disturbing interplay of hidden purposes, too subtle for ready analysis, complicated by centuries of oppression. This lends a gargoyle externality to Mexican thinking and art. This grotesqueness of conduct and aesthetics results from the unruly surge of forces beneath the crust of political disorder—a baffling labyrinth, a jungle of cross-purposes, a wilderness of wheels within wheels: Indianism, land-communism, oriental fatalism, genesiac grotesqueness, all shaken up with Spanish-Roman ecclesiasticism, feudalism and pomp; the entire melange now being broken apart and rehammered by American industrialism. There are no permanent alignments. The challenge of the hour is, in a general way, the handicraft aesthetics, communal semi-oriental psychology, and Latin flamboyance versus the mechanistic power and the aggressive industrialism of Europe and the United States. An indigestible cake iced over with Moorish-Spanish, French, and United States' cultures. A series of blistered layers of so-called civilizations holding down the seething native life, which ever and anon like a boiling lava flow bursts to the surface and flows over government and institutions, leaving long black scars on the surface of the national habits.

2

The Indian regimes, rooted in a long, obscure, but dignified past were, at best, tribal-communistic, with a gaudy overgrowth of feudalism and regality. They had already blossomed into factitious civilizations. Many of the people had become city-dwellers. Though the Mexican nation had not yet been born, the native cultures had produced a calendar as accurate as the one we use today in these United States of the eight-hour work-day and buy-a-book-a-week. The Mayas, the Texcocans, the Nahuas, the Tarascans, the Mixtecs, and Zapotecs had created memorable monuments, great temples, auditoriums, pyramids, fortresses; they had installed ramified irrigation systems, had established equitable produce distribution and possessed many far-sighted laws. The remnants of the Texcocan literature reveal true loftiness; it had even reached the Omar Khayyam satiety point; Toltecan and Mayan and Tarascan art was as sophisticated and startling as that of the Etruscans and pre-Grecian epoch. The admirably impressive stone gods, Huitzilopochtli, Tonatiu, the Tlalocs, Tescatlipoca, Quetzalcóatl, conformed to an aesthetic which, if bizarre, was highly developed and subtle; and these gods represented the power, stability and grotesque glory of the native mind and institutions, plus an abjectness not remote from Christian humility. Their great religious ceremonies and sacrifices were symbolic, poetic, intricately organized and represented philosophical and theological conceptions aeons ahead of the brute lynch-mind of our own South.

Colonial rule, Spanish rule, imposed a super-feudalism: grandiloquent Spanish-Roman church, grandiloquent language, grandiloquent government, Western art-realism, the economic instrumentalities of subjugation—Colonial exploitation, trade-acts a la Colbert, rich land and labor grants (encomiendas, repartimientos). The Conquest grafted itself upon the existing stock. Here it disrupted, there it destroyed, elsewhere it promoted, if in somewhat different guise, existing native cultural strains, especially superstate rule. Both the Aztec and Catholic faiths knew incense, holy waters and holy oil, penitence and fasting, flagellation, confession, charms, amulets and scapulars. In general, Colonial control provided cement to hold together the existing warring nations. Under the viceregal administration, force, language, Church, improved communications, more widely organized industry, tied the country into something of a unit. Obversely it gave many elements, peculiarly the worst elements of the native society, those elements relating to governing power, greater kinetics and flexibility when carried over into the Spanish overlordship—Huitzilopochtli girded in mail and stuck on a horse. The Spaniards, the hated Gachupines, achieved a temporary synthesis that the empire of Moctezuma was, perhaps, on the eve of achieving.

Independence undid this effort; it was the heel that powdered the molded clay. From this angle Independence was a retrogression. Spanish rule was replaced by the more meddling, directly selfish Creole rule, the rule of the native-born

Spaniards. The lower classes and races were thereby deprived of all the beneficent protective laws of the Indies, and their *ejidos* (village commons) that bulwark against exploitation, relegitimated by Philip II, were again menaced. Independence deprived the Indians of that occasional Crown intervention which, like a swift-falling sword of justice, cut the worst knots of servitude, restoring the conquered for short periods, to a measure of dignity. Independence destroyed the protective sympathy of the Church. Bishop Bartolomé de las Casas had even declared the Indians had souls (though most of his confreres graded the indigenous ghost stuff from zero to fifty percent); and he crossed the ocean fourteen times to plead for a square deal for the Indians. The Independence-rule of a retrogressive Creolized Church, of an anarchistic Army, of feudal Landed Proprietors resulted in a most hectic interplay of rapacious cross-purposes. The new Punch and Judy show was called Republicanism—Huitzilopochtli wearing the toga but no less eager for his "due meed of innocent blood." Naturally in this endemic confusion, the Army gradually gained the upper hand. Time and again it hammered the helpless country on the anvil of its villainy, creating—scrap-iron. The Mexican nation had not yet been born.

The jealous quarrels led the various aristocratic factions to resort to popular shibboleths to gain their ends, and to keep the Mestizos and Indians under heel. Yet inevitably these "Liberty" catch-words gathered content. Creole rule was ultimately ripped apart by all the restlessness growing out of economic exploitation and out of unsuccessful racial and cultural fusion. The *prietos*, the dark-skinned, the sandal-shoed came croaking up, like so many Nicklemen, from the slimy depths of three centuries of spoliation, dripping with the weeds and scum of a servitude as degrading as that of the Roman slaves, which had now been made completely intolerable by Creole excesses.

Benito Juárez, Mexico's Lincoln, in the 'fifties, for a short time broke the organized power of Church, Landowner,

Army, and super-class State, putting into operation the reformation constitution of 1857 and the Reform Laws of 1859, only to see his work largely destroyed by the Spanish-French-English intervention (leagued with the disinherited Creoles and the Church) which imposed Emperor Maximilian.

In the 'seventies the toga was seized by Porfirio Díaz, the one-man dictator, the military hero—the new Huitzilopochtli demanding his "due meed of innocent blood." Santa Anna, the picturesque, unprincipled "hero" of the early years of independence represented the Army run amuck. Díaz represented the Army disciplined into the supreme governing power. Church and Landed Proprietor were now definitely in the background, though still powerful factors as is shown by the rapid enclosures of the village *ejidos* and the absorption of the peasant by the large haciendas. But industrialization was clanking over the land.

This sort of rule facilitated industrialization—the overwash of American post-Civil War industrial development into Mexico; to quote a native writer, "the devil-fish of foreign capital clutching out for control of the vast national resources"—a new, more powerful, more sinister Idol than any preceding. Railroads were built, mines opened, oil-derricks flung into the jungles, peons herded from the haciendas into the factory-gates at the point of the rifle. Yet capital in Mexico, being foreign, split among various nationalities and a dozen relatively non-related industries, has never been able to become the direct governing power—at best a meddling *Deus ex machina*. The result has been more disorder, failure of the Mexican nation to get born.

Thus Mexico, toward the end of the Díaz epoch—featured by the decline of the older governing aristocracy and institutions, by the putrification of the Army—was left without any well-knit social group capable of directing the State, and this at the very moment when the country's social and economic life was being disrupted by new alien forces. Nor was

there any outstanding political personality to whom the people could turn—no Lenin, no Mussolini, to bridge the gap. Díaz was the only demigod and he belonged to the Götterdämmerung—an old man over eighty, surrounded by Methuselah cabinet ministers and gray-bearded generals, all nodding wearily over the political chess-board. After them—the deluge!

The revolution of Madero happened. It happened because Díaz crumbled and because Díaz crumbled at practically the time when the whole center of economic and political gravity was shifting; when the modern Socialist movement was agitating the world-mind; when the old creeds were perishing; when the prestige of the Church was perceptibly on the wane; when the feudal hacienda, through an anachronism, had buttressed itself up by wholesale land-seizures; at a time when industrialism was injecting the virtue of a new, non-regulated, rampant, and predatory activity into the veins of the nation. The break-down of the old governing aristocracies, the rapid enclosures, the intrusion of disturbing non-Latin, non-Indian industrialism—all made possible the violent Madero upheaval, with its pink-lemonade slogan of "Effective Suffrage No Reelection," with its unimpressive Idol labeled "Political Democracy"—made possible all its noble aspirations and terrible consequences. These conflicting forces needed to find an equilibrium. The explosion came before equilibrium was achieved; the explosion was part of the effort to achieve equilibrium.

3

Madero had a vision of democracy, a politically free people. An incompetent dreamer, he ruled the State by mystic communings with spooks and the planchette and impractical worship at the clay feet of his Age of Reason Janus, "Political Democracy." Through the American Government, misrepresented by the charlatan Henry Lane Wilson, buzzed about his ears like the proverbial gadfly, Madero was singularly unappreciative of how terrifically foreign capital, on one hand, and Marxian and Bakunin doctrines on the other, were undermining the social stability of his country. Too, his ears were plugged against the racket of the race and cultural forces he had released.

Democracy! As though volcanoes know ought of democratic behavior! Yet the Madero revolution made "Political Democracy" its "Big Idol." Neither then or since has Mexico known political freedom, any more than a life-long blind man has ever fainted at sight of Ziegfield chorus legs. On every official document, right next to the red seal and the flourish, appears "Effective Suffrage; No Reelection." But there has never been an honest election in Mexico. Most elections, not fixed beforehand, consist of swiping ballot-boxes, Hallowe'en style, plus pistol shots and broken heads. The side collecting more urns and fewer mortalities declares its candidates elected. Mexico hasn't the racial homogeneity for the proper uniform genuflexions required by democracy; it has too great diversity of social classes, too many warring economic ingredients. It has no straight-jacket education, hence no Ford-part minds. Mexico lacks the first essential of a functioning political democracy à la the United States—the political party. Political parties in name, yes; but without the game, of no truly national significance; except perhaps the short-lived Labor Party, side-shows run by the main-circus militarists. The popular will, the mass race-will has ever worked through the freedom of citizens dancing around in white hoods or sticking ballots into boxes on election days. Rivers flooding into the seas, not Holland canals. And though the Madero revolution began by worshipping the red-nosed, club-footed Idol, "Political Democracy," the militarists, the politicians, the laborites, the peasants, the Indians—all have mutilated this along with a hundred other lesser foreign gods. Political democracy found no real popular echo; the social,

41

economic, educational and collective bases were non-existent. They perhaps cannot be created until the warring racial, cultural, and industrial forces of the era find some equilibrium.

4

Madero went smash. The dream of political democracy went smash. After Madero came Huerta, the bloodthirsty drunken troglodyte; Villa the half-savage bandit Socialist; Carranza the stately obstinate Caesar; Zapata, idealistic, crude, despotic; Obregón, the plump card-sharper of ambitions. After Madero came a cyclonic upsurging of ambitious personalities, primitive cruelties, Boxerism, social frenzy—and Mexico hit the nadir of indecency and disorder; an epoch replete to bursting with bloodshed, fantasy, plunder-lust, an epoch so terribly monstrous that it could have but one answer: the old, crude military tradition reasserted itself with a bang. The Army, swelled by the wild hordes of bandits, troglodytes, yahoos, pariahs, uncivilized Indians, criminals, and adventurers, reasserted its sway. After the last of the bouffet-opera series of presents and pseudo-presidents and would-be presidents, i.e., by the close of the term of the bearded, blue-spectacled Carranza, Mexico was exhausted, bled white, apathetic from so many gory trapeze artists and bestial profanations.

The military elements held the double-bit to the abused country, and if they still cried "Democracy!" with every blow of the quirt, they were merely utilizing tricks learned from a century of brutal domination. Carranza's Administration fell into the hands of the Junkers, a military plunderbund. Their spurs were long-roweled; their greed deeper than the sea; their creed blood, gold, and women. Carranza, obstinate, well-meaning, stubbornly blind to realities, was undermined by his own orgiastic military party.

Obregón appropriated the military spurs and bit. Through eight thousand miles of bloody campaigning he learned to master the brutal master. Putting a curb on its insatiable plunder-lust, he made of the reckless, pillaging, violent, unpatriotic, Hydra-headed Army an approach to a political party, liberalized it, gave it a soul to speak, though a rather Troll-like soul. Even before the flight of Carranza in 1920, Obregón had coalesced the more flexible military elements into a group with some scant respect for the revolutionary principles that had so agonizingly given them birth—established filial respects in the prodigal. He hammered his wing of the Army into organized purposefulness and unity, and when he came into power in 1920, and again during the De la Huerta trouble in 1923-24, and during the Gómez-Serrano uprising in 1927, he stamped on recalcitrant trouble-makers as on the head of a snake. The Army remained supreme, but a Pride's Purge Army, the New Army, the pseudo-revolutionary Army. The best in the old military tradition, in the tradition that had surged up through the feather-decked brigades of Moctezuma and the Tlascalans, through the feudalism of the Conquest, through the epoch of Creole domination and the dictatorship of Díaz—respect for personal leadership, if not for the nation—he reestablished. The crass militarist tribe, curse of Mexico's century of independence, was, for the first time since Díaz, given discipline.

43

Under Díaz the Army had been disciplined for oppression. Under Obregón it was disciplined for the realization of the "ideals of the revolution" until it can once more become the instrument of tyranny or be amalgamated with some other power—some civil power. Thus the twentieth century break-up in Mexico saw a childish Santa Claus "Democracy" strangled, first by the treacherous militarism of sanguinary Huerta, then by militarism run wild (Villa, Zapata); then lawless militarism officialized (Carranza); then the semi-disciplined militarism (Obregón).

But Obregón has gone! Calles, in a moment of panic, went back to the Madero credo of democracy. Fatal retrogression! Meaningless rhetoric! But the disciplined Army was still there under the guidance of Joaquín Amaro. Will it discipline itself into the traditional superstate? Or will it discipline itself into retirement as one of a number of national institutions?

5

Obviously, all during the Madero-Obregón break-up some criterion more modern, more realistic, than that of Alcibiades or Rousseau, was needed, badly needed. Most revolutions have been the chicks of definite ideologic hens. The French revolution was the philosophy of Voltaire and the Encyclopaedists,

44

pricking the shell. The Russian soviet revolution was out of
Marx and Engels. The Fascist revolution, if less obviously
possessed of ideology, owed much to Sorel, Corradini, and
Pareto. But the Mexican revolution had as dubious a philosophical heritage as Attila or the outbreaks of the Helots.
No criterion existed, only a heterogeneous job-lot of marked-
down imported plasterparis doctrines that fell to pieces under
the blows of the revolution. The theories of the native "cogi-
tators" Caso, Reyes, Vasconcelos, Atl, Acevedo, are a ludicrous patchwork quilt, concealing rather than revealing the
brutal dynamic forces at play. The Mexican revolution had
no prophet and no body of positive theory; it was obliged to
formulate its own ideology and own program as it went along,
a halting, fumbling misdirected series of experiments that
have brought the masses little but a sense of freedom—a
freedom not too easily demonstrable. Papini has declared
"True revolutions begin in the head not at the barricades."
In Mexico, the head never caught up with the barricades.

Nevertheless, with the death of the idol "Political Democracy" the lower classes, the Indian race-groups, the handful
of proletariat, all became more and more imbued, as time
went on, with sentiments of Marxian class-consciousness,
much in the same way that flappers bob their hair and have
petting parties—a la mode. As a result there was hatched the
scraggly duckling of a labor movement (Mexican Regional
Confederation of Labor; Saltillo, 1918. National Agrarian
Party; Mexico, 1920. Mexican Labor Party; Zacatecas, 1920.
National Peasants League, 1926).

The new movements quacked all the Auld Lang Syne songs
of labor the world over. But Mexican Labor has had as little
respect for "Political Democracy" as the Army. It has, wherever it could, used the same old strong-arm, bureaucratic
superstate tactics. Mexican Labor became the conspicuous
new Idol in Mexico. The workers movement, semi-artificial
though it is, became like the military caste or the Church

of the Conquest, something of a common denominator, a new cement—most important in a land lacking national consistency and order. It represents the coalescing of the more mobile indigenous elements under the bitter blows of foreign exploitation, a coalescence facilitated by the temporary tolerance of the military superstate elements menaced by the same foreign invasion. Yet this labor unification, like all other emerging castes in Mexico, has been on the fringe of the true Mexican nation. Already it has passed its zenith.

The peasant revolt, in spite of land reform, a really deeper stirring of the indigenous culture, never really materialized. Except in connection with the mobile labor of the haciendas, it remained vague, inchoate. More basic than laborism, like all things basic, it was ignored, toyed with, betrayed. It was never able to coalesce. Its most emphatic expression was the ready rifle hid in the palm-thatch of the *ramada*—quick retribution, feather-shanked aggressions, disorganized seizures of ancient patrimonies.

In Mexico, capital faces similar dilemmas. As yet capital has been unable to create the social unity characteristic of the modern industrial nations with their closely woven economic and financial organization. Capital in Mexico suffers from the heterogeneousness that is characteristic of Mexico—be it geography, climate, race, religion, or politics. Capital cannot achieve the concentrated power once wielded by the Church. Capital is foreign, non-nationalistic; it is atomized, divided among many diversified interests: mining, petroleum and railroading are American and British; hardware and machinery, German; large-scale factories and department stores, French; the henequen industry is in the hands of the Yucatecan aristocracy. A coffee grower does not see the point in linking up with a petroleum producer; the henequen-grower does not realize his interdependence with the copper-mining of Sonora. Capital is split among many nationalities with conflicting interests, imperialistic and otherwise; divided by

46

the walls of many unrelated industries. Each of these industries, for the most part, has had more direct contacts with the foreign world than the center in Mexico City.

But the growing predominance of American capital provided a semi-unity which for a brief time gave Mexican Labor anti-imperialist credos. Labor at least has the common coefficient of an empty stomach; it was united by all the bitterness of centuries of exploitation; it is composed, in large part, of indigenes who, though once separated by racial barriers, found a common race-affinity in their struggle with the white man.

This has made labor groups outspokenly nationalistic. Labor, if it has trouble with a foreign employer, immediately demands not merely better wages or conditions, but his expulsion as an undesirable alien. Many subterranean racial and agrarian and nationalistic tendencies have therefore flowed into the so-called proletarian movement. Thus the labor movement is, in large part, but a new-named instrument for working out many old cultural tendencies, for satisfying an elementary landhunger, for Boxerism, for national integration. Indeed a Labor movement in the American or French sense does not exist. A dozen extraneous tendencies have canalized into it; national and racial and cultural possibilities unknown to our labor movements are latent in it. Yet it remains on the fringe; it is a splintering off from the main current of nationalism. The peasant movement has yet to grasp for its place in the sun. The race soul has yet to find outlet. The Mexican nation has yet to be born.

Labor leadership, at its strongest movement, was permeated with the old-time vices and traditions of cast dictatorship. By the time of Calles, most of the labor leaders had come to batten at the Government tables, all city-dwellers. They used the worker in the same way that the earlier caciques used him, in an arrogant bejewelled overlordly manner; just as his inflated Spanish conqueror used him. Most of the labor poli-

ticians, to advance their power, accepted the proletarian slogans, even hearkened to hoi polloi demands whenever to do
otherwise would prove embarrassing. They passed factory
regulations which were not enforced. In a lackadaisical manner they cut up trifling portions of the large estates to restore
a few thousand villages *ejidos*. They tried now and then to
found cooperatives, always according to some pet intellectual
scheme, rarely attempting to graft them on to the old ejidal
practices.

Take the cooperative town in Chapingo (twenty-five miles
from Mexico City). This town is laid out in American ready-
made tin-can style, dotted with cigar-box bungalows, provided with a community assembly hall and a community
kitchen, uglified with an inartistic statue. Saloons and
churches were taboo. Through the center runs the Street of
Social Foresight, the Street of the Proletariat, the Street of
Worker's Savings. The place was stocked with prize peasants
and workers on the easy-payment plan. Strange to say, the
dwellers one by one slipped away, not content with their
cheese-boxes; the atmosphere choked them. Now grass grows
in the revolutionary streets. The vacant windows stare for-
lornly, targets for the rocks of passing urchins. And the
care-taker has built himself an unsanitary adobe hut with
flowers trooping over the door and children sprawling in the
dirt in front. Even he will not live in one of the immaculate-
conception bungalows. Yet undoubtedly this pathetic pater-
nalistic experiment was an idealistic outgrowth of the popular
need for economic and spiritual expansion. But it teaches that
cities and ideas must grow out of native soil and out of
native needs and be breathed upon by the community life.

The price of this lack of realism was, by the time of Portes
Gil, a smashing of the politician-captained official labor
group as previously organized. A house-cleaning for the purpose of reintrenching the militarist super-state and destroying
all free popular expression.

48

Thus the labor movement has been another lava flow leaving another scar. But it is neither the fuel, nor the cauldron nor the contents. The peasant movement, rooted in the indigenous culture stuff, worshipping semi-Oriental communal idols has yet to have its say.

6

In this I have used the word "Huitzilopochtli," the name of the Aztec War God, first, as a symbol of the old tyranny of the pre-Conquest regimes perpetuated down through the ugly centuries of Mexican history in a dozen different guises; second, as a symbol of the vitality and survival value of the native cultures; and third, over and beyond both of these uses, the word "Huitzilopochtli" shadows forth the strivings and aspirations born of the native desire to be free of the very ignorance and superstition and servility that Huitzilopochtli typifies. "Huitzilopochtli" is thus both a static and a fluid symbol; it represents historical survival, also the evolution of the indigenous culture. Through more than three centuries the native peoples have suffered from dislocation and exploitation. Though persistent, their culture was accordingly modified; here degraded, there fortified, else-

49

where redirected; but with the exception of the backward northern districts, always representing a mass resistant power.

The culture of the Mexican elite is European, as was that of the United States prior to the arrival of Walt Whitman; but the true Mexican culture, the mass-culture, though traced through with a dozen foreign designs, is obviously, predominately Indian, the modified Indian of today. And it is surging up and over the imposed Latin practices, creating a new unsettled complex of traits, vaguely shaping themselves into what will be in time a national mode of expression.

Idealism constantly thrusts the people back, bleeding upon the thorns of reality, or into a warm poetic love for the simple intimacies of nature; fatalism expresses itself partly in the vast stolidity of the people, in their brooding watchfulness, their long intricate silences, and equally in their recklessness of means and of ends. They believe in the Supernatural; they flirt inconsequentially with life and its terrors, always *La Vacilada* will to kill or be killed in any way that seems elegant, humorous or original. This psychological complex at its worst expresses itself, logically enough, in lack of loyalty, frequent treacheries, brutality and cruelty.

Artistically the people express themselves, in an original symbolic æsthetic. Even the most ragged *pelados* are sensitive to form, color, composition, rhythm. The handicraft tradition is ancient and unbroken. A stream of legend and popular fantasy empties into the national literature creating a new unsettled complex of traits, vaguely shaping themselves into National Expression.

The native tongues of the Indians enrich the vocabulary, and make more flexible and musical the Spanish of the Hidalgos; totemic symbolism flows over into new rich connotations.

The politicians of the capital speak sobbingly at public banquets of "Us Indians and our age-long sufferings;" and in the next breath patronizingly, of the necessity of regenerating the Indian. They build futile model towns; they

drag Indian children to city schools to learn things they never will use. But out in the *pueblos,* in the "provinces," Indians more and more are capturing the local governments. Recently I met the mayor of Tepoztlán, Morelos: he was barefoot but shrewd; and he knew the needs and beliefs of his *vecinos.* More and more, men of Indian origin, retaining their native psychology, sagacity and integrity, are forcing their way into the higher posts of the Government. The native tide is sweeping up higher and higher over the bulwark of the state, with its outworn bureaucratic ramparts. All this complicated Indian revival, shot through with Iberianisms, Creolisms, Gallicisms, Americanisms, is evolving into a new intricate national life. For a time this process may be checked by the new drive of foreign capital and the new subservience instituted by Portes Gil and Ortíz Rubio. But until this process reaches an equilibrium the Mexican nation cannot be born.

And so on down the list: the native culture is wrapping its arms about the newest industrialism, modifying the methods of work; remoulding the aims of the schools for example in ("Missionary" teachers, handicraft schools, *ejido* schools, Institute of the Indian). The Church is absorbing pagan motives, dramas, dances; regarding the Family, the native cooperative love-relation is constantly treading on the heels of the stilted Spanish institution.

Whatever Mexico's ultimate language, and it will probably be Indianized Spanish; whatever its future biological composition, and it will probably be brown-skin mestizan; whatever its final cultural complex—and all will be amazingly different from what we know today, the indigenous culture still has the superior assimilative potentiality. In a hundred years, the percentage of whites in Mexico has declined from 18 percent of the total to 7.5 percent. In spite of centuries of spoliation, in spite of aristocratic preoccupation with European Art and Government, Mexico's great reservoir of culture is Indian. Land is enclosed and distributed and re-stolen; the Church teaches the catechism but not the use of soap; foreign capital hollows the hills for gold; but the native life continues to crystallize with ever new facets of social liberty, ever new radiations of beauty. It is contributing ever more formidably to the national development. It is integrating itself into national power. The revitalization of the multi-form Huitzilopochtli and not the worship of the Idols "Bolshevism" or its counterpoise "Democracy" is for me the most significant aspect of the 1910-20 overturn and its present reconstructive epilogue. Both Capital (in the Mexican case, a revolutionary factor) and Bolshevism (here a conservative factor) are borne along on the crest of a long and deep racial and national wave. The white content diminishes biologically and culturally.

Thus, the native culture is the deep-seated driving motor. The various petroleum laws, sub-soil laws, foreign-property laws, forestry-conservation laws, irrigation laws are but expressions of the renewed dignity, the stubbornness and independence of the downtrodden races who have, from the days of Cortez and Alvarado to Doheny and Hearst, regarded the intrusion of the foreigner, particularly the white man, with suspicion and hostility. The native races have ever demanded, now mildly, now in the strenuous tongue of armed mass-action, a curtailment of the ruthless exploitation that so featured the Colonial, Creole, and Díaz epochs. They have demanded this, not for Socialistic or proletarian reasons, however utilized those adjectives, but because of the great urge toward group and racial and national self-preservation. The native peoples, instead of being herded into reserves as in the United States, are endeavoring to set up one vast national reserve. Calles toward the end of his regime, then Portes Gil, and Ortiz Rubio, swung away from this process. They will have to return to it or be swept aside in bloodshed.

When the past and present rulers of Mexico are long forgotten, and the present catch-words of liberty have become rubber stamps, there will be remembered in Mexico the names of its Indian heroes: Cuauhtémoc, Juárez, Altamirano, Zapata, Villa, Carrillo, who, in their various ways, oftentimes brutally and crudely, managed to breathe upon the old race traditions and fire anew the dreams of the indigenous masses. When Calles and Portes Gil are but dust in the irritated eyeballs of posterity, people will still go to the walls of the public buildings to marvel at the powerful paintings of Diego Rivera and Clemente Orozco, who with the earlier Indian sculptor, Istolinque, have been among the first to express the sorrows and patience and strength of the native races in a truly national art. Thus behind the whole Mexican scene still towers the grotesque fanged shadow of Huitzilopochtli, no longer a menace, no longer demanding his "due meed of innocent blood," but convertible once and for all into a symbol of a people emerging from superstition and servitude to found one of the most fascinating civilizations of modern times.

III

GUADALUPE HIDALGO:
RELIGIOUS CAPITAL

Dᴇᴄᴇᴍʙᴇʀ twelfth, the na-
tional religious holiday of Mexico, is celebrated in the national
religious capital, the town of Guadalupe Hidalgo, some five
miles north of Mexico City. This Mecca clusters about the
hill of Tepeyac which commands the high Anáhuac valley
for miles about. On this hill on that day, more than three
centuries ago, the Holy Virgin appeared to a credulous Indian, Juan Diego. This was the first time, legend declares,
that she set foot on the western continents. A cathedral rose
on the summit of Tepeyac. The faithful flocked to the spot
by tens of thousands. And thus Guadalupe Hidalgo on
December twelfth is the longed for goal of every religious
heart in Mexico.

Many a December twelfth I have walked down the long
road, lined with black and white poplars, that leads out from

Mexico City to the little town. On December twelfth this road becomes a river of bobbing sombreros, is jammed with hilariously eager pilgrims, from coal-eyed *niñas* in dust-dragging skirts to swart-faced adults. Once this vast Romería was made slowly and on the knees, with lengthy prayers before each of the fourteen chapels along the route— the ever celebrated fourteen stations of the cross—but now it is made with song and jostling and jest.

Last December twelfth, a friend and I started out at dawn. The whole road was lined with venders of *dulces* and candied fruits. Cheap jewelry, long barbaric earrings, amber beads, fire-glistening combs, necklaces, bracelets gleamed from the road-side stands. Red lemonade, "cured" pulque slaked the thirst. Piled high were bananas, from Tabasco, sugar-cane bunched like wigwam poles, drunk sapotes that seemed all juice, "popcorn" made of tiny grass seeds and brown syrup, and pineapple sliced into golden wedges. As we neared the densely crowded town, religious objects predominated: man-high candles, garishly twisted, decorated with miraculous Biblical scenes or pictures of the Santissima Virgin; *gorditas de la Virgin*—"little fat ones of the Virgin"—holy sweet-cakes, almond-sized, made from the meal of the big Cacahuazintla corn; rosaries of carved wood, of glass, of silver, even of the fretted gold work from far-off Yucatán; aluminum medallions stamped with the Virgin; tiny carved opera glasses of bone, no larger than a penny slot and with pin-hole openings revealing magnified images of picturesque local panoramas.

Here and there we saw incongruous pre-Cortez objects: "deer-eyes," with scarlet strings and bits of gnarled pine-wood stuck in the edges, to be hung about the neck as a protection against the evil-eye; oranges wigged with red corn-floss, the pagan offering to the local Indian goddess Tonant-zín; carved serpent canes from Apizaco, once the somber fasces of an ancient ceremony.

Straight down the road, looms the pink Cathedral built in

1792. Above it, on the site where the Virgin Mary revealed herself, on the high-walled hill, terraced with the tombs of the Tepeyac cemetery, a white wind-worn chapel pierces the turquoise sky, 7,000 feet above the level of the sea. And still higher, on the hill behind, are three gaunt crosses—the eternal Calvary.

At the lower church, a crowd of rag-tail Indians battle around the iron grill along the imposing atrium. Whining festering *léperos* hold out their claws for alms, there beneath the up-shooting columns that support the niched facade with its saints and bas-reliefs which tell how nearly four centuries ago on this spot the Virgin miraculously appeared to the poor Indian Juan Diego.

On and on through this swirling ragged tide, we struggled to reach the lofty green and gold interior, vibrant with the echoes of Aztec splendors and Spanish might. Enormous brass texts, with tipsy letters hug the walls beside dim ascetic saints. Through frames made by the ponderous Corinthian piers, we stared at huge historical and religious paintings done by the foremost artists of the Colonial period. The light sifted down to us from the grotto-circled brown lantern of the cupola and glistened upon silver gates and balustrades and shining candelabra suspended by massive chains. Where the light passed through drifting spirals of incense it crystallized out into solid metal bars—quivering hot-white shafts. Oriental profuseness and mysticism! Egyptian massiveness and fatalism! In one of the aisles we came upon gorgeously attired feather-decked native dancers clogging away to the melancholy screech of a single-stringed violin, and armadillo guitars. The swaying throng eddied about the saints, the holy-water basins up and around the white portal of the altar with its four tall columns of Scotch granite.

For the miraculous image of the Virgin is there. Neophytes in vivid red and white aid priests in golden robes performing high mass with much droning and shin-digging and tinkling of bells.

The advance into the depths of the Church became sweltering. Huge sombreros rasped our faces, pyjama-clad Indians shuffled their *guaraches* and flung their sarapes tighter across their shoulders. Little islands of kneeling women in very long calico skirts, black *tápalos* tightly clutched over their full breasts and about their plump olive cheeks, blocked our passage. A woman, surely eighty years old, wormed along on her knees. A mangy dog slunk by with a helpless yap. A peasant beat his head three times upon the pavement. An urchin chewing peanuts knocked his heels on the edge of a latticed confession stall. Through this great unwashed that knows more of catechism than of soap, we elbowed, pushed, perspired.

With real relief, we sank into the stalls of the carved sillería. These canonical chairs are embossed with saints and female martyrs in high relief. Here, in the transcoro, the church was much dimmer; the Byzantine splendor of the forepart of the nave and the shafts of sunlight from the lantern and open portals were toned down to drowsy sombreness. A subdued dazzle of rainbow colors fell on the checkerboard tiles within the silver and bronze grill of a tortured Saint Stephen. The gold-red panels of carved gray stone were softly harmonious.

Beyond, in the chapel dedicated to the Holy Founders of Religious Orders in Mexico, a wheel-window gleamed with a stained-glass representation of Santa Teresa. Her fiery yet restrained sensuousness shed a new glamor. Her full firm lips which betray the tortured grandeur of her struggle to submit body and beauty to her creed, seemed to be saying once more with a slightly ironical tilt: "*Que es Díos muy buen pagador!*"—"God is a very good paymaster."

Teresa, of all the female saints, is most Mexican in spirit. Her mysticism, like that of Giovanni della Croce, is a glamorous, star-pulsing faith; and the Mexican world ever expands from song and color and art into mysticism and from mysticism subsides into brooding beauty and intense gray-gold passion. Teresa's mysticism, her intense desire, her sensuousness, her vision of a world bathed in blood and fire, her drowsy luxuriousness—these things are part of Mexican character, inlaid into the very soul of the people.

Yet, in many respects, the Mexican world is outside of her ken:—primitively elemental, despite having almost incomprehensible variety. Mexico, more than any other Latin country, has achieved the impossible of being at one and the same time subtle, desperately persistent, delicate in its emotional and intellectual nuances, yet vigorously crude, fearlessly garish—be the manifestations good or evil.

This Mexican duality was most vividly revealed to me by the pictures which the visiting worshippers had plastered along the staircase leading down into the Guadalupe sacristy. Every inch of wall is covered with *retablos*, harsh home-made paintings of miraculous salvations: Here, an auto struck by a train; the occupants, who cried out to the Virgin Guadalupe, escape unhurt; the whole episode is depicted in brusque oil on a cigar-box cover. There, a man escaping a firing squad in front of the Palacio Nacional. Here, a woman surviving a Caesarian operation. These paintings set forth painstakingly all the gruesome details, yet with sweetly simple fidelity of emotion.

Indeed the real beauty of the Mexican world, where its more joyous pagan characteristics appear side by side with its mysticism and patience, is to be found in those minute handicrafts of native communal life, as much a part of Mexico as the trees and stones and interminable cactus of fields and dry hills, and which shed color over the life of the most despicable, tattered *pelado*.

But yet, these things too would have been alien to Teresa's understanding. These expressions of the Mexican spirit are unsophisticated, with pure lines and elementary colors, while the world of Teresa was complex, touched with the Baroque, consciously flamboyant. Teresa was too perfected, too refined; she is the sister of Anatole France's Thaïs. To Teresa the world seemed stained with sin; yet, above all, it was a perfected world, an orderly world, nicely tabulated, pigeon-holed, with post-office efficiency—each human trait, each emotion, each sin carefully labelled and pinned in its hierarchical place: Hell, Purgatory, and Heaven, as methodically arranged as in the *Divine Comedy*. Other-worldliness is her creed; peace is her dream; death her desideratum.

But Mexico *lives* in the here and now—and its living is never mechanistic, rarely efficient. Mexico is ever throbbing with too much vitality, greedy for life, reckless of means, unable to confine its boundless energies within any predetermined mold. Similarly, Teresa's love of the sanguinary side of the crucifixion is the tempered decadence of Baudelaire and Flaubert, not the Mexican rawness and unruly passion. Here in Guadalupe in this temple at the base of Tepeyac, the blood that drips over the bony Christ cries out with the same terrorizing intensity as the blood shed by the devotees of Huitzilopochtli when the living hearts of human offerings were torn palpitating from nude breasts and held up smoking to the sun-god in mighty invocation. Here are grotesqueness, terror, sublime frenzy, little of the tempered texture of the Old World which refines even its atavisms.

Yet, at times, Mexico gives the illusion of refinement. This is because it has absorbed from so many cultural founts. It is a whirlpool into which has been sucked every sort of jetsam. For in society, in government, in industry, in religion, Mexico is confused, complex—but a raw bleeding complexity, an ulcerating complexity, as a wound infected with many germs. Mexico has cultural layer plastered on layer, shaggily after the fashion of the feathers on the humming-bird shanks of the old Toltec God Quetzalcóatl; civilization has been ground into civilization, world into world, idea into idea.

And yet, in a sense, all this is superficial; one never discovers the true heart of Mexico, that pulsing center which has whirled this nation into one of the most tragic and bloody destinies recorded in history. There is something savage, untamed, perhaps untamable, at the source of Mexican life. The very marrow boils. And yet this has meant no suffocating of the aesthetic. The sense of form, color and rhythm is innate in the Mexican's being; and if the expression seem to us at times garish, the vitality grips one the more intensely. And, paradoxically, subtlety is never absent. The native harshness had been subdued in the handicrafts; it is struggling into mature artistic expression in the Diego Rivera school of painting and the music of Ponce and Chávez. And yet perhaps all which may be termed refinement in the Old World sense, other than dilettante aestheticism is found focused in Guadalupe Hidalgo. Teresa is most at home there.

For Guadalupe Hidalgo is the greatest remaining center of the religious afflatus of the old race which swept on, slightly modified and softened, into the channels of Catholicism. Puebla, the second mecca of Mexico, a creation of the Spaniards, is crudely colonial, sentimental and shoddy modern. Cholula, with its star-jabbing Pyramid to Quetzalcóatl, dozes in forgotten isolation. The Sanctuary of Ocotlán, beyond Tlaxcala, is hidden in a relatively inaccessible mountain-ringed valley. Indian and mestizo Mexico turns to Guadalupe Hidalgo; here lies the mythical center of all miracles, the dreamed-of goal of every religious heart, the faithful guardian of noble and ignoble superstititions, of beggars, flies, raw sores, glory and resurrection.

Inevitably this place will become an important religious center. Tepeyac is the nearest imposing outcropping of hill near the capital. In the old days it overlooked imperial Tenochtitlán, citadel of Moctezuma. Through the long pulsing ages it has commanded an unbroken view of volcano-rimmed Anáhuac Valley. And from time immemorial, men have flocked to such places to found their temples, their forts, and their palaces.

Even in ancient Indian days, Guadalupe Hidalgo was a great religious center. Near here on the adjacent Yoaltecat Hill, every year in the month of Atlocoalco (which began on the twenty-second of our February, the dry, dusty part of the year) the Aztecs sacrificed children to the Tlaloques, the midget gods of rain. The sacerdotes laid the victims upon the sacrificial *techecatl* over which waved black, color-rayed banners. With razor-sharp glass blades they slit open the tender breasts and offered up the smoking hearts of the children to the gods of rain. And on Tepeyac hill itself, once stood the ancient *cu* or temple of Tonantzín, protectress of the Tononqui Indians, on the same site that Cristobal de Aguirre subsequently erected the chapel, *la Capilla del Cerrito*, which he endowed with a fund to commemorate annually the apparition of the Virgin.

Tonantzín was the goddess of Earth and Corn, the equivalent of the Greek Ceres. Also, she was Coacíhuatl— "Snake Woman" and "Our Mother." Being a Virgin, she became Mary. Being associated with that original oriental and primitive religious symbol, the snake, she became "Eve, our mother, who was tricked by the serpent." Legends cluster about her. She dressed, as a rule, in white, with her hair done into two small horns on her forehead. Across back and shoulder she carried a cradle in which slept her divine son. This cradle she would leave in the buzzing *tianquiztli* in the care of the village market women. Later, when Tonantzín failed to return and they would look within, they would find a hard stone, shaped like a lance-head. This would subsequently be used to sacrifice the human offerings in the *cu* on the summit of the hill. "And all this was a sign that Tonantzín had been among us."

We passed up to the hill chapel through a twisted lane of green and pink houses, ascending winding stone steps. Pausing in the shade of a carved stone sail set in the wall by sailors saved at sea by their appeal to their native Virgin, we gazed down upon the outspread town. Its flat, many-colored roofs are cracked, eaten into by cactus and chayote vines. The rolling *techo* of the cathedral, with its four towers, is picturesquely framed in false-pepper branches. Narrow streets ray out in all directions.

We continue to ascend. The vast city of Mexico stretches out toward the south. The huge cathedral on the *Zócalo*, the largest church in the two western continents, pokes above the plain imposingly. At the opposite fringe of the city is set the rusting dome of the unfinished Palacio Legislativo, a symbol of the shattered dreams of the great Porfirio Díaz.

The whole sweeping panorama of the Anáhuac Valley unfolds. To the west are the remote frosty peaks of Popocatépetl and Ixtaccíhuatl, dim in the glimmering horizon haze. Closer at hand extends the arching shore of Lake Texcoco, its unruffled surface changed by divine alchemy into pure silver. Near the chapel is the crowded Pantheon of Tepeyac in whose neat parterres the elite for one hundred pesos are laid out to rest *para eternidad.*

From here, over flights of stone steps and time-stained roofs, we see winding lanes and little villages tucked in the rolling hills. A crumbling Spanish aqueduct crawls along the sedgy shores of another lake. Its massive arches frame the iridescent glints of the late sun. High steel towers (with seven-petticoat insulators carrying heavy wires that send light and power humming to the capital) seem hurriedly striding across the marshes. Everywhere are sarape-clad Indians, burros stepping deliberately with twitch of ears down shale shelvings, tinkling herds shaping and reshaping on the hillside like the fluid letters of some mystic prophecy of doom.

This native life is so patiently persistent; no wonder the crafty bigot, Bishop Zumárraga, found difficulty in converting the people. Ultimately he had to make use of the Indian faith by identifying the Virgin Mary with the pagan goddess Tonantzín. The excuse for the erection of a Christian chapel was found in the experience of the credulous Indian Juan Diego.

Juan Diego, crossing the barren cactus slope of Tepeyac, suddenly heard the most harmonious music. Out of the hill sprang a brilliant-colored arc, in the radiance of which appeared a lady of exquisite face and form. *"Hijo mío,"* she called, reassuringly, and informed him she was the Virgin Mary and that he was to tell the Bishop to build a church on the spot. Bishop Zumarraga gave no credence to Juan's story. But when the Indian returned to Tepeyac, the Virgin again appeared. Once more Juan went to the Bishop. This time the prelate instructed Juan to demand of the apparition a sign of her divinity, and sent two spies to follow him. But as Juan approached a small bridge, he miraculously disappeared from their sight. In reality he had continued on his way. Once more the Virgin appeared, telling him to come back the next day. But his uncle being dangerously ill with *cocolixtle,* a native fever, he did not obey.

Two days later, when hurrying along the base of the hill to secure a priest for his dying relative, a small fountain bubbles out at his feet, and the Virgin descends the hill in a flame of light. He falls upon his knees trembling. The Virgin again reassures him, announcing that his uncle is well. "Ascend the hill," she commands, "and gather roses."

"What, in that barren spot! Why there are only rocks and cactus!"

She chides him for his skepticism, bids him obey. And there on the summit, which had never known flowers, he finds a beautiful garden riotous with roses. After filling his *tilma,* or apron, with them he returns to the Virgin. She presses the flowers to her bosom and then bids him take them to the Bishop.

When Juan Diego displayed the roses, the Bishop was amazed to see painted upon the *tilma* the shimmering picture of the Virgin standing in the cup of the moon and surrounded by a gold and red aura—a young woman with breast-folded hands and inclined head, black hair piously parted in the middle. Her symmetrical face was sweet; her downcast eyes half-hidden by full soft lids. Around the waist was a narrow violet *nelpiloni* confining a rose-colored gold-flecked tunic from whose lower hem peeked out one gray slipper. A Nile-green cloak fell from the crown of her head and, catching on her left arm, hung in voluminous folds to the cloud-wafted cherubim at her feet.

As a result of the enthusiasm engendered by this miracle, a cathedral sprang up at the foot of the hill, on the summit, the chapel. To enclose the gushing fountain was constructed a most delightful symmetrical church, a perfect gem of Mudéjar art, with yellow and azure tiles set about a circular stucco-carved entrance with deep star-shaped windows. The interior is less satisfying: a ceiling bubbling with cherubim; El Anima Puro, a pale youth unconcernedly burning in livid flames; gory images and garish Nile-green Baroque altars.

To this enclosed well come the halt and the maimed and the blind. The sulphurous waters gurgle up near the tiled floor; they are drawn forth by a steel chain and a copper bucket. The sick drink; the syphilitic pour the precious fluid over their sores, letting the residue fall back into the well; the crafty fill numerous small green bottles which they peddle in their home towns at extortionate prices.

But though churches have sprung up and miracles have been worked, and are still being worked, which astound the credulous, the old rites of Tonantzín linger on. The twelfth of December is, perhaps, the fourteenth day of the month of Atemutzli of the Nahuatl calendar, when primitive dances were held and native festivities aroused joy and passion. Similar dances survive today. They are now spontaneous without the old pagan satraps to direct them, being organized as a rule by neighborhood groups probably once upon a time consanguineous. Sometimes these groups consist of a handful of people, sometimes they include several hundred persons from black-eyed three-year-old tots to grandmothers and great grandmothers, as though to fulfill the old Talmudic proverb that "the woman of sixty runs to the sound of music like the girl of six." The dancers wear bell-decked sandals, short, bright-colored tunics, embroidered blouses, and elaborated headdresses of silver beads, mirrors, feathers and popped corn called *monochtli,* which is "like a snow-white flower." At their belts dangle clinking tassels of shells, miniature cooking utensils, magic wind-pebbles of the wind-god, Ehecatl, carved obsidian, bits of claw-like jade. Music is provided by one-stringed violins, *teponastles* (queer drums), and armadillo guitars. Special caricature actors clog in the center of a large ring. These wear odd headdresses and skins of animals: possums, bears, leopards, lions, coyotes—perhaps the remnant of village totemism. A sort of black-faced monkey called a *huëhuë* scurries around tripping up the dancers, swishing a lash at stray curs, beating off the urchins with a pig's bladder, and destroying the solemnity of the affair—somewhat after the fashion of the *marshillih* at medieval Jewish weddings. The onlookers laugh uproariously but the dancers obviously try not to be amused; when they fail, they too feel the *huëhuë's* lash. Hour after hour these dances continue—slow, solemn, a round of melancholy, unmelodious rhythm.

Here in Guadalupe are all the greatest popular venerations. Every child knows the story of how, when a copy of the painting of the Virgin of Guadalupe Hidalgo was shown to Benedict XIV, he exclaimed, *"No fecit Taliter omni nation"* —"This was granted to no other people." For the Virgin of Guadalupe is the Joan of Arc of Mexico. Her image blazed on the banners of the patriot-priest Hidalgo; she led the armies of independence to victory. The Spaniards, to counter her influence, chose as their patroness, the Virgen de los Remedios, and so the battle of independence became also a battle of faiths. In old Europe two villages frequently battle over their saint and their patrons, even to bloody death—as D'Annunzio tells in his *Tales of Pescara,* and Blasco Ibáñez in his *Blood and Sand* of the conflict in the streets of Sevilla. But in Mexico, superstition and benighted bitterness were lifted to imperial dimensions. Today, as a result, the Virgin of Guadalupe is the heroine of Mexico, more popular than the independence leaders Hidalgo and Morelos.

And so, the town of Guadalupe Hidalgo, the ancient Quatitlapán of the Aztecs, is to Mexico what Lourdes is to France or Loreto to Italy. It is to modern Mexico what the great Cholula, with its four hundred flaming pyramids looming over the Puebla plains, was to the early Toltecs.

It is the Mexican Toledo, for in Guadalupe Hidalgo every religion and every culture that has reached the upland plateau has left its trace. Here passed the Toltecs, and the Chichimecas, and the Tlaxcalans, and the Aztecs proper. Here the Spaniards fought the Tepeyaqueses to make secure their communications with Vera Cruz; here Sandoval, the doughty lieutenant of Cortez, cut off the rear of the Aztecs during the second attack on Tenochtitlán. In Guadalupe Hidalgo was signed the treaty of peace that gave to the United States half of old Mexico; and here the French intrenched themselves during the meteoric career of Maximilian.

In later days Guadalupe Hidalgo became the seat of ecclesiastical intrigue. As in the days when Cardinal Cisneros of Toledo arrogantly defied the Spanish state and crown and saw his commands whirled over the land, so at times in Mexico's history, the Prelate of Guadalupe turned the scales of native history, and worked his insolent will upon a nation. Guadalupe is the second capital, the religious capital of the country.

Today when Mexico is seething with modernism, with revolutionary restlessness among the proletariat and peasants, and the Palacio Nacional is the scene of shifting military and popular control, Guadalupe Hidalgo, but a few miles distant, remains primitive, unchanged, the stubborn center of a stirring Indian life and a politically discredited religion, the center of an invisible empire. Juárez broke the power of the Church by wrenching away its mortmain estates; the recent revolution completed the process, but the invisible theocratic government still persists, and still focuses in Guadalupe. The

Indian religious tide is struggling into a new integrated life, still swirls in Catholic channels, still swirls about the base of Tepeyac hill, about the site of the ancient *cu* of Tonantzín.

True, the stream of people is not so great; many of the worshippers not so credulous; the churches not so clean or so meticulously preserved. The robes of the neophytes and priests are frayed and spotted; their faces weary and cynical. But in the eager eyes of the gay holiday goers still shines the love of the bizarre, of rite, of pomp, of splendor—the heritage of Latin and Aztec; the priests in robes of tawdry gold perform high mass according to the ritual of Rome, but the populace weaves on to the edge of the religious ceremony its own quaint memories. In the common heart still abides a child-like passionate faith in miracles and phenomenal cures; and so, around the base of Tepeyac in the dreamy glad little village of Guadalupe, the spirits of air and earth and water and fire are still strangely potent. Here *El Gran Pescador*, as Santa Teresa was wont to say, still dips His hook and line into the vast pool of superstition and faith and fanaticism, and His catches are wondrous to behold.

True, the life of the town flows quietly beneath the wide-spreading oaks and poplars. Ice-cream venders, carrying their freezers on their heads, call in musical crescendo; tin-type men in the dilapidated plaza take pictures of Indian women from Tehuantepec, from Guerrero, from Nayarit, gayly dressed in embroidered *huipiles* and golden necklaces. Bright incidents, these, that accentuate the leisurely dreaming of the place.

But once a year Guadalupe Hidalgo becomes boisterously choked with pilgrims. They come bringing their babies, their blankets, their cooking utensils. In every angle and alley, they squat down, unsling their fibre-woven *ayates*, unpack their *jarros* and *ollas*, set up their tin *braceros*. Over charcoal fires they cook brick-colored stews, zipping hot with chile, brown beans, and tomato-flavored rice; and they pat moist ground corn of the most venomous greenish hue into thin crisp *tortillas*. When they have eaten, they crowd along the streets and slanting paths, into the chapel, the Pantheon, the red-and-white gambling tents, the festooned pulque shops. They elbow before the tissue-paper decorated refreshment stands, guzzling down drinks made from a dozen mysterious tropic fruits; they crush in front of the *puestos* that bulge with nicknacks and curios.

Once a year ragtail and caballero, harlot and housewife, thief and honest man, swirl through the iron grill of the atrium, into the cathedral, around the slippery stones of the holy well, beneath the horse-shoe facade of the Capilla del Cerrito. Poor and rich, they are holy and hilarious. Awe and jest clash in a dozen dialects—Otomí, Tarascan, Aztec, Zapotec, Huastecan, and all their variants. This is Mexico's greatest fiesta. Guadalupe is still the hub of the Mexican religious wheel. Its spokes are Tlaloc and Tonantzín; Guadalupe, Moctezuma and the Pope; high mass and feather-decked dancing; holy-water and deer-eyes. Guadalupe is the religious capital of Mexico.

IV   TLAXCALA: ANCIENT REPUBLIC

MALINCHE,—guide, interpreter, and bed-companion of Cortez during his ascent to the capital of Mexico—has her *memento mori* in the sharply triangular snow-clad peak, bearing her name, which lords it over the fertile valleys of Apam. Around its sun-kissed holy slopes are scattered the villages of the people she helped Cortez to conquer, still speaking the Nahuatl and other tongues which she translated four centuries ago. Across the plain, in the opposite mountains, lies the rugged but productive state of Tlaxcala, occupying practically the same confines as the original Tlaxcalan Republic which so violently battled Cortez and earlier had defied the ponderous armies of the Aztec emperors—a tiny oasis of independence in a domain which stretched from Nicaragua into the United States. And to this day the state of Tlaxcala seems almost as uniquely self-sufficient as those tiny republics in the Pyrenees.

To reach the capital one leaves the train at Santa Anna, a quaint town where a barber-shop finds itself so important as to merit advertisement in huge letters across the main-street, a la Gopher Prairie "Welcome to Our City." One boards El Rapido, a miniature one-car train, pulled by a consumptive gasoline motor. The line uncoils through glistening valleys—green, peaceful, prosperous; the motor roars over sharp ravines where women are spreading out bright-colored clothing on maguey thorns and sage-brush. Ahead looms a long *loma*—a brown ridge above which floats the hazy white outlines of Ixtaccíhuatl, the "White Woman," the great volcano whose crest in its far grandeur seems quite disembodied from anything of earth. To one side rises the snow-capped cone of her consort, Popocatépetl, the "Mountain of Smoke." Over the far side of the *loma*, the two white bell-towers of the renowned Sanctuary of Ocotlan stick up like Egyptian obelisks. As the train winds nearer, these become two twisted candles, finally, before disappearing, are blunted to two circular white bee-hives. The metaphor is appropriate. The train shudders to a halt on a siding; a happy buzzing fills the balmy air: the gurgle of brooks, the rustle of leaves, the tinkle of herds, the low of cattle. One appreciates why this region is called Tlaxcala—"the land of corn"—synonymous in Indian phraseology with Paradise.

El Rapido swings around the *loma* and drops upon the state capital which bears the same name—Tlaxcala. The ancient town is set so snugly in a little circle of terraced hills that its sudden appearance partakes of the miraculous. The thudding gasoline motor pants into the plaza, a neat little tree-filled square fringed on one side by long cool arcades. The peaceful spirit of the place sets one instantly at ease. The patios and gardens of the town dream quietly. They are cluttered with pepper and herbs and pansies; with magueys, plums, and *capulines*; with black sapotes whose flesh looks exactly like axle-grease but is intoxicatingly sweet. The houses seem comfortable, and the encircling hills are dotted with churches of every tint, size, and shape; their tiled domes and white facades gleam in the sun; their bell-towers poke above the trees. In every direction the streets leap up toward these sanctuaries with almost lyrical eagerness.

But the town as a whole lies compact and contented in the embrace of its hills. One feels that Tlaxcala should have a lid; and though the sky, because of the proximity of the hills, seems higher than most places in Mexico, the impression is given that the Great Pigeon-Holer of Destinies had temporarily lifted the cover from something precious but that he will replace it and turn the golden key, and that Tlaxcala will go dreaming on. For though the streets and lanes leap up to the hill-perched churches, Tlaxcala lacks the animation of most Mexican towns; it seems sunk from sight, held in eternal enchantment—a Sleepy Hollow indeed. Everything important or noble has fled Tlaxcala. It is a republic no more; the warlike spirit of the Tlaxcalans has vanished; they take little part in the upheavals in Mexico (the new more untutored races furnish the sinews of these periodic convulsions); even the seat of the bishopric has gone to Puebla. Yet the people of Tlaxcala are sturdy in their very humbleness, and their peace, as they were once great in government, in war, in religion.

I was looking over the shoulder of Don Romueldo (a friend whom I had made in Panotla, one of the nearby hill-villages), a tall man built like a temple, so finely sculptured are his face and body. His finger was tracing out on a map the little state of Tlaxcala, surrounded on three sides by Puebla. He remarked facetiously: "Tlaxcala is entirely too small. We ought to be more patriotic. We'll make you a general; I'll be your aide and we'll take half of Puebla. They robbed us of our Bishopric, we ought to take half their state in return. . . . But while you organize the army, I'll go out and feed the pigs." This is Tlaxcala. It is feeding its pigs, watering its gardens. It is content to be forgotten, to be provincial.

"You were once a great people," I remarked to Don Romueldo.

"Yes, but now we are the most *humilde* people of Mexico."

Humble, resignedly ready to face either life or death. In

the olden days, death was a gala occasion—the dead went to
the hereafter in all his finery, and his departure was followed
by twenty days of dancing, feasting and enjoyment—a
pleasurable custom blighted now by the sorrowing hand of
Catholicism.

Nevertheless, though *humilde,* the Tlaxcalans have a most
avid curiosity about the outside world, a curiosity that
would have pleased Matthew Arnold. For even though this
trait has all the naïveté of a small boy pestering everyone
with absurd questions, it bespeaks largess of vision. Yes, blood
counts; and even in the decay of Tlaxcala a real sturdiness of
spirit persists. Tlaxcala somehow is impressive in its negation,
sturdy in its abnegation.

The old pre-conquest days may be visualized by ascending
any of the nearby ridges. Grim precipitous mountains loom
up at the back gate of the town. Those mountains, against
whose shakeless walls the Tlaxcalans placed their backs and
fought off foe after foe, are barren, harsh, chalk-white in
places, though in the old days they were covered with fine
timber, the beautiful carved timber that beams the ceiling of
the nearby Monastery of San Francisco, the oldest church
founded on the American mainland, and the timber which
provided the sturdy planks for the brigantines which Cortez
used against Tenochtitlán.

Centuries ago the Tlaxcalans, part of the Chichimeca race
group, were close neighbors of the Aztecs; for once upon a
time they inhabited a part of the Anáhuac Valley, that upland plain where so many races have contended for mastery
in their endless migrations toward the south. But the uncom-
promising spirit of independence possessed by the Tlaxcalans
(then known as the Teochichimecas), the spirit which so
characterizes them to this day, aroused the enmity of surrounding tribes. It is said that the Aztec Monarch Quinantzín
tried to force them to leave their favorite cliff dwellings and
build cities in the low lands. At any rate the Xochimilcans,
the Colhuas, the Tepanecas, and the Chalqueses gathered to-

gether a formidable army; but the Tlaxcalans, though a mere handful, met them on the plains of Poxauhtlán by the shores of Lake Texcoco and crushingly defeated them—this the Tlaxcalans at any rate claim. So furious was the fighting that from the town of Cohuatichán to the town of Chimal-huacán, through all the marsh and along the lake shores, there was nothing but streams of blood and dead bodies. The lake was a sea of scarlet. The natives believe that a certain edible shell fish of a vivid red, called *izcahuitli*, which is found here in great quantities, was created from the spilled blood of that battle.

The Teochichimecas promptly determined, with that high intelligence that forever featured their boldness, to leave an unprotected place, where they would live constantly under the shadow of war. Their god Camaxtli advised this course: *"Oncantonoz, oncantlahuiz, ocanyazque ayamonica"*—"Go forward, not yet is this the place of your glory." And so about 1351, in the year Ce Tecpatl, they divided into groups and treked west. The largest group, skirting the shore of the Texcocan lake and passing through Amecameca and near Cholula, settled first on the sun-warm slopes of Malinche. Here on the summit of a crag they established themselves and at various elevations they constructed five fosses over fifty feet in width overlooked by as many fortifying walls. The dirt and rock of these walls was secured by digging out great caves high enough for a mounted man carrying a pike. Later, to serve as fortified retreats against the Aztecs, the Teochichi-mecas constructed similar fortifications in Tlaxcala, on the mountains of Matlacueye and Tepeticpac.

But near Malinche, in spite of their intrenchments, the emigrés were constantly harassed by the Olmecas and the Xicalancas; and so they withdrew into the opposite mountains. This was about 1380.

In these new, virgin, fertile, wind-protected valleys they prospered and developed those institutions of liberty for which they are famous in the annals of Mexico. Tlaxcala—

they called the spot—Paradise; and soon they became known by the name by which they were subsequently known— Tlaxcalans, Dwellers in Paradise. They developed into a mountaineer and hunting people, worshipping in splendid isolation their great war-god Camaxtli, he of the two-headed deer whose great teocalli was higher and more magnificent than that of Huitzilopochtli in Mexico City (Tenochtitlán).

Under Camaxtli's auspices, they knighted the sons of the leading houses and all those distinguished in battle. The candidates were shut up to fast in the temples for sixty days. They had no intercourse with human beings save their servitors. After their abstinence, they were taken to the major temple, where they were advised as to the doctrines of life they were to uphold. At the same time they were insulted, laughed at, and struck, even on the face, to test their restraint and stoicism. Blood was then drawn from their noses, ears and lips to be offered to the gods. At last, publicly, they were presented their weapons, bows, arrows, spears, shields, etc. From the temple they were conducted with great pomp, rejoicing and solemnity through the streets and squares. They were now fully and gorgeously accoutred, weighted down with armor, weapons, and bijoutry. Gold pendents hung from their ears, gold rings hung from their noses. They wore carcanets of the bones of tigers and lions and eagles.

With such customs and such independence a mountaineer comraderie grew into being. This their government soon reflected. Each valley chose an independent chief; these various groups then united into a loose federation—a sort of Aetolian League, with a representative government, the principal arm of which was the famous so-called Tlaxcalan senate, a most flexible instrument, composed of the chiefs of each group.

The Tlaxcalan Senate was based upon four principal *cacicazgos*, or lordships: The local annals relate the order of their establishment: "Tepeticpac" was founded by Culhua Quanez; "Ocotelolco," by a brother of Culhua Quanez named Cuicuitécatl; "Quiahuztlán" was a union of numerous smaller nations and from the beginning it was governed by election from the leading houses, Mizquitl being the first ruler. The last *cacicazgo*, "Tlaxcala" (which ultimately became the most important, for it was ruled by Xicontencátl, president of the Senate and friend of the Spaniards), was founded by Tepolohuatécutli. Noble-sounding names, these!

But even in their mountain fastness the Tlaxcalans were now and again menaced and sorely tried. More than once they had to call upon Camaxtli to come to their aid.

Camaxtli was distinguished by his long brown hair. His forehead and nose were tinted black, as though wearing a mask. His impressive crown was of blue and gold eagle and quetzal feathers. In the cartilage of his nose he wore a transparent stone; around the biceps of his arms, several bracelets each crossed with three arrows; and on his breast a rabbit's skin. In his right hand was a basket in which to carry lunch to the mountains; and in the left, bows and arrows. His loin-cloth (*maxtli*) was most elegantly knotted, hanging in front almost to his knees. His sandals (*cactlis*) were exceedingly ornate. From neck to ankle, his body was decorated with vertical white stripes. Opportunity soon arose for this wondrous personage to aid his people.

Shortly after settling in their new home, the Tlaxcalans were attacked by Xiuhtlehuitécutli, the king of the nearby Huejotzincas, who gathered together an enormous army with Aztec allies.

Declaring a siege, Xiuhtlehuitécutli quixotically informed the Tlaxcalans of the day set for the assault.

The newly arrived Tlaxcalans were in difficult straits. They implored Camaxtli to aid them, placing upon his altar a great quantity of grain, jars, vases, glass bracelets, feathers, and all the necessary materials for the making of arrows.

"Our enemies have come upon us when we are unarmed, Oh, Camaxtli; and only through your intermediation can we obtain sufficient weapons to defend ourselves. We are able

arrow-shooters, you well know; but we have no arrows. Oh Lord, come to the defence of your people."

The voice of the God answered: "Do not be cowardly for I shall be with you and aid you to triumph over your enemies. All that is necessary for you to win is that you have faith in me and that you execute my commands to the letter. Listen: put a drop of human milk in the sacred vase of ebony, and it will save you."

The Tlaxcalans marveled. They did not see how a drop of milk could save them, but having faith in their god, as people are wont to do in times of war, they decided to carry out his instructions.

They led to the temple a beautiful girl. She had one teat larger than the other, and by giving her a certain national medicinal and magical drink, they succeeded in obtaining from this teat the drop of milk demanded by the god. The drop was then reverently placed in the sacred vase and covered over with laurel leaves. The materials for making arrows were placed before it.

Three long days they waited, making many sacrifices of snakes, rabbits, and quail; giving offerings of holy paper, thorns, tobacco, and perfumes. The sacerdotes performed all their rites meticulously with great devotion. But nothing extraordinary took place. The drop of milk dried up to a small white flake.

Arrived the day of the battle! Panic struck the Tlaxcalans!

But before the attack was launched the head sacerdote noted with great surprise that from the sacred vase now bubbled a frothy liquor which ran down abundantly over the altar. At the same time, he observed that the god had provided arrows. There they lay on the altar in place of the raw materials brought by the Tlaxcalans. The news of this miracle reanimated the Tlaxcalan warriors.

On the arrival of the Huejotzincas, the besieged went forth valiantly to the encounter, leaping over their trenches and advancing spiritedly. With the very first blows they succeeded in taking a prisoner. They led him immediately to the altar of Camaxtli to be sacrificed. His heart was offered up to the god.

The body was then flayed, and one of the sacerdotes dressed himself in the gory skin and presented himself in the battle front. Putting himself in full view of the enemy, he frightened them greatly and this at the moment of the most furious combat.

The air was filled with the cries of the combatants, the discordant noise of the tambors, the trumpets, the sea-shell cornets, the wooden flutes. A rain of arrows and a hailstorm of stones darkened the air. The fighters reeled together, dealing out blind blows and inflicting terrible wounds.

The leading sacerdote prayed fervently to Camaxtli, then taking up the sacred vase, flowing over with foam, he harangued his people:

"Soldiers of Camaxtli," he shouted in stentorian voice. "Forward! Fight with valor! God is with us! His protection is manifested in this sacred vase. Behold! This is the white unguent of death for our enemies!" He poured the white liquid over the sacerdote wearing the skin of sacrifice.

"And now behold, the miracle is complete! The god has sent us enchanted arrows."

Taking one from the altar and putting it in his bow, the priest sent it whizzing toward the enemy.

A miraculous moment! The rest of the arrows, moved by some occult mysterious force, lifted from the altar and flew straight toward the Huejotzincas. So many were the celestial barbs that sprang from the altar of Camaxtli that in half a second they formed a dense cloud over the field of battle, obscuring the sun itself. The Huejotzincas were mowed down wholesale. Great gaps were torn open in their ranks. Obviously, it is wise to have god on your side!

The assaulters were staggered. Blind with fury and stupefied amazement, they became so confused that they attacked each other, comrade slaughtered comrade. As though the wounds caused by the divine arrows were not sufficient, they hacked away at each other as if suddenly gone mad.

Finally, in complete rout they ran over the rocks and hills, falling into the deep ravines. The sides of the mountains were carpeted with their bodies. Blood ran as though a red rain had fallen from heaven. The few surviving assaulters fled utterly panic-stricken from the horror of their own work and that of Camaxtli.

To celebrate the victory, the young Tlaxcalan males organized a chase. Before dawn, they dressed themselves as hunters, armed with bows and arrows. About their eyes and mouth, they painted chalk circles; their bodies were decorated with white stripes. Head and ears were adorned with red plumes; their hair was knotted with red leather thongs, from which were suspended down the back beautiful eagle plumes. They went nude except for their *maxtli* or loin-cloth. Thus bedecked they formed a squadron at the base of the temple of Camaxtli—then, at a given signal, the hunters ascended the mountains, with loud cries and nimble leaps, and in such good order and so closely united that not a single animal could get by them.

Afterwards they descended, arriving triumphant at the temple where they laid their trophies before an old man, attired to represent the god. The animals caught alive—deer, rabbits, hares, quail—were the holy victims. The hunters immediately sacrificed them to Camaxtli.

In spite of such attacks and occasional internal discords, the Tlaxcalans prospered. They built up their new territories on the basis of industry, order, and justice. Soon they were trading with the remotest peoples, from the furthest mountains to the sea. From Cempoalla, from Tuxtla, from Cohuazacoalco, from Tabasco, their merchants brought back gold, cocoa, cotton, clothes, honey, wax, precious plumage.

But as the Aztec Empire reached its tentacles out over the length and breadth of Mexico, the Tlaxcalans again found themselves menaced, this time more seriously than ever before. The Aztecs sent them a brusque ultimatum to come under the hegemony of the empire and pay the customary tribute or have their cities razed to the ground.

Haughtily, the Tlaxcalans replied, "Neither we nor our forefathers have ever paid tribute nor shall pay it. If our country be invaded, we know how to defend our homes and our institutions."

Though it is not recorded that they were particularly interested in making the world safe for democracy, doubtless they were quite convinced that their democratic institutions were, above all else that ever happened on this planet, quite worthy of perpetuation. With this laudable patriotic belief they organized their forces and constructed defenses. On the east they built forts and trenches; on the west they closed a six-mile gap with a massive wall. The system of defense was so well planned as later to arouse the admiration of Cortez, doughty veteran that he was and skilled in superior ways of war.

For more than sixty years the Aztecs maintained an economic and military blockade of the little Republic. There were no imports or exports. Essentials of life were scarce or entirely lacking. There was no cotton with which to weave clothing, no gold, no silver for ornaments, no precious feathers for gala occasions, no cacao, no salt. Even to this day many Tlaxcalans do not use salt.

But during this long trial, here to Tlaxcala flocked all the enemies of the Aztecs—the Xoltocamecas, the Otomies, the Chalcas, peoples recently subdued by the Aztecs—to help the Tlaxcalans maintain the unequal struggle.

War preparations were continuous. And so, when Axayacatl, the Aztec Emperor, finally sent a powerful expedition, the Tlaxcalans—with the aid, especially of the Otomies, that rude but vigorous nation to the north—were sufficiently well-prepared to drive the invaders back.

The Otomies, as a reward, were given the right to man the frontier forts, as a sort of Tom-Sawyer-paint-the-fence privilege—but buffers have ever been the final word in human intelligence. Certainly the Otomies were proud of their trust, so that when the furious Axayacatl sent out a second and more powerful expedition, they broke the first fury of his assault, giving the Tlaxcalans time for escape.

When the emperor's cohorts finally swept down upon the garden-like republic, the Tlaxcalans—resorting to the tactic of the Russians when Napoleon crossed the snows on the steppes to Moscow—slipped up into their mountain fastnesses. And when the Aztec soldiers were feasting and clashing their spears in triumph in the Tlaxcalan capital, the mountaineers poured down upon them, massacring the flower of the army and sweeping the broken remnants forever from Tlaxcalan soil.

Proud, fearless, super-intelligent, thus the Spaniards found the Tlaxcalans. For by 1520 the Tlaxcalans had prospered. Their cities and villages were densely populated; the four main valleys contained more than a hundred and fifty thousand houses; the fields were blooming; the independence of the little republic was everywhere admired and respected. Its laws were just and vigorous. Said the old chronicler Muñoz Camargo, there in Tlaxcala "men kept their promises and fulfilled their contracts punctually and faithfully."

At the approach of the Spaniards the Tlaxcalan Senate gathered to discuss the best way of confronting the new menace. This stormy session (so vigorously depicted by the native painter Rodrigo Gutierrez), finally resolved to accept the offers of friendship made by Cortez, but at the same time to send the forces of the Republic against him. In case of victory, the Tlaxcalans would be secure in their homes, while their reputation for courage and independence would resound throughout the native world; if defeated, the blame would be thrown upon the general in command, and the way would be still open for rapprochement.

In four bloody battles, the Tlaxcalans, though they almost broke the spirit of the Spaniards, were defeated. They were quick to turn the other face. They offered themselves as allies to Cortez; and that extremadurian genius, always ready to adjust himself to means rather than harbor personal grudges, seized upon Tlaxcalan offer. Forthwith, the four patriarchal senators of the republic were baptized in a fount which still stands in the chapel of the Third Order of St. Francis on the hill above Tlaxcala. 1520 is the date of its inscription; and it reads that Xicotencátl, the president of the Senate, was baptized as Vicente by the chaplain of the Spanish Army, Don Luis Díaz.

Xicotencátl, since he possessed more than five hundred women, had innumerable sons, all armed and knighted. One of the most important, Ayacatzín, was subsequently put to death by Cortez, who hung him in Texcoco. Ayacatzín, who had led the Tlaxcalan allies that accompanied Cortez, had a secret love affair with a local ruling princess or *Cacica*. Three times he slipped off to visit her. Cortez suspected treachery rather than *amor*, and complained to the Senate. The Senate, since the youth's intrigue was an unpardonable violation of the Tlaxcalan military code, delivered Ayacatzín to Cortez for punishment. The episode is typical of the Roman character of the Tlaxcalans.

Yet the Mexicans to this day are strenuous in their denunciations of the Tlaxcalans as the traitors of Mexico, as the *canalla* who sold the country over to the hated white *Gachupín*. But the reasoning of the Tlaxcalans was sound. Previously their armies had defeated the finest phalanxes of the Aztecan empire; they had maintained their independence in the face of the greatest power in the native world; but those same armies went down in defeat before the Spaniards. The military superiority of the new invaders had been clearly demonstrated. Furthermore, the Spaniards guaranteed the Tlaxcalans their liberty and institutions, insured them their status as copartners in the conquest of a hated enemy. The burden of blame rests upon the Aztecs, not upon the Tlaxcalans.

The Tlaxcalans are not half-way people. Not that they are so intensely passionate, so zealous, so emotionally direct as most of the races of Mexico; rather are they a people of strong decisions. Their face and skull contours denote intellectual capacity, coupled with stubbornness. And as soon as they had dedicated themselves to the Spanish cause, with the exception of a few remoter chiefs, they espoused that cause loyally, indefatigably, without complaint; they provided everything demanded of them. The recently shattered armies were reorganized and marched by the side of the cross and the red-and-yellow Spanish flag to the conquest of the Mexican empire.

And once having accepted the Christian baptism, churches were forthwith built on every spur and *loma*, the same churches that still fringe the valley—set down on a hundred hills: La Trinidad, El Santuario de Ocotlán, the Church of los Reyes, San Miguel, San Nicolás, the Sanctuary of Tepeite, La Defensa, San Juan, San Hipólito—the names tick off a long list of the saints. This did not entirely prevent a backward look at the old faith; food (as is told of in *Marius, the Epicurean*) was still put out for the old gods. The supposed cinders of the great god Camaxtli were long and reverently guarded by Tepanecatl, Chief of the nation of Tepeticpac. Yet Jehovah was royally accepted—as part of the existing Pantheon.

The oldest of the Christian churches, the Monastery of St. Francis, still stands close at hand, reached by a short ascending street bordered with ash trees. At the brow of the hill one passes beneath a strong beautiful triple-arch, flanked by a stone bell-tower whose square sturdiness typifies the Tlaxcalan thoroughness. Beyond are the ragged gardens of the atrium, dating back four centuries. From their crumbling balustrade one looks down upon the plaza, patio, and flat red roof.

The church itself is high and airy, beautifully beamed, slightly reminiscent of Santa Croce or San Miniato in Florence. It is rich with retablo work, brimming with paintings, scalloped with chapels, the two largest of which, up near the altar, take the place of a transept. The one to the right, the Chapel of the Third Order of St. Francis, contains the pulpit from which Padre Díaz preached the first Catholic sermon in America, and the basin where were baptized the four senators.

About these various churches soon clustered the Tlaxcalan legends. Here is celebrated (by a curious association of ideas) in the sentinel-like Church of the Defence, in a far ravine, the festival of the old days when the Tlaxcalans withdrew into the mountains to elude the Aztecs. There in the shadow of a white-backed spur where one giant outspread oak stands in solitary grandeur visible from any point of the lower lands, the Tlaxcalan warriors combatted the further advance of the Aztecs. From that narrow gorge, when the Aztecs were stalking the streets of their capital, the Tlaxcalans swept down in avenging fury and wiped them from the face of the earth. And so today, on the twelfth of October is celebrated in the little church of La Defensa, which for the rest of the year stands lonely and unattended, an elaborate festival in honor of the greatest victories of the Tlaxcalan Republic.

Independence is their creed. Tlaxcala was the first state during the revolution of 1910-20 to gain back the *ejidos*, the village common lands.

I passed a ruined hacienda castle in the company of Don Romueldo's son, Antonio. He pointed to the cracked walls.

"There we worked before the revolution for thirty centavos a day. Now we till our lands. We are free."

And having obtained lands, Tlaxcala promptly forgot the revolution and began cultivating them—with care and pride.

As in the old days, Tlaxcalans want as little to do with the Center as possible; they are suspicious of all things Federal.

Sunning myself at the gate of the main church of Panotla, in the company of a group of Indians. A man in khaki with leggings passes with a tripod and camera over his shoulder.

85

"A soldier *here!*" exclaimed one of my "pyjama"-clad companions. "We ought to kill the dirty *cabrón!*"

"*Tonto!*" exclaimed a second, "he's not a soldier; he's a photographer."

"Well," said the first stubbornly, "we ought to kill him just for dressing like a soldier."

On a hill to the right of that where stands the Monastery of St. Francis, but further from the town, rose one of the most famous shrines in all of Mexico, the Sanctuary of Ocotlán. It is reached by a dozen winding paths. An imposing structure. Its white bell towers are first seen over the *loma* from the opposite side, on the approach to Tlaxcala; and as El Rapido plunges into the winding streets of Santa Anna, they are the last remainder of this land so strangely apart from Mexico.

The snow-white facade of this sanctuary gleams dazzlingly in the late sun. It has a design that plays around a huge shell whose lips extend up and out and whose ribs have pleasing fidelity. Authorities declare that this facade is flavored with the architecture of Puebla as are many of the tiled Talavera Poblana domes in the vicinity. Certainly the Tlaxcalans, for all their proud independence, were not bigotedly patriotic; they were ever eclectic, willing to experiment. But though the Sanctuary of Ocotlán may have hints of Puebla art, in ensemble it is delightfully unique. The facade is set between two circular piles of red pentagonal bricks which support the white, white bell-towers. These (top-heavy though they seem) have a lofty isolation there on the high hill. They even typify the whole of Tlaxcalan history, they are so proudly alone and erect, dominating town and valley. The interior of the sanctuary is also significant. Apse and transept have the most elaborate Plateresque retablos in all Mexico. The nave is plain blue and white but one cries out with genuine pleasure as he steps on into the wilderness of gold work—scrolls, flowered designs, cubic perspective. It seems like entering a grotto, rich with glistening stalactites and golden moss

—and this, too, is another typification of Tlaxcalan isolation
and pride, as though the people had worked out in miniature
here the dream of splendor and luxury they would have
wished to see carried into reality in their independent grotto-
like world.

This church, also, was grafted on the Indian legends; it is
situated on the site of the palace of Maxicatzín, one of the
old Tlaxcalan princes. It is the Guadalupe Hidalgo, the
Lourdes, the Loreto of Tlaxcala. Every first Monday in May
its miraculous Virgin is carried down into the town. The
story of her original appearance is similar to that of María
Guadalupe, the national Virgin of Mexico. A poor Indian fled
from the virulent Spanish plague, the small-pox, which had
laid its hand of death on the entire countryside. He was
perishing from thirst on this hill when the Virgin miraculously appeared; and, even as Moses of Old, she opened a
seam of rock from which gushed a fountain. At the same
time she ordained that a church be built on the spot. The
church is there, glistening white, and to this day no Virgin in
Mexico is more efficacious in warding off pestilence than the
Virgin of Ocotlán.

Thus the great festival of Tlaxcala is the joyous spring
festival, the May festival. For this reason, and also perhaps
because the religious center of this region has drifted to
Puebla, Holy Week is not brilliant; it is celebrated in a quiet
way. On Ash Wednesday the people become more *triste* than
usual, and come out of the temples with their heads stamped
with an ashen cross in sign of an ancient suffering. On Holy
Friday the venders make *muéganos*, little cakes of unbaked
flour and eggs and milk and sugar which they coat with sweet
brown *piloncillo* and sell in the hope that they too will become rich as did the poor Puebla Indian and his wife who
invented these confections and sold them to travelers crossing
the bridge near their home. On the Saturday of Glory the
burros come plodding into town loaded with pig-bladders

tight with pulque; and tail and ear and back are gay with many-colored tissue tassels and flowers.

Holy Thursday I celebrated in Panotla with my good friend Don Romueldo. Like his handsome face and body, his house, though small, is solid and picturesque. Its porch opens out on a hillside rectangled with maguey fields and *huertas* of sweet limes and zapotes. He is poor, but good animals are in his corrals, and in the backyard are a finely constructed well and a native *temascal*. This is a low conical brick bath-house, carefully calcimined inside to keep out water. One crawls through a low door; a fire-box heats the whole structure till the walls become too hot to touch.

But I had been especially interested to see *Las Tres Caídas* —the three "falls" of Christ when carrying the cross—which are celebrated in the town church of San Nicolás every Holy Thursday. Above the heads of the packed congregation, whose dusky faces flicker with the gleams from a thousand candles, was a platform sustained by six powerful Indians. It served as a stage for an emaciated statue of Christ (robed in ludicrous purple) who with the aid of a Roman soldier in helmet and armor was carrying a huge pasteboard cross. The face of the Roman soldier, who was quite alive, was covered by a black veil, for who in the village would care to be recognized as the villain who lashed Christ on to his death? The emaciated Christ, over whose sickly green face streamed the blood from his chaplet of iron thorns, was attached a long hook manipulated by a boy beneath the draped platform. At the proper moments, this boy pulled the helpless statue down upon its nose with a terrific jolt. Between times, this urchin played a weird flute. Preceding the float, dressed in outlandish armor and carrying every fashion of medieval weapon, marched the Roman soldiers. There went all the historic characters; the Roman centurion, the Jewish constabulary, the soldiers who diced for the seamless robe. One individual clanked a heavy chain, another skirled a *matraca* —breaking the bones of Judas; an old fellow, perspiring

89

copiously, peered over his spectacles at a text from which he chanted lugubriously. Behind him on another platform came a most piously sorrowing Mary. She was held aloft by four silk-clad Indian girls with glistening black hair and tear-streaming eyes. From the apse came the thin clamor of holy music made over into Indian monotony, the quarter notes of the Indian scale wailing freezingly, rising, breaking, sinking, then flowing into a rich mood of the long pure Gregorian intervals.

The old festivals hereabouts linger on, but the glory of the local congregations has gone with the passing of the Bishopric to Puebla, where, in contrast, one finds a people nose-pointedly religious, though in everything else they are dowdy and drowsy. Even the celebrations of Holy Week and similar festivals have, in Puebla, a note of cheap tinseled prosperity. But here, in Tlaxcala, in Panotla, everything is toned down to the *humilde* spirit of the people, incongruous if you wish, often lacking in dignity from a purely material stand-point, like this petty drama of the Three Falls; yet, though things are drowsy in all Tlaxcala, tasks, be they religious or otherwise, are done with pride, with due respect for the solidity of character that is Tlaxcalan. Blood tells.

The super-intelligent adaptability of the Tlaxcalans, coupled with their habitual integrity of spirit, has made the blend of things native and things foreign less unlovely here than in most places in Mexico. The result here seems more harmonious; the discords have been eased down into keeping with the snug little town and nation; nothing, at first sight, seems exotic. And yet even here the seething melange that is Mexico swirls and eddies in the lives of these dwellers. As everywhere else, the ingredients have not really blended. A thousand antagonistic forces are struggling, elbowing, jostling side by side. In general these forces polarize about things Indian and things Spanish. Though in some places American industrialism and haste furnish a third even more disturbing factor, refracturing the still unset bones of the social skeleton, here in Tlaxcala the general alinement is dual. The villages have two names: one Spanish, Christian; the other—Mexican, pagan: San Nicolás Panotla, Trinidad Tenexyecac. . . . But one of the two names lingers on the lips of the people—the Indian name; the other, though the pious try to keep it alive, is tacked on for special occasions. It is a holiday name, a Sunday-best name.

This cultural conflict, so glossed over here in Tlaxcala, becomes more obvious when one probes the thoughts of these people. Here, as elsewhere, the Mexican mind is bristling with the most desperate ideas—the people have porcupine minds; they are scintillating with ideas drawn from every nook and corner of the world—Europe, the Orient, Russia. A pulque shop even carries the name of a little lake in Siberia. The street that leads to the Monastery of San Francisco is called Pestalozzi; adjacent is Xicotencátl street. The discrepancy intrudes into the very speech. On the consonant-loving native tongues, the soft Spanish "aire" becomes "aigre" (as elsewhere in Mexico) suggesting "ogre" or "tiger," anything but the bland breezes that traverse this upland corner of the world. And in the hearts of the people reverberate skepticism, agnosticism, doubt of the Christian faith; in another corner of the same brain will be blind acceptance of set ritual and of all things Catholic. Don Romueldo assured me that "he wasn't anything," but when we began discussing religion with freedom, and I had convincingly proved that the Christian faith covers only a portion of the globe and stimulates but a minority of its inhabitants he waved the evidence aside with a casual "Yes, but Christianity is just about everywhere," and told me with a quick vengeful gleam in his usually gentle eyes that God had killed all the Jews, which was very good because they weren't "Christians and had crucified *Nuestro Señor*."

Superstitions, too, they have, with mild skepticism. "The ignorant say," declared Don Romueldo, "that when the *tecolote* hoots over the roof-tree the Indian dies—but that is superstition, is it not?"

I nodded.

Yet Don Romueldo shook his head a bit doubtfully and lugubriously, "Why then does the owl cry that way—perhaps after all there is some reason? Why does he cry?"

"Because he can't laugh," I replied smartly.

Don Romueldo chuckled. "I really don't believe the yarn —but still, I hope *Señor Tecolote* keeps away from my roof-tree."

Science and mechanical efficiency play a small part. Only as a last resort do families call in a licensed doctor; they go to their local *curanderos* who paste nasturtium leaves over their fevered temples, who give them native herbs—*ruda* for headaches and *romero* for skin-trouble, and *toronjil* for stomach-ache, and bright berries of the *colorín* for a diuretic. *Manita*, the red flower like "a little hand" cured heart trouble long before the scientists used digitalis.

And always the people are *humilde* with a slight ironic mockery, nothing boisterous, just a subtlety of humor that one would scarcely expect in a people close to the soil. But this attitude masks sadness.

"Once," said Don Romueldo, when he and I were on a high crest from which we could see the bright pointed summit of Malinche towering above the rolling hills of the Apam plains, "once we were resentful that Malinche, a native woman gave herself to Cortez and aided him even though we, as a people, did the same thing. But she suffered and was betrayed and crucified. Perhaps the Spaniards even crucified her on that mountain," he suggested, with a wave of his long brown hand. "She suffered the same betrayal that all the people of Mexico have suffered. We are too proud to admit our suffering; too proud to admit that we are less noble, less instructed, less wise than three centuries ago when the Spaniards first came, but in our hearts has long been the sadness of a vanishing race. But at night when the *tecolote* wails

92

over the roof-trees, bringing its tidings of death, we say that
Malinche has come again, the betrayed one, the great *Llorona*,
the crying one, who goes wailing down the night highways;
only we now bear her resentment, even though she bring
death, for we know that even death is inevitable, perhaps
there is no heaven of reward, perhaps that too is a lie. But in
spite of this sadness there is sprouting in our hearts a slow
hope; we have discovered our own persistence. Even in being
humilde we are persistent, patient—and you, all you other
people, you are not patient. We are brothers to the rocks and
the soil; we listen to the morning bray of our burros, to the
call of our fowl, to the restless feet of the river, and we
know that we shall persist; even being *humilde* we shall in-
herit the earth. You have never learned that lesson, though
you have mouthed it for centuries. We have learned it because
the iron crown of thorns has been on our brows; we have
learned it because we have been so close to the simple things.
We were proud, and we have been humbled. But we Tlaxcalans are Tlaxcalans still."

Yes, blood counts.

V AMECAMECA: TOWN OF DOOM

ONE spring day I was riding horseback northeast from the Mexican upland town of Amecameca to attend an Indian fiesta in a pueblo at the foot of Ixtaccíhuatl, the White Woman. Half way there, I was robbed by bandits, stripped to my shirt. A whole week's wait for funds in the little Sacred Mount Hotel in Amecameca. For the first two days, aside from flirting with an actress of a stranded travelling troup, there was little to do except stare desultorily from the window of my second floor room. Occasionally a funeral procession, carrying flickering candles or ocote torches passed toward the high-perched cemetery. Morning and night the gaunt shrill wind whirled over the sear upland fields. Towards each day's end the long gray-green twilight shadows deepened on the nearby Sacro Monte, a curving hill of sacred miracles on whose crest two churches notched the gloomy sky.

But on the third morning the sun came out brilliantly, and the two enormous volcanoes, Popocatépetl and Ixtaccíhuatl, towered above us—white, majestic, clear-cut in the rarified, turquoise atmosphere, seemingly close enough to be touched by the hand, yet splendidly remote. That day, walking in the town plaza or sitting on one of the carved stone benches, I watched the light dance and gleam on their lofty summits. The afternoon passed away in subdued glory. The flame on the volcanoes died slowly: amethyst, rose, heliotrope, lavender, violet. In the hushed evening, soft-sandaled Indians slipped past me in their red and blue sarapes; the town clock glowed like a full moon through the thick-clumped cypress trees. Toward the opening west country, set in a Colonial horseshoe arch, could be seen the humped outline of Sacro Monte. Its wind-bent trees marched like an attacking army, like Burnam's wood itself, against the high-perched tilted churches. In front of the big cathedral, on a mound dominating the plaza with its mongrel collection of Indians and holiday booths, with its wailing music and dancing bonfires, was a flight of stone steps leading to a triple arch of classic continence. In the flicker of the evening light, the panorama enclosed by the arch was hazy—like an incense-blackened Perugino tryptych against a crumbling wall. But the two imperial volcanoes refused to fit into this curving frame; they towered from every angle, over and above church and town. As the night deepened and the chill intensified, the lofty mountain outlines faded away—all but the gleam of the snow, two rifts of icicle blue embossing the black sky, two rifts that linger on until dawn, when the two peaks become silver, pure, hammered silver.

I have seen the sky-defiant outline of the Alps from the northern Lombard plain; I have been through the Rockies by numbers of routes; I have tramped the Apennines and the Pyrenees, and they are mountains to live with; but I know of no more intensely overpowering spectacle than these volcanoes, Ixtaccíhuatl and Popocatépetl, which lord it over the upland plain of Mexico. Fujiyama must be much the same as Popocatépetl, with its sleek, swift-rising, sunset-flaming slopes. Like Fujiyama, "Popo," the Smoke Mountain, is sacred to the native religion. Equal to it in grandeur and only second in holiness is Ixtaccíhuatl, "The White Woman." The summit of the latter is formed by three peaks that give the unmistakable outline of feet, breasts and head—a draped female figure sleeping in eternal white. Someday, say the natives, the Smoking Mountain will awaken her, and they will go away to a heaven sweeter than any known by man; for were they not once lovers, of a valiant, handsome race that has long since disappeared from earth—set above the world

by the greatest of the gods as a reminder of the glory of a time that is no more?

The lives of the quiet people of Amecameca, their simple circumscribed existence in their adobe houses, their flower-filled patios, their corn-planted *milpas*, bear the impress of their intimacy with the two mountain spirits. The late dawns, the early twilights, the lost wind-soul that wails eternally through the gap, make men shudder and children whimper. The voices of women in the low doorways sink to whispers; the children suddenly stop startled in the midst of their frolicking to glance about fearingly; men turn uneasily in their sleep and breathe deeply—for hooded witches flit in the dark; and the awful Nahuatl, the animal soul, slinks past, and black spirits ride the restless air; and the ghosts of ancient cloaked kings stalk the streets. The owls hoot over the roof-trees, and then the Indian dies—*"Cuando el tecolote llora, el indio se muere."*

The people seem singularly apart at such taut, fear-clad moments—impenetrable. And the mere flirt of a sarape over the shoulder becomes a baffling gesture. Nowhere else in the world can that gesture be imitated. It makes one suddenly look back into the abyss of centuries when the old Toltecs and Chalcas swept over these upland regions. Yes, just a gesture; but it sets this race æons apart from the rest of us; for that motion was moulded before the white man put foot on this continent: the arm and neck muscles subtly adjusted from infancy, habit irrevocably engraved and handed down from generation to generation, until now, the flaunt of a crimson sarape has become a symbol of a mystic people. It is a proud yet sad, fatalistic gesture. For there is a fatalism peculiarly Mexican—a fatalism compounded of his Oriental, Moorish, and Latin psychical heritage. Here, in Amecameca, that fatalism is stronger than in other places in the fatalistic land. Here in Amecameca a whole village has resigned itself to ultimate extinction; and the knowledge has wrought in the people an ironical ease; has built in their inner conscious-ness a frescoed chapel of assured indifference.

The very word "Amecameca" means "A town upon a town." Once the arbitrary God of the Smoking Mountain grew angered with his people and hurled poisonous smoke and burning stones and boiling lava over the llano floor, wiping them out in a single night. The legend reads that some day when these new ones that now worship at his feet grow sinful, he will bury them from sight in the same way, that they may write in eternal torment in the bowels of the earth. This de-struction is to be periodic, linked by superstition to the great fifty-two year cycle of the Nahuatl calendar. In the old days this coming of the dreaded end of the *Xiuhtonalli*—as the cycle was called—gave rise to propitiary rites to ward off the terrible catastrophe—a festival known as the *Toxiuhmolpilia*. Then the despairing Amecamecans broke their dishes, their furniture, destroyed their clothing and flung their small beloved household gods of jade and woven straw and bamboo into the stream. All the kitchen fires were put out—for of what use were all these things if the cataclysm occurred? And at sunset the sacerdotes, dressed with the insigna of the gods, made a procession up the Sacred Mount in the same manner the Aztecs had made customary up the Hill of the Star above Ixtapalapa near Mexico. The file of sacerdotes wound round and round, up and up, arriving at the hill-perched *teocalli* of Tlaloc, god of rain, exactly at midnight, which hour was determined by the position of the Pleiades. Surrounded by the breathless, fearful people, they paused there a solemn heart-breaking moment in the oppressive, still darkness. They then set to work with sticks to make new fire. If they were successful, then Amecameca was good for at least another fifty-two years. On the instant the New Fire burst forth, it was seized to light a great pyre upon which was flung a sacrificed victim. With flambeaus in hand priests and neophytes raced down the hill, with shouts of gladness, the long flames streaming, their long robes flying.

But some day the God of the Smoke Mountain will pour forth his wrath, over the Sacred Mount and the town, blotting out the waiting multitude. Long after, when the lava has cooled, Xochiquetzal, the Goddess of Flowers, and Tlaloc, the god of the rain, will come strewing white lilies and bronze violets; and the lilies will be the women breasted like the sun, and the violets will be men with tireless loins; and thus shall be created a race more splendid than has ever trod the seamed weary crust of the earth. Then Amecameca will be a kingdom of peace; then will come to this guarded nook of the world, the golden ears of plump corn and fat deer,

and the days will be filled with magic music. Then the Great
Smoke God will waken his sleeping consort, and they will
vanish from the eyes of mankind—like all things enchanted.
But until that Elysian time, the people of Amecameca live in
the shadow of imminent destruction, with ever an apprehen-
sive eye for the trailing funnel of smoke that hangs over the
vast cloudy brow of the God of the Mountain; and they
chant an ancient hymn:

> O great God of the Mountain of Smoke;
> O dweller in the Realm of the Eternal Sun;
> Be merciful to Thy People;
> Spare us yet a while;
> Not yet have our lives grown sinful;
> Spare us yet a while.

But when the morning sun strikes its silver flame upon
the two white mountains, the fears of the natives fall away;
then men walk with quick elastic stride, proudly calling
themselves the "Sons of the Smoking Mountain." At such
times a superficial brightness and business rustles like the
autumn leaves through the twisted streets. Long trains of
burros come jingling and braying down from the mountains,
dragging enormous timbers slantwise, or staggering beneath
sacks of brimstone from the crest of the crater. The lanes
echo with the clear echoing yodel of muleteers. Bent Indians
dogtrot half a day with hundred-kilo sacks of charcoal
strapped to back and brow; at night the blood-red fires of
their kilns may be seen far up on some wind-swept ridge.
The town itself is criss-crossed with deep-cleft gleaming
arroyos; streams of crystal-clear water gurgle down the center of the streets; and women in bright wondrously embroidered *camisas* scrub clothes on slabs of gray *tezontle*. Geese
scold stray pigs, and coal-eyed *niños* ride mythical bamboo
water-steeds. Then the sun-white Mountain God smiles be-
nignantly; the Sleeping Woman turns on her bier with a half-
sigh of contentment—or is it only that eternal breeze through
the cypresses?

At other times the very grandeur of these two mountains becomes oppressive. Then the people look with relief to the small Sacro Monte with its two rose-colored churches, its soft Italian profile set against the pastel-shaded sky. It would seem, at such times, that Nature had planted the Sacro Monte there at the backdoor of the town to be a kindly solace to a people knowing its ultimate doom; and indeed the goddess who once abode on its wooded slopes was less feared but more companionable than the two mountain spirits.

True, all these olden native legends were disrupted by the advent of the Spaniard and Christianity. The reckless energy of Cortez and his followers turned itself into too pragmatic channels to resign itself to drowsy awe or queer dreams of disaster. From ancient Cholula, the holy city of the snake-sheathed Quetzalcóatl, they whirled up over the enormous divide between the two volcanoes and down upon the town. The clang of their armor shattered the quiet and peace of twilight and dawn; and the breath of their virile passing still eddies here in this hollow beside the Mount of Sacred Miracles. On that Sacred Mount, the Conquistadores planted the cross of the Roman Church and the red and yellow emblem of the Catholic monarchs. The little band even swept up to the summit of Popocatépetl, the third highest peak in North America, not with any remarkable reverence, but to wrench out great chunks of sulphur from the crater, which they slid down the snowy slopes on straw *petates* in order to feed the ravenous maws of their cannon.

And even the holy Fray Martín de Valencia, one of the early twelve apostles of the Franciscan order, who took up his abode in a cave on the Sacro Monte, must have been a practical man, worshipping his abstract God in wise appreciation of means, cleverly bending the natives to his creed. In 1524 this Fray Martín de Valencia, the Superior of the Spanish province of San Gabriel, and his companions sailed from Spain and landed at the sinister Vera Cruz fort—San

Juan de Ulua. As evidence of their indomitable purpose, they walked from the coast to the plateau, skirted the Texcocan marshes, and reached Mexico within a month. Fray Valencia, "Father of the Mexican Church," though an inflexible patrician, said to have destroyed with his own hands over a hundred thousand idols, was not merely a blind fanatic. Though his burning zeal was in acid contrast to the passive native fatalism, it was not a zeal without intelligence. In Amecameca, as in so many other places, a Catholic temple rose on the site of the destroyed shrine of Tlaloc.

A native tale is told of the origin of the shrine. Muleteers from villages to the south were carrying images to be sold in Amecameca. Twice, a mule broke away and ran up the Sacro Monte to the cave. The second time, he refused to come away. On undoing his load, the muleteers found that he carried their own image of the Christ and this was deemed evidence of a divine desire for a chapel to be founded on the spot. Today it bears an inscription by the poet José Joaquín Terrazas:

Asilo dulce, soledad dichosa
Donde extasiado en religiosa calma
Olvidé la morada congajosa
Que aprisionaba en la ciudad la alma.

Sweet asylum, happy solitude
Where ecstatic in religious calm
I forgot the harsh walls
That imprisoned my soul in the city.

Above, on the crest where once stood the temple of Teteoinán, another legend has it, the Virgin Guadalupe first appeared, even prior to her advent in Guadalupe Hidalgo. But as only a thatched *choza* was built for her worship, she went off indignantly to Guadalupe Hidalgo where a magnificent cathedral was constructed, and she was honored as the national virgin of the country.

101

The Amecamecans, duly chagrined, hastened to construct a proper edifice and sent a valiant volunteer of the community to steal her back again. But though he carried her part way down the Tepeyac hill of Guadalupe Hidalgo, she soon grew too heavy to be carried farther, and mockingly returned to her place. The mortified Amecamecans redoubled their prayers and offerings and finally she relented, promising them that every year in September, on the day she originally appeared on the Sacred Hill, she would come among them again; and this, too, corresponds to a day once famous in the pagan religious annals.

The Indians soon learned to turn their worshipping feet to this church and above all to the kindly hospice of good Fray Valencia, who knew well the value of easing their pagan fears of the great Smoke God; and if he made the Christian Hell equally vivid in their hearts, he also pictured for them a paradise no less Elysian than that of the golden age of the chosen race which was to come when they should be blotted out and forgotten.

Mexico's greatest writers, from Mendieta and Motolinía to Altamirano, have chronicled the legends of the early father. He was a local Saint Francis. When praying, he ascended slightly from the ground in a dazzling halo. He once resuscitated a child "just because it had died on the road as a result of its parents having refused to baptize it." And Mendieta tells how the Fray went out every morning to say his Paternosters under a tree, to which immediately flocked thousands of birds whose eager singing woke echoes far down the hill-side, but that after he died, "they came not there again."

On the hill in his cave, now enclosed in a camarin, is his burial place; a sculptured image (that may well be of him) kneels before a glass-cased image of a miraculous Christ— *El Santo Entierro*. This image is of the pith of maize sculptured in the Tarascan manner—singularly light (one Indian

can carry it on his head), so that its frequent jerky pere-
grinations through the water-washed, wind-swept town still
console the fearing people—now that the good Fray is no
more.

Holy Week overtook me in the hotel. Pilgrims approached
the shrine of el Santo Entierro on their knees, or crawling in
the dust. They had come, as the old song *corrido*—with a
Whitmanesque flair for rhythmic names—tells us quaintly,

> "From Mexico and from Toluca,
> From Tenancingo and Pachuca,
> Amecamecans and townspeople."

Nor did they forget to come:

> "From Cuernavaca and from Iguala,
> From Zacualpan and Agangüeo,
> Those from Taxco and Tetecala,
> From Ixmiquilpan and Quetzala,
> All weeping they go,
> From Yautépec and Amatlán."

On Ash Wednesday, the miraculous Christ was lifted at
the head of a long garlanded procession which wound down
stone-hewn basalt steps and a zig-zag road to the toan, to the
wailing of Indian music: the great to-to-co-to-co-ti of the
teponaztle music of *tepehuatzin* wood, alternating with the
tan-tan of the *huëhuëtl*, a great drum, and accompanied by
the garrulous shrill melodies of the *chirimía* flute—the same
music with which they had greeted the great God of Rain
centuries ago. And in the afternoon, shrine and image serve
for the setting of a semi-pagan Passion play. Every year on
this night, the spirit of the good Saint Valencia walks abroad;
but no one knows with whom he consorts. For on this night,
Teteoinán, the Nahuatl Goddess of Cleanliness, passes over the
face of the taut earth like a cool wind, fresh from the mountain snows. The Indians hang their dirty clothes on the trees
to be blessed—queer bat-like effects among the spidery

103

branches, touched with fugitive color as the *ocote* torches of the worshippers flit along the twisting hill-paths. The goddess in her headband of thread-wrapped spindles and her broom of grass comes sweeping the earth; she cleanses the garments, purifies the air and wards off disease; and her passing lightens for many a day the leaden melancholy that hovers over Amecameca.

That night, as the hour grew late and the town clock chimed softly, lingeringly, the crowd thinned, the torches went wavering down the slopes. I slipped along up to the higher sanctuary with its Campo Santo where haphazard graves tilt and hump in the dark, and queer black crosses tumble and point at a thousand stars. There on the edge of the hill, under a writhing, wind-bent oak that leans over the steep descent, I had gazed that morning at the massive immovable mountain gods across and above the town. There, that evening, I found a tall old Indian, gnarled as the trunk by which he stood, as though both had been distorted by the torture-instruments of the Inquisition itself. He was planted with one foot on a raised grave-slab, eyes peering out across the dark at those two vast guardians, now but blue rifts floating frostily in the black fluid sky. He was muttering, muttering—perhaps an ancient prayer. . . . Like Mitya in *Brothers Karamazov* he seemed "one of those who don't want millions but an answer to their questions"—or more likely he was wrapped in pure wonderment, close to the great mystery which makes even questions superfluous.

"Great things are done," said Blake, "when men and mountains meet." True! The village of Amecameca weaves the days into simple mechanical routine; the corn sprouts in the *milpas*; the women (when the Goddess Teteoinán is not abroad) wash their clothes on the stones at the edge of the snow-cold water that ripples down from the mighty heights; the church bells call to early mass; the people gossip and jest in the stores; but I knew, as I watched that gnarled figure that here in Amecameca, for all the simple routine, even in the humblest heart, "great things are done." And I doubt not that more than one wrenched soul that night of Ash Wednesday turned away from the weird festival on the Sacro Monte with a quick pang of misgiving to consult those greater arbiters that stand so inscrutably watching the human comedy, ready to accord or chastise.

I, stranger to this place and race, will never feel the heavy clutch of foretold doom that tightens upon the hearts of these people. For me, these majestic, immovable, immaculate peaks had become a symbol of peace, that matchless peace that has no reason to doubt its own righteousness, a peace which for us mortals must remain the unattainable as surely as we value our souls—the peace of last perfection. And yet, there that night, I, too, was anxious to be reassured, anxious to see them on the morrow, as I had so often seen them— silver-white against the dawn.

But by morning the wind-spirit was wailing through the gap, rattling his bony hands against the window-panes, shaking the trees in his fleshless teeth; and an enormous belt of heaving gray cloud swirled in the east, billowed, slipped down over the thatched and tiled roofs of Amecameca in a smothering blanket. Easy to image that the final doom of the town was at last arriving!

When I said goodbye to the arrogant little actress (whose painted pouting lips and sinuous blue kimona set her a trillion miles away from this myth-magic place) and went down to the railroad station, the heavy damp had made the town im- palpable, the figment of a vanishing dream. The waiting Indians had gathered their sarapes close about their faces; passing saddle-horses moved stiffly, and the silver braid on the pantaloons of their riders returned not a gleam; the tired flat-roofed houses huddled together fantastically. Over one of them circled a lugubrious black, red-headed buzzard, a *zopilote*. The fields, where little puffs of vapor formed and reformed or scurried off among the trees, were more sear than usual.

Not until the train had swung around the Sacro Monte did I again catch a glint of sun—on a yellowing ridge, far across the llano. But the Smoke God and his sleeping consort still hid their faces in a mantle of impenetrable gray.

VI   MILPA ALTA: GRAY PEACE

MILPA ALTA—High Corn-
field—crowns the Valley of Mexico. It is a gray stone Indian
village, relieved from drabness by its weathered tiled roofs.
The town is perched on a northwest declivity of gray lava
crags, whose jagged outcroppings are crisscrossed with golden
cornfields and hit or miss rows of fantastic silver-green
maguey plants and twisted thorny cactus. The lanes zigzag
up and down steeply between lead-colored lava walls, over
patches of solid rock worn deep and smooth by the age-old
passing of countless sandal-shod feet, by cows and burros,
by goats that have left their marble-like droppings everywhere and an acrid perfume sensually disturbing, as of something pagan, festive, and all but forgotten.

Formerly, Milpa Alta, though but twenty miles from the
capital, was rather inaccessible, approachable only by a rocky
burro road, which crossed through the village from the canal-
bound town of Xochimilco, to the valley-walled empire city

of Tepoztlán. Now there is a modern macadam road, and the villagers own a cooperative auto-bus to carry themselves and products to the municipal markets. In Carranza's days, the village was a stronghold of the agrarian leader Emiliano Zapata; his rebel watchfires gleamed impudently night after night on the high ramparts of Milpa Alta, clearly visible from the National Palace, where sat the constitutional rulers of the land. Tomorrow, very likely, Milpa Alta will harbor the stone chateaux of the *nouveaux riches* of the revolution it helped to create.

But in spite of incident and change, Milpa Alta still remains a world apart.

Its people are Nahuatl Indians. They speak their own tongue, usually called "Mexican," not Spanish, which they find difficult, for they cannot pronounce "R" for which they substitute with an "L" sound, like the Chinese.

The village slides along in the groove of customs which existed long before the white-winged boats of the Spaniards hove to in Vera Cruz to set ashore the terrible white god of battle, Hernán Cortez. Why should Milpa Alta change until it has to? Its volcanoes are the same as centuries ago; so, too, its gray walls, its foot-worn paths, its living maguey and cactus fences. The same god-like sun wheels overhead; the same cold winds strike down from the heights. Habits, attuned to the smell and growth of cornfields, to the swing of the seasons, the glow of charcoal fires, still persist. The sons of the same ancient people still weave on ancient looms the old embroidered sashes or *fajas* which circle the loins of their fecundity.

Since the Conquest, new animals rub the posts of the corrals; a new ritual (but not entirely new) satisfies their religious instincts; but the same old spirits walk abroad in the night, for are there not tuftings of red and green wool on the trees at the entrance to caves? In those caves, in the spring, the wise men of the village, and all keepers of supernatural knowledge, sit down and banquet over tiny calabashes and

young corn and foods unnamed. In low voices, they determine the fate of the tender corn shoots, freshly mantling the drab earth between the gray out-croppings with delicious green. Above, on the jagged heights, known as La Lux, dwell the witches, who for fees in kind, perform good and evil deeds. Milpa Alta is still a world of animism and fateful mysterious happenings, adventurous with spiritual chance, as should be the world of any good polytheist.

Even the sharp gray stones are holy. They are potential deities, ever ready to stir, to walk abroad, or leap starwards to their brothers of the Milky Way, that path of flame left by the victorious Tezcatlipoca when he whirled over the heavens after replacing the sun in its place. For, once, the mother of gods gave birth to a silex, which so chagrined her brothers that they hurled it to earth. The fragments buried themselves in the mountain slopes of Milpa Alta; and some day the god-head of these sleeping stones will reassert itself. Milpa Alta is truly a holy place; its ways are holy ways. Why should they change?

Not that the people refuse all new things; they seize upon many of them all too eagerly, be they Christian baubles, kewpie dolls, or powder puffs. For a time such things stick out like sore thumbs from the powerful palm of the village; but in the long run, such intrusions are converted into symbols and subside with artistic deftness into the native pattern. Polytheism is receptive and accepts new gods easily and gracefully, baptizing them with slight change of garb into the existing hierarchy. The art of living is similarly tolerant. Often I have seen in pottery and weaving designs, French flags hailing from the days of the imposed Emperor Maximilian; or pagodas, telling of the Colonial Chinese-Spanish trade which passed through this village from Acapulco; or a reproduction of a futuristic modern magazine cover—yet for the most part these had been reduced to poetic Indian symbols; subdued by the abiding spirit of the place, fully harmonized with the indigenous aesthetic, which permits many bastard details to flow into a quite universal unity. A French flag, believe it or not, can be made to stand guard without artistic incongruity over the harsh features of a rain-bringing Tlaloc. The teeth of Mictlantécutli, Lord of Death, grin admirably from the center of a cross. The cross becomes a symbol of historical experience, freighted with a double consciousness of suffering; a symbol truly native. Promptly the stiff phallic rigidity of the Christian cross disappears; the machete-hewn arms curve and bulge slightly. The base expands until it suggests the human torso; the native cross becomes sensuous, pagan, living, vital. Then Death—native Death, Mictlantécutli!—He peers through the very heart of the thing, as though piercing through the essence of a soul to be conducted with his red dog to Mictlán, across the fearsome river, over the mountains jagged with sharp obsidian blades; through the ravines swept by winds that are ten thousand knives. Milpa Alta Indians could well understand Bunyan's Pilgrim's Progress, as simple people close to poverty and the caprices of nature have done the world over. Brer Rabbit and other European folk-lore personages, now have adventures in Milpa Alta with crickets and cacti, with maguey plants and stone metates. Just at first they are strange—then they grow quite at home there.

Esperanza introduced me to Milpa Alta. It is her native village. Her family still live there; so does she intermittently. During the years, Esperanza has grown portly, but once she was a sturdy country Indian girl of magnificent bearing and build. Her deep bosom; her ample, perfect shoulders; the perfect texture of her copper skin; her big black eyes and straight black hair, long drew admiring glances. An artist discovered her in the Mercedes market of Mexico City, selling some wares; and thereafter, for most of the painters of the capital, she served as model in typical native costumes. When such work was not available, she hired out as servant for more Bohemian American bachelor girls, who enjoyed native food. When neither of these things presented themselves, she retired to Milpa Alta and wove bright-hued embroidered sashes, or made spangled China Poblana dancing costumes, in great demand among foreigners. She is saving money to buy a house and garden in Milpa Alta.

In the course of the years, she acquired a child. The man was crazy to marry her, before and after; but she would listen to no proposals of marriage. Not that she is burdened with any modern theories. With her, this course was purely rational, the logical decision of one who had learned to live independently in two very divergent environments.

"I love him. I am glad to have the child. But as a husband, he would be useless. Married to me, he would soon tire of me. He is shiftless. I would have to support him. I am glad to support his child, but not him. Besides, we would quarrel because now I am accustomed to do as I please."

When Esperanza wrote to Milpa Alta that she was arriving with a child but no husband, her mother promptly disowned her. The codes of Milpa Alta and especially Esperanza's people (from one of the historic and leading families of the region) are strict. Not that couples may not live together; but at least there is a responsible man; and it is assumed that some day, when the couple can afford it, they will be properly married. Besides, except for entertainment, there is no particular cost, attached to the native marriage.

Usually the native marriage is preceded by the customary church wedding, where rings are interchanged, the golden sash is laid on the celebrants, and thirteen pieces of money are placed in the hands of the priest. Then the couple is conducted directly to the Indian bridal chamber—a special lean-to built against the side of the bride's home, provided with a new petate mat, still smelling fresh from the river reeds. Here the couple kneel and the elders exhort them to be faithful, to be industrious, to be fruitful—a rising crescendo of emotion that precipitates everybody into tears.

Esperanza has ignored these cherished ceremonies. But she

could not lose Milpa Alta. She was determined to have her child baptized in no other place. She chose several foreigners as god-parents. Generous people, they also helped to give cast to the child. Boldly, simply as a matter of course, she returned to her village. Well enough, she probably knew, she would easily sink back into the native patterns, with its limitless capacity of absorbing bastard details into its unified aesthetic. Patiently, for two days and nights, she sat on her mother's doorstep, waiting for maternal displeasure to weaken.

Traditional hospitality finally forced her mother's hand. The white foreigners arrived, and they, of course, could not be excluded. Iron-bound social custom, where foreigners are concerned, can rarely meet all contingencies. And if the white foreigners were not shocked—perhaps . . .

Anyway, Esperanza was admitted to the parental roof-tree, and tolerated. For several years she was merely tolerated. Her mother, a wiry Puritanical person, frequently reminded her daughter that she was a lost soul. But now Esperanza is past thirty, buxom and maternal, she is economically independent. She lives her own life. She is part of the pattern again.

When the baby was several months old, I began taking Aztec lessons from Esperanza. Often I joyed in the simple beauty of her nursing of the child. Without the least embarrassment, quite naturally, she unfolded her dress, exposing her lovely sculptured brown breast. The child sought the nipple with eager smacks and sucked greedily, contentedly, while Esperanza told me the "Mexican" equivalent for "I go to your house," "He goes to your house." Occasionally she interrupted to whisper endearing phrases in "Mexican" to her baby, or to give it gentle little spanks.

Esperanza took me and some friends to the religious festivals celebrated in one of the smaller churches, a gray stone Franciscan edifice with one tower shot away by cannon during the revolution.

113

Mass was supplemented by an elaborate "Dance of the Moors." The participants dressed up in regal medieval garments and wigged themselves in long black beards. One with such a long false mattress looked decidedly ferocious in a French brass helmet tufted with black horse hair, red coat, white trousers, and puttees. And he carried a French flag! Later, having removed his costume, he proved to be an exceedingly mild, gentle-faced Indian, clad in white "pyjamas" and sandals.

It was the historic combat between the Spaniards and the Moors reduced to symbolism. Actual combats were typified by three sharp clashes of opposing blades. Spanish royalty sat arrogantly in an elaborate Fourth-of-July pavillion; the Moorish kings sat glumly on native leather *icpal* chairs. Each king, in turn, was lugubriously overthrown, after long preliminaries of singing and discourse in "Mexican"—a five-hour drama.

The children, too, danced, boys and girls facing each other, in bright red kirtles and spangles; a slow weaving in and out, with simple stamping foot movements to the tune of wailing native music, without melody. The climax came with the rapid setting off of dozens of home-made *cohuetes*, or willow-shafted rockets, a deafening uproar.

Later we were taken to a private house, and fed with *atole*, a thick corn-milk gruel, and rolled *tacos*.

What a gracious formality attends all Indian hospitality! I have traveled much among the peasants of Spain and Africa, of Italy and Russia, but none equals the Mexican Indian peasant in hospitality. The Spanish peasant, perhaps, has more consciousness of his essential manhood; he can be arrogant and self-assured in beggardom; but none possesses the exquisite Oriental courtesy of the Mexican lower classes. One might consider this an indication of long oppression, a hypocritical self-protecting device for treating outsiders, did they not treat each other with the same grave dignity.

In our wordless ignorance, we must have seemed a bit

boorish to these poor, illy-clad people. The stranger is welcomed to the Indian house with a series of formal addresses, which are then replied to in similar formal phrases, with a long clasp of hands and a deep searching glance of eyes. I cannot reproduce the words, and they lose some of their dignity, even when spoken in Spanish, but they run something like this: "It gives me deep pleasure to receive you in this, our humble house. This dwelling is poor and inadequate for the honor you have shown in visiting it. But we place ourselves and all we have at your disposition. You have but to command, and everything within our power will be done

to fulfill your wishes." And the polite person (which none of us were) replies: "We are sensible of the great courtesy you are showing us. It is enough that you desire us to come; your generosity and cordiality have already more than repaid us for our visit. We ask nothing but the privilege of conversing with you and feeling the warmth of your friendship."

Soon Esperanza led us up to the zig-zag shelvings, between the lava walls overhung with yellow *tejocote* fruit, to the main church with its communal well and stone Tlaloc, graced with geranium and calabash vines (the latter a sacred flower among the Nahuatls). We went on past open doorways, odorous with fruit and chili and fresh leather. In one a group of men were sitting around a terra cotta vat of wild honey, pungently sweet. Twisting the honey on to clean sticks they thrust them into their mouths—as though committing suicide with beams of golden sunlight.

We reached the stone house of Esperanza's family. Here in the smoky interior, sat her mother, like some sorceress in a circle of red ollas with simmering strange brews. Before her was a *metate*, a grinding stone hewn from lava, for making corn tortillas which she was busily toasting on a tin *comal*.

Horrors! Our atole and tacos had been but a *merienda*—a light repast. We were obliged to sit down to a table spread with native green glass and glazed red terra cotta dishes, decorated with animals and flowers. Again we gorged, the *piece de resistance* being *mole de guajolote*, turkey cooked in some twenty spices.

We left in the twilight, clambering down the stone lanes. Soft-sandaled feet slid past us in the semi-dark, and a musical *"Buenas noches"* came from shadowy figures, dusky faces indistinguishable under broad sombreros. The gray of Milpa Alta became a caressing velvet. The air was a balmy liquid that flowed about us like some sea perfumed with spices. The animals made homely sounds in the corrals. Far below us lay the vast bowl of the Valley of Mexico; and in its hollow, glowing like a mass of living coals—Mexico City, another world. In that world one found everything of note called modern: there were its rushing lighted streets; its restaurants and saloons and cafés; luxury riding on cushions through an atmosphere tainted with dust and smoke.

Here in the peace of this upland village, for one with somewhat jaded city appetites, it became quite too easy to sentimentalize, to romanticize over these Indian peasants in their stone-walled dirt-floor dwellings, sleeping simply on woven *petates*. Certainly poverty exists in Milpa Alta; sanitation is left to God; and superstition rules these souls; black magic abounds, and spirits dwell in every tree. Yet whatever physical and intellectual limitations rule their existence, a quiet grace adorns these lives, never swept into the stream of what the world calls progress. The dwellers of Milpa Alta do not argue with their own quaint beliefs; they are willing to call all outsiders "*gente de razón*—reasoning beings"; they prefer, simply, to live, leaving logic to habit. There is a beauty of daily existence we can never know. Life swings through its elemental cycles; the blood answers the rhythm of the days and the rhythm of the seasons. Milpa Alta stirs with the chickens; it sleeps at the fall of night. There is a true inwardness of spirit in the people; they are content with little, even in the way of food. They will spend hours making beautiful things which have scant market value. There is pride of workmanship. There is the satisfaction of working well with simple tools and materials, of creating objects which require much calm and patience. The people have fortitude. They are not weighted down by a frenzied desire to improve their standards of living. They are not envious of those endowed with this world's goods. They are not burdened with consciousness of their poverty as is the European peasant; they do not fret because they do not sit in the social sun; nature's sun is sufficient.

Is this too placid an existence? Perhaps. Yet they are far happier, I am convinced, than a New York office clerk, cogged in eight hours of routine, flinging his pleasure into evenings that have no coordination with his day or his tasks. The American lives in compartments of uncorrelated action. The Mexican peasant's life is one texture. Work is pleasure; and pleasure is work. The day, for him, is woven into a unity, satisfying in its completeness.

Is this too animal an existence? Certainly it is elemental, but not animal. The Indian's handicrafts, his love of mystery, his courtesy, his fearsome poetic awe of all things on the face of nature—these tasks and emotions are, as far as we know, not animal in their nature. He asks little of the universe and receives much.

His island universe, probably, is doomed to extinction— and soon. Yet somehow, sometime the world will have to re-

discover, in new form, the essential values which he knows
and cherishes. Essentially his is a far richer world than the
world of automobiles, radio sets, telephones, and busy social
preoccupations. Sixty miles an hour may mean a sluggish
mind, unseeing eyes, and a dead soul. Gasoline speed carries
no nobler aims than does the Milpa Alta burro. We Americans are interested in new toys; the Indian peasant is interested in new beauties. Our lives are largely external; his is
indwelling. He needs no religion because he lives religion. We
put our religion into a compartment. Work is one compartment, pleasure is another, religion is another. But for the
Indian, work, pleasure, mind, home-life—these are all part
and parcel of a religious experience. Perhaps, when we are
wiser, when time has stabilized our mad rush for progress,
the gewgaws of our frenzied industrialism, for which we
now sweat and slave, will become as beautifully commonplace as the petate of the Indian; perhaps they will sink into
a cultural pattern, giving background to our lives but not
absorbing them, rather freeing them. Now, we are more enslaved than poverty-stricken Milpa Alta.

The machine age gives little promise as yet that the work
of our lives will ever provide us with creative passion; perhaps instead of allowing ourselves to be enslaved to disagree-
able routine which permits of no individualized expression,
in time we will finally master the machine and relegate it to
a more automatic process, requiring little extended attention
from the mass of human beings. Perhaps we can then dedicate
ourselves to creative tasks, which will prove more satisfying
even than those of the Indian. Perhaps, on a more sophisticated plane, we can recapture what our age, for the present,
has lost, and which the Indian knows instinctively. Until
then, were I not already the slave of the machine, I should
prefer Milpa Alta.

There is something Oriental in the Indian, at least in his
patience, his renunciation of too much worldly endeavor; yet
there is also something more truthful and wholesome in his

life than in that of the East. We Americans shut out the roaring tide of life by externals, by living outside of our bodies and minds, by conquering nature instead of ourselves; the Oriental escapes the roaring tide of life, by shutting out the world, by conquering himself instead of nature. But the Indian lives close to the spirals of nature itself. There is a healthy interpenetration of himself and nature. The American lives for the future, he divides his life into time units; the Oriental destroys time; the Mexican peasant is time, in its Bergsonian fluid essence. The American is practical, the Oriental metaphysical; the Indian poetical. We live for action; the Indian for aesthetics; the Oriental for thought or religious ecstasy. The super race, perhaps, will be that which combines all three successfully. Action is birth; aesthetics is content and form; abstract thought is death. All three might make the rounded culture. Perhaps no people can achieve such a culture permanently. Perhaps, rather, for a brief moment in their history, this is the gift of all peoples whose careers are not aborted.

Returning in the soft lingering twilight of Milpa Alta down a winding path, where echoed the laughter of a group of girls in bright dresses hurrying among the straight dark trunks of some willow trees, we met a shepherd with a live lamb hanging about his neck, exactly after the fashion of a relief of Hermes, protector of flocks, that I once saw in the Barraca Museum in Rome. The shepherd was standing on a high ledge, patient in his strength, outlined against the gray shimmering sky.

Here was a man untouched by the spirit of Oriental renunciation, by the spirit of struggle in the ideal meaning of the word, by scientific understanding, or by conscious creative effort. Thus most of the human race lives. And yet, in this man's life, even in its ignorance, its limitations, its lack of self-consciousness, undoubtedly plays the whole gamut of racial and emotional aspiration. The lives of such as he are unconsciously closer to the fourth level of human activity than are those of many who strive for creative comprehension and achievement. The round of existence for this lone shepherd is instinctively creative, one piece with the life-stream that flows through the centuries, fundamentally unruffled by political upheavals. In this stream is snuffed out the smoky torch of renunciation. Its waters flow with immutable serenity over the violence of the too-ambitious and over the bloody struggles of those who clutch at power. Science and learning cannot alter its fundamental routine or change its eternal rhythm. And in this stream we all have birth. To this stream, when our conscious creative striving has scouraged us down some bitter cul-de-sac, we all return. Here is the current on which civilizations drift to their cyclic destinies. From the rooted life of men close to the immediacies, to the elementals, to the soil, great leaders step forth, great families arise; and to this simpler realer world, their grandsons and great grandsons return. So it was with Benito Juárez, the great Indian leader and shepherd from Oaxaca; so it was with Ruben Darío, the Nicaraguan poet, who blossomed from the homely soil of Metapa.

We stood only one last minute in the soft night of Milpa Alta. Far across the plain streamed the lights of a train—at this distance a toy train; the moon silvered the crest of Ixtaccíhuatl, the White Woman. Nearer at hand were the dark outlines of five truncated cones, attesting to the violence which had prepared the peace of Milpa Alta aeons ago. Came autos snorting up the hill road, attesting to violence to come. For even peace, it seems, must be struggled for in some form. The battle for peace is the most terrible of all battles. But Milpa Alta, for the present, knows nought of this.

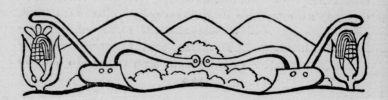

VII TEPOZTLAN: THE LIFE AND LEGEND OF A PUEBLO

1

MY HORSE carried me from
the railroad station of El Parque along a mountain skyline
that commanded the majestic panorama of the Mexican state
of Morelos. After a few miles the trail dipped sharply around
the brow of the rocky range, and I dropped down, down
among pines to the town of Tepoztlán, a glowing gem, set
in a circle of embattled cliffs at the head of a long sweep of
wedged-in valley-floor. Though I had just descended thousands of feet, the village seemed perched at the tip-top of the
world; for it looks down through enormous volcanic gates
upon the vague haze of the city of Cuautla and the wide
meadows of the Yautépec River. Far beyond, across the vast
sun-sweltering llano, the state of Morelos fades into Michoacán and Guerrero, and both fall away to the Pacific. Tepoztlán, the mistress of this untamed empire, is throned on basalt,
robed with the royal purple and gold of her imperishable
heights and with the green of her lavish vegetation.

The very next morning, before daybreak, I climbed the

broken mossy tower-steps of the cathedral (one of the seven crumbling local churches) and edged across the roof, a veritable sea of spherical angles, to the massive battlements of this huge structure, that so defiantly sneers down on town and plaza. I gazed out at the distant mountain darkness, edged with gold, soon shivering into color. A clinging mist mantled the dim valley lands in silver folds. As the light filtered through the rifts of vapor toward Cuautla, as purple faded to blue, to rose, to amethyst, the fog magically vanished, leaving in its wake shimmering gray pools that changed to skeins of silver cob-web quivering among the chinampa and mango trees thick-clumped about the brown adobe houses. The mountains still loomed dark and ominous; distant black clouds scowled over their jagged turrets. Suddenly the world grew lighter, an uncanny tremulous pallor—lyric with pregnancy of day. The sun leapt out—a hot round disk, shedding an almost insupportable dazzle over valley and height. El Cerro, the high-flung crag that spires directly back of Tepoztlán, reflected a ruddy flame from its crystal facets and from the broad band of stone where stands the ruined carved temple planted on that burning crest ages ago by Tepozteco, patron god of the town. The Cyclopean mountain walls gleamed with a hundred delicately erratic tints. The morning glowed.

The cathedral roof becomes oppressively hot. Down in the shaded cobbled streets, in the damp, leaf-massed gardens, in the sleeping plaza, it is cool. I lie on my back in the tall grass among dandelions, gazing at the azure sky. The hours glide by like a song. By ten o'clock the mist drifts back along the face of the far cliffs. I watch El Cerro; its glow fades. Billowy milk folds shroud it like some pagan shaman. The serried rocky summits of the encircling mountains look like turbaned Hindus. The vapour settles lower and lower. The bronze naked precipices become completely cloaked in full-flowing snowy caftans; and the peaks, gleaming all morning in the sunlight, are blotted out.

The mist crawls nearer, envelops the village, turns into rain. Not a dark drizzle but a cleansing shower, opalescent with faint pallor from the hidden sun. The slanting needle-shafts of water scintillate; the shower glistens, like a tune that plays brightly and yet sadly, between smiles and tears.

The rain has spilled itself out; and mist has disappeared. Noon sun beats hot upon me; and Tepoztlán steams; the earth smokes, exhaling long undulating scarves of whitish moisture. The black soil stirs beneath the blazing rays; strange things worm into life; taking shape as out of prim-ordial chaos; the corn leaps inches; the mangos turn golden, and fall; the bamboo shudders; and the chayote vines wrap eager tendrils about trellis and branch.

In the afternoon puffy clouds advance along the high horizon, in fantastic confusion; purple shadows fall upon Tepoztlán, bloated monsters with myriad arms. Gradually the clouds expand into yeast-like masses that churn in the heavens, then flow into one consistency of gun-metal gray. A wind shreds the trees; the cliffs ring like a bell; and at twilight *"el agua viene"*—water is upon Tepoztlán again; this time, hammering floods of it, a storm of Titanic spite. Awed, I stand under the cavernous arcades of the cathedral sacristy, staring out across the round burial grounds at the jagged storm-shaken heights. Livid arms clutch at the throats of the mountains; long lances tipped with fire dart through the night. The battle extends. Sheets of flame ripple around the horizon; the thunder of smashing clouds descends in avalanches of terrorizing uproar upon the plaza. The bold stone escarpments of the mountain seem outposts of destruc-tive malice, as if Tepozteco in his impregnable teocalli on El Cerro had seized, in his mailed fists, sheaves of lightning, and boulders of thunder, and buckets of boiling oil-like water to hurl upon the huddling valley-dwellers—bent upon destroy-ing his people. The storm swoops across the plaza, across the graves, full upon me. I cower under it.

But the straight-stemmed, taciturn Indian, wrapped in his

mystic red sarape, hidden under his broad sombrero, stands under the straw decked *ramadas*, motionless, like a rooted tree, suffering, unafraid, noble. He knows that this destructive upheaval is only illusion, drama; that ages ago the great god Tepozteco lifted these granite walls to protect his people. Tepozteco's mountain phalanxes, in their castle-like rock formations, are interposing dun-studded shields to the thunderbolts and the lightning; his eagles are tearing the storm clouds into tatters. Tepozteco is there, battling for the town, saving it. The solemn Indian knows that these ringing crags have made Tepoztlán, have protected it, have drawn from the turquoise skies from time immemorial the floods which make this tight-woven, casket-shaped valley an eternal Eden.

2

Tepoztlán is scornful of outsiders. It boasts of no hotel, no restaurant, no doctor, though every other place of its size in Mexico would have all these things. Tepoztlán is content with the venerable ways of its fathers. The people cling proudly to their ancient gods, their old medicine-men. They weave the simple fleeting moments of their lives into intimate local legends dithyrambic with poetry and color. Tepoztlán is a

Mexican Florence. It exemplifies the classic unities; it breathes of the city-state tradition; Aristotle would not be lost here.

The people of Tepoztlán—Nahuatls they are, cousins to the intrepid Aztecs—claim to be a race of princes, descended from the gods. They are unwilling to admit their lives are shaped by force and historic tides not of their own will. But their checkered history is shattering their illusions. The past, though it had its glories, has left deep scars upon Tepoztlán. In the days when Tepozteco planted his triumphal temple on the high windy edge of the beetling crags of El Cerro, Tepoztlán, though the proud ruler of many cities, nevertheless had to beat off enemy after enemy. She suffered from war and plague and death. The present is no kinder. In these years her closed basalt walls have served as a vast crucible for tragedy. These walls have become fused through and through by the hot blasts of combat and revolution, or have resounded with sporadic inbursts of so-called modern progress. Kinship with the gods has not saved Tepoztlán from "the fell clutch of circumstance."

The seven churches, the great symbols of Spanish conquest, are scars. They mar the even tenor of the valley; they break the velvet contour of tree and meadow and rock. But for the churches, a traveler along the mountain crests might pass this valley by, knowing not that a village lay in its compact depths, for the low house-roofs are humbly concealed; the shivering palm, the bellying banana fronds, the writhing honey-suckle vines, the chirimoya trees, cast a green mantle over the town. But the old Spanish churches, gray, cracked, somber, poke their staggering campaniles above the restless sea of plant life. Even the lofty cathedral, if viewed from some distant height, for all of its majestic proportions, seems like a welt left by the lash of some lightning-whip; viewed closer at hand, like a fantastic animal humping its turret-shaggy back, crouched to spring upon the village, but frozen into impotent rigidity.

These seven churches are deserted now. Though they once

promised to bring religion, art, and exaltation, yet they never integrated the lives and habits of the people; now they are but hollow shells. Tepoztlán seems eternal, determined to last forever, but the old Spanish churches crumble. Their interiors are smoked and shattered by the blasts of twenty years of revolution; their walls are broken, rotting with moss and weeds. Bats gibber in the chapels, scorpions creak in apse and transept. The Spanish churches are scars.

Walking down the steep cobbled streets along the stone walls shaded by century-old plum trees, I find more recent mutilations: houses blackened, falling, crushed—though over these the quick gourd and chayote and trumpet vines have flung concealing arms. For Tepoztlán—peaceful, continent, industrious Tepoztlán—strangely enough, became the very breeding ground of the long Mexican revolution; and the storms and counterstorms of war all but wiped it from the face of the earth. Here Indianism suddenly uncoiled itself and thrust out its hot fangs at Porfirismo, at industrialism, at the mestizo-ruled nation of which it is physically a part. Here the Zapatistas plotted and swarmed and swept over the mountains on their wiry ponies, mammoth felt sombreros bent low over saddle-bows, racing quirt and spur and cry of liberty down upon Cuernavaca, upon Cuautla, upon Yautépec. And down upon Tepoztlán swept khaki-clad Federals. During the time of Carranza, the terror struck Tepoztlán. Men were dragged from their beds and murdered, houses were smashed like paper bags, and horses were stabled in the chapels of the main cathedral. Cannon answered the thunder of the crags and even an aeroplane or two frightened the eagles of the Nahuatl gods and the sons of the Nahuatl gods.

There are even newer scars—only some men call them symbols of progress. But to me this progress is so alien, so utterly apart from the town's real existence—from this Tepoztlán so proudly different. There is a white-washed "Biblioteca Pública" glaring among the green mangos, vaunting on its painted shelves the "Dialogues" of Plato and "Don

Quixote" and "Les Précieuses Ridicules" of Molière. And
near the plaza a galvanized roof has made its appearance, and
barbed wire in the park, and bottled beer in the *cantinas*.
And here and there an Indian slips past in corduroy and in
cheap "Excelsior" shoes instead of in comfortable "pyjamas"
and easy, thong-bound *guaraches*. Serenading lovers forget
the old Indian *canciones* and sing cheap popular tunes:

> *Si Carranza se casa con Villa,*
> *y Zapata con General Obregón,*
> *si Adelita se casa conmigo—*
> *pos se acabara la revolución.* . . .
>
> If Carranza would marry Villa
> and Zapata General Obregón,
> if Adelita would marry me,
> why, revolution would be gone. . . .

Even Bolsheviks! They make parades and wave blood-red
banners and shout the names of Lenin and Trotsky and
"Libertad ó Muerte", fully believing that Liberty is something you can carry home in a little wooden package.
"Chivos"—"Goats"—my eighty-year-old friend Don Vicente calls them and sneers in Nahuatl and laughs. He is a
bitter Porfirista, a lover of the good old times of Díaz. But
Don Vicente has known what revolution means. Twice he
was stuck up before a firing squad for refusing to be a
Zapatista and once for refusing to be a Carranzista. His house
was burned and two of his sons murdered; yet he has lived
through it all with a tang of humor and the courage to
rebuild his home and plant new crops. . . .

3

Don Vicente's youngest son, eighteen-year-old Wenceslao,
and I hired horses, not too *briosos*; but even the few jolts and
spirals proved a primitive wooden saddle to be a poor
protection against the sharp-ridged spine of my beast. We

filed over the divides toward Yautépec, galloped down into
a sea of valley-fog, crossed a stream in a wild hoof-flung
shower, visited an hacienda where seventy thousand pesos
worth of sugar-refining machinery lies rusting under the
open sky, then cantered leisurely back in the heat of the day.
On the outskirts of Tepoztlán we swung off our horses before
an adobe *jacal* where a wrinkled Indian sat smoking a bamboo
pipe in a low, vine-tangled doorway. To his cheery *"Buenos
días"*, I replied in the quaint Nahuatl: *"Tehuantin n' apiz-
miqui*—we are hungry."

The gentle response: *"Axcan quena*—now naturally. . . .
It is the hour of meal-taking. . . . Come in . . . and see
my lovely garden and I shall give you some flowers and
plums . . . and we shall eat."

I asked about things *mexicanas*, things native. "Who can
tell me stories and legends in the Nahuatl tongue?"

He shook his white head sadly. "The *viejos*, who knew
those things, have gone. Even our language, since the revolution, is *muy champurrado*—hashed up. These have been
hard times. The rebels burnt my house and livestock. For
seven long years I hid in Hidalgo. Now I've come back.
Yet things aren't what they used to be. Everything is
changed, everything. Our young men have ridden in the
revolution. Our families are scattered—like mustard-seed."
He waved his gnarled brown hand. "We love our Tepoztlán,
and we are sad, for the old life is no more."

But the old Indian is wrong. The past is assertive. Its
beauty is continually stirring beneath the newer crust. The
sound of rushing waters, the tinkle of cow-bells, the crisp
pat-a-pat-pat of tortillas in the early morning, the whisk of
soft sandals on the stones, the great shadow of the ever-
spiring cliffs—these things are of the very blood of the people,
part of a fine-textured, centuries-old existence. Something
in the people, the traditions, the integrated setting, is remoulding the community life to its old-time unity. In other

places in Mexico, the Spanish language, the Church, the Roman-Spanish code unifies the people. But here things Indian give coherence; here, this cupped-in valley compels unity. For Tepoztlán and its dwellers to survive—now that the wounds of conquest and revolution are being healed—the things of the outside world, the modern oil-can progress and mechanical perfection, must be woven gradually and appropriately into the native social texture, which is lovely and classic as the blue and gold bead work (*mullo*) that the women weave with their deft brown hands.

The old life intrudes into the language. If the Indian tongue is *champurrada*, so is the Spanish; both are in the melting pot, waiting the birth of a true Mexican speech which some day will emerge not only in Tepoztlán but in all Mexico. And the old life intrudes into things Christian. A hulky cross in the shattered Campo Santo of the cathedral (where the Zapatistas pawed around for buried gold) has, on the ends of its arms, pagan dogs' heads snarling at the would-be defiler of the remains that it guards. Another cross bears the carved relief of the Nahuatl god of death, frowning between Christian palm-leaves. Upon the soft brown, sandstone facade, with its carved stuccoing, may be seen Aztec symbols; the sun, the stars, lightning-darts. The Virgin Mary stands upon the moon, not in pious medieval fashion, but in the Aztec manner of an earlier goddess. The stiff cubic formality of the wings of the angels is reminiscent of the humming-bird feathers on the shanks of the white-faced Toltec god Quetzalcóatl.

The Padre, a sympathetic studious man, who thinks more of his eighty-five year old mother in Mexico City than of his parish, shakes his head sadly over the prospects. "Behind the most popular altars, I find the idols of ancient gods. What am I to do? If I take them away, the offerings cease, the people depart. The last time I was off in Mexico City, old Doña Rosa of Santiago (a nearby pueblo) dreamed that Tepozteco had come back to his ancient temple on El Cerro. So the villagers made a pilgrimage. Of course they did not find him. A half-witted boy here, a sort of Velasquez' Bobo, of whom they are much in awe and whom they superstitiously call El Tepozteco, said the god was on the eagle-crag on the opposite side of the Valley. So they made another pilgrimage. You see, even here we have our story of Moses and the golden calf, however . . . time . . . time . . ."

But he speaks doubtingly, sorrowfully, for this, his church, has had nearly four centuries, yet stands bleak, half-empty, walls stained, the graves torn up for treasure and the bones scattered about, the courtyards ill-kept—a mere handful of melancholy worshippers beneath the battered Franciscan arches.

My Indian friend, old Don Vicente, told me the story of the Tepozteco pilgrimage after his own fashion: how the villagers flocked up the slot-like trail to El Cerro beating their *teponastles*, Indian drums, and chanting magic charms. And added he:

"We went to pray for rain."

"And did the rain come?"

"Ah, yes. In three days a great tempest that made the hills rock—Tepozteco, laughing . . . laughing . . ." Then, darting me a quick glance of mistrust, he added at a breath. "Tepozteco told us to buy a new jeweled robe for the Virgin to replace the one the impious bandits stole during the revolution." Mumbling something about "Christ, our King", he hurriedly shuffled away, his manzanita cane tapping on the flaggings.

Another day he told me of treasure, the fabulous treasure of Tepozteco buried under the temple. He drew his coal-black brows down over his gleaming eyes and, leaning tensely forward, pointed a long bony finger at me and said in a dark mysterious whisper: "Sapphires there are, and emeralds, and rubies, and flying wheels of beaten gold, and chains of silver." His voice sank lower: "But no man dares touch it; the spirit of Tepozteco jealously guards it eternally."

4

Not until Wenceslao and I struggled up the steep trail to El Cerro did I get the full story of the hero-god who had saved the town from its enemies. The stone cliffs, but an arm's width on either side of the trail, leaned in upon us, ready to clap together and imprison us forever, along with Tepozteco's treasure, as in some fantastic Arabian night's tale. A golden-green macaw screamed at us from a sapote tree. The narrow gorge dripped moisture. The walls were matted with moss and ferns and aerial plants; the tree trunks were bursting with scarlet fungus; the coffee berries glowed like rubies. Above us stood Tepozteco's three silent body-guards—three crags shouldering the turquoise heavens. Ahead loomed the huge boulder which Tepozteco used for grinding his corn. The hardened remnants of his *maza*, still waiting super-human hands to pat them into tortillas, were massive knobs of granite and chrysolite which protruded from the canyon walls. Crowning all, aloft on the summit, his pyramidal, stone-carved temple! And I pictured the ancient days, the Indians staggering up this tortuous trail under the weight of enormous slabs of stone for that monument to their patron god, a long file winding up to that towering apex, dark against the dawn.

Fired by this shrine of his fathers, Wenceslao told me the story of Tepozteco and his temple. "Tepozteco was born of a virgin. His father was the frolicksome god of the wind. The mother, hard put to keep track of such a spouse, in her shame left the baby in a maguey plant to be devoured by wild animals, in a maguey plant she left him." Wenceslao's dexterous hands, as he uttered the quaint Nahuatl repetition of phrases, suggested the gentle enfolding. "Next she placed Tepozteco in an ant-hill. But the ants covered him up and fed him, the ants they fed him. At last she flung him into the river. Tepozteco turned into a bright blue fish. An old man hooked him out. Tepozteco turned back into a baby. The astonished fisherman adopted him."

Wenceslao paused to roll a corn-husk cigarette and went on to tell how in those days the kings ate old men. The time came when Tepozteco's protector was demanded for the pot. The old man "tore his long white hair in despair; he tore his hair." Tepozteco, now a stalwart lad, insisted out of gratitude on going in his godfather's stead. He was led "up and up and up the mountain trails" to the king's palace. The king was enraged when he saw Tepozteco instead of the old man, but nevertheless ordered the youth cast alive into the boiling pot. Three times the royal chef scampered to the pot to serve up Tepozteco. Three times the royal chef lifted the lid and blew away the steam. The first time, he jerked back from the snarling head of a tiger; the second, a hissing snake; the third, Tepozteco himself, laughing and unharmed. Now kings are impatient. His Majesty ordered Tepozteco brought in immediately and swallowed him at one gulp. But Tepozteco found the king's stomach a dark and dismal hole, so with a sharp obsidian blade, he cut his way to liberty.

"He was pursued down many valleys, down many valleys they chased him." And the quaint aeteological account told how, near Cuernavaca, he threw away his mirror, and a wide lake spread out before the feet of his pursuers, a lake that glistens there to this day. Again hard-pressed, he flung away his hair-brush, and a mighty forest hid him from sight. The third time, he threw away his comb, and amber-hued ribbed cliffs sprang up, these very cliffs which overlook Tepoztlán century after century, "these very cliffs on which we are now lying."

And indeed these splintered crags do spire up like the teeth of a gigantic comb that shreds the thick clouds into rain and the blue sky into shadows.

Wenceslao cupped his chin in his hand and stared out over

the sun-weltering empire towards the violet mountains, mile after hazy mile beyond distant Cuautla. Then, reverently raising his arm toward the crumbling shrine, he continued his story:

Ages ago it was that Tepozteco built his temple here where it overlooks the village in the snug valley below. Under his guidance Tepoztlán became conqueror. Then came the hosts of her seven vassal cities, "galloping . . . galloping . . . galloping over the hills with hoofs of thunder to destroy Tepozteco's power." They hammered the pillared base of the cliffs and cried out tauntingly: "Of dust and earth art thou, oh thou who dwellest in the mountains of the wind; and to dust and earth we shall return thee."

Tepozteco shouted back his joyous defiance and hurled his lightning at them; and, frightened, "they rode away, the seven vassals, they rode away. . . ."

Regretfully Wenceslao and I bade farewell to Tepozteco and his temple and dipped down to Tepoztlán. That night El Cerro was a flaming beacon, for once a year the villagers light up the soaring crested height in honor of their vanished but still potent protector, who, properly propitiated, will some day return in person to his despoiled people.

The night after, a Saturday night, I witnessed the elaborate annual fiesta in Tepozteco's honor. There in the plaza under a *ramada* of ash-branches, among the candles and peanut venders, and the dried meat of open-air butcher shops, and starving curs, and silent Indians, we waited for the twilight storm to spend its fury and the festival to begin. All around us the lightning flashed, and the silhouette of the mountain danced in our eyes with jagged brilliance. Then darkness and rain, and the glimmer of an *ocote* torch in the hands of a *rebozo*-hooded woman hurrying across the wide plaza in front of the cathedral. The cathedral itself loomed large and sinister, its bell-tower sticking up like a black finger. Earlier I had attended mass the Padre gave to the almost empty nave. He had hoped that litanies and candles

134

and incense and his holy procession before all the saints would dampen the Indians' zest for the pagan festival. He refuses to realize that the rites of Tepozteco have more vitality than all the ceremonies of the mouldering church.

When the Spaniards came to these parts, they tilted the stone image of Tepozteco from his high temple. A delegation of Catholics met with the native king and his priests in the holy place. The Catholics argued that this stone image was not a god at all. "Throw it over the cliff, and you will see that it will break. Has a god power if he can be pitched over a cliff and broken?"

The Indians acquiesced, because they had to; but they knew that Tepozteco was as powerful as his rock-ribbed mountain; that he would punish his defilers. In spite of their protests, the monolith was dragged from its stone platform and hurled crashing into the gashed ravine. But Tepozteco did not break; he settled heavily and whole among the houses below.

The Catholics then sawed him in four, each piece being used as a cornerstone for the cathedral.

Tepozteco was quick to revenge the insult. For days he could be seen burning in the clouds, now as a serpent, now as a tiger, occasionally as a man—his three-fold form. White worms gnawed the maize roots. Drouth struck a flat fevered hand on the valley. The crops perished. And the church was obliged to bow to Tepozteco being worshipped on the same day as the madonna.

The bleeding Christ and the holy madonna of the high altar are now almost abandoned. Here in the rain-ragged plaza stands the whole village, every eye fixed on the lofty central pavilion where is to be enacted the drama of Tepozteco. The rain is over; the spectacle begins. Tepozteco (a tall lithe Indian) and his followers, armed with sheathes of arrows and beating their drums, mount the pavilion. Its red and green bunting bellies in the wind and catches agile serpentines of light. This high platform is El Cerro brought into the plaza—the god's ancient throne, his temple, and his fortress. Once more Tepozteco is reënthroned, in the eyes of his people. The warriors of the seven vassal city states, bells jangling on their steeds, whirl through the dark, shouting curses and raining blows with sharp copper machetes against the high wooden supports of the pavilion—as of old, they hammered the base of the cliffs. The god and his guards drive them off with fire-arrows and mocking words; and the eagles of Tepozteco whirl down with beak and claw. The last retreating hoofbeats die away in the wet pulsing night. The victorious Tepozteco and his cohorts stamp a wild exultant dance on the rocking floor to the galloping thunder of drums that had been before ever Cortez crossed the seas in his white-winged boats. The dancers shout; their short green and scarlet tunics jerk and glow in the flame of pine-fed braziers; the bronze faces flame with conquest. . . .

The spectacle on the pavilion has merged into the vast setting; the last great glimmer of lightning running around and around the high horizon; the rain dripping from the roofs; the *ocote* torches flashing in the dark; the huge cathedral, somber, sinister, at our backs; and men shaken and scarred by years of fiery revolution, standing there, solemn, silent, tense, only occasionally breaking into low-voiced comment. . . .

5

Tepoztlán is not merely "another village." It is a place with a tempered soul, with an iron-forged, beauty-moulded past. Here between its gargantuan, beetling, overshadowing mountains, here at the head of its sweeping valley floor, here looking down upon Cuautla through its Cyclopean basaltic gates, it broods over its legends, its traditions, its history. The sandal-shod Indians stand solemnly erect or slip past softly. Life flows on quietly, restrained, self-sufficient. The people plan and work and play. They go on simply, fulfilling their destinies, building their adobe houses, planting their corn, picking their fruit with long bamboo nippers, combatting the pests, raising their babies and telling them strange sweet stories; and when they are sick in flesh or in soul, the *curanderos* stroke their limbs with magic eggs, rub their bodies with thyme and sweet-smelling herbs, and send them out to lay their foreheads in the grass and stones of far canyons; and they get cured and come back and tend their gardens and their tinkling herds.

In the quiet *huertas*, glistening with chirimoyas and plums, under the leafed ramadas, in the lee of cactus fences, down the brooding vistas of vine and lane, are sun and shade, the sun and shade of the overpowering grandeur of the spot in which they dwell; the easy-going picturesque life; the shadows of the wheeling eagles of Tepozteco; the shadow of alien culture that ruffles their inner harmony and sullenly struggles for its place. And the freshly seared scars of revolution! And the ugly touch of modernity! These brusque, uprooting factors are well concealed, but bit by bit the stoic, stark independence of the inhabitants is becoming darkly overcast. In the brimming cup of their normal unaffected lives whirls the backwash of the tempest of the changing world. They feel subtly, uncomprehendingly, the tug of these conflicting influences; yet they little realize how much they are the puppets of grotesque gigantic forces, forces that are shaking them down into that enormous bag which the giant Destiny carries upon his shoulder for the seeding of the vast fields of some future epoch.

Tepoztlán! Will you be as self-sufficient, as heroically beautiful a hundred years from now? If I read the god-like palm of your destiny aright, you will forever cherish your traditions and your loyalties. For in the shadow of these Titanic mountains, here in this rock-hollowed nook of empire, in the warm profused luxuriance of the rainy months, in the glare of the earth-shaking tempests, or in the parched brilliance of the hot dry months, only a proud, self-reliant, soil-wise people can survive. Indianism has here adapted itself to its epic setting; the eagles of Tepozteco still whirl down from El Cerro on wings of thunder; and the heroic legends are still told in low-voiced wonderment under the thatched eaves and tiled *techos* by a people whose persistent lives have been ennobled by simplicity.

The old churches crumble; the gourd vines fling fuzzy arms over blackened timbers; the wind-spirit rattles the galvanized roofs; the *"chivos"* dip their blood-red banners to placate strange gods; the cloud-bannered crags hurl their lances of lightning—but Tepozteco stands unshaken upon his ancient outposts in the mountains of the wind, hearkening to the welcoming drums of his people.

VIII   VALERIO TRUJANO: BLACK JOY

From the biting cold of Tejotépec, a Cuicatec Indian town perched on the crest of the Oaxaca Sierras, we had descended for seven hours at a steady trot and gallop along an old abandoned *camino real* through a tangled wilderness of parched mountains to the heavy tropic heat of Dominguillo, held in the fructifying embrace of the Thin River. Through vast cool timber lands of pine and mahogany, we had dropped along mangy ridges of yucca and cactus and mesquite, to the dense bower of fruit trees and vines that shade the wattle-woven thatched houses of the river pueblo. Here, at the muttered invitation of the lean, black, sour-faced Municipal Agent, suffering from malaria and yaws, we had slept in the city hall—on clean straw *petates* spread on the red brick floor.

The following morning we toiled along the low valley lands. Our yellow-shirted guide led us through the beautiful green cane meadows of Chilar, the abandoned communal lands of San Pedro Chicozapote, and on through the desolation of organ cactus, sand and rocks of the steep-walled

139

Cañada. The stale heat of late noon, charged with choking dust from our horses' hoofs, seared our nostrils, as we plodded up a low ridge blistering in the incandescent sun.

Half turning in my saddle, I could see the sheet-iron roofs of the dismal station town of Tomellín. Beyond, to the left, towered the red cliffs of Cuicatlán, Place of Song; and to the right, the purple haze of the gigantesque mountains we had descended the day before—harsh, sharp, uneroded crags with a fantastic crumpled-saw outline.

Topping the ridge, we straightened up gladly in our saddles, laid hold of our lax reins. The little village of Valerio Trujano lay below us, another bower of trees and houses. On beyond it, stretched long meadows of sugar cane, sloping north and east to the foot of the desolate high mountains of the Mixteca Indian region. Tall cocoanut palms waved over the greenish church dome. Massed about the low dwellings, were buxom *tempezquixtle* trees (the native olive), mangos, chirimoyas, sapotes, oranges, lemons (sweet and sour), bananas, mameyes.

We wound down to the pueblo among organ cactus, nopales and the *cardones*, those gigantic gray-green candelabra, which produce yellow-white flowers and the red fruit, *pitahaya*. The "Bad Woman" trees, with their pure white blossoms and serpent tangles of jointed branches, menaced us with their poisonous spines, "which strike pain clear to the heart."

These fantastic desert trees, caricatures of real vegetation, thinned to less extravagant growths. Soon the yellow flowers of the *tepeguaje*, with its pencil-line leaves, competed with the yellow blossoms of the Mulato trees, red, onion-skin barks peeling to nude silver. The gray-frost branches of the Popotl or Cotton Ceiba, were exploding white silk puffs. The *linaloe* trees crouched with broken backs as though expecting ere long to be distilled into precious perfume.

Soon these trees mingled with the dense fruit orchards of the town. We crossed a silver-splashing mountain stream and straggled through a lonely alameda under the yellow-gray

arches of a Colonial aqueduct, La Rueda; 5000 varas long, built in 1700, which still carries water to the adjacent sugarcane hacienda. Independence Street, shouting its freedom from a nationalistic red, white and green plaque, led us into an unimproved plaza, where stood the adobe, tile-roof school.

We drew to halt under the welcome shade of a ceiba. Hardly had we swung from our horses than the municipal president, an alert square-jawed man dressed in white, greeted us in company with the school-teacher, Angelina Chiu, her name and features indicating part of Chinese blood, a serious little woman in her early twenties.

We were led off for cool drinks to the mayor's little store. Presently we waded through undulating heat waves, along a stony cactus lane to a meal on the cool piazza of a hillperched adobe house. Chickens flew from the big brick charcoal stove to balustrade and table. A mouse-colored burro brayed a cracked welcome. Nearby razor-back pigs grunted theirs.

Our hostess was a pleasant slender mulatta with graying kinky hair. Our host, a thin mulatto in an ash-colored shirt. We were introduced to a buxom barefoot daughter of compelling voluptuousness, sultry passionate features, and goldlooped earrings.

A school festival is staged for us. The children have turned out in their glad rags. A tiny girl in beaded blue silk, black hair plastered smooth about her round, velvet, chocolatecolored brow, recites a monotone welcome with stereotyped gestures. The crowd of village spectators are chiefly women; their men are in the fields. For the most part they are clad in gingham blue, with blue striped *rebozos* setting off their dusky oval faces. Again I notice the predominance of negro blood, in every conceivable combination with Spanish and Indian, here just a hint, there black skin, kinky hair, full apricot lips.

Music strikes up—guitar, banjo and *cántaro*, played by

three old men, the youngest, seventy-two, the eldest over eighty, magnificent, hale bearded types. Two have mahogany complexions; the *cántaro* blower has kinky hair and an ash skin. The *cántaro* is a fat, narrow-mouthed, black terracotta jar (made in the style of Coatépec pottery near Oaxaca). Kinky Hair blows into it lugubriously, an ominous African undertone for the tinkling strings, a sound that rises and falls like lost winds in the jungle, like the far roll and beat of a night sea.

Presently they strike up the typical song, *"Los Enanos,"* (The Midgets). Our old lady hostess picks a partner. They shuffle dance to the weaving notes, her long, wide flounced ruffle skirt swinging like a ringing bell over her bare black toes, a swaying motion, graceful as a birch tree in a slight rotary wind. She wears a red embroidered *huipil*, bosom cut low, arms nude. One of the ancient musicians sings in full baritone:

> "Ay, how beautiful 'The Midgets'
> When the Mexicans dance them;
> They are, they are, they are the Midgets.

> "These Midgets aren't from here,
> They're from the plains of Potosí;
> They are, they are, they are the Midgets.

> "Now these Midgets are angry,
> Because they've pinched the old lady;
> They are, they are, they are the Midgets."

> (ad infinitum)

Not a true translation, because *"son"* (they are) puns with *"son"* (sound or tone) and corresponds to a vigorous sweep of the strings and a deep hollow blowing on the *cántaro*, followed by a wailing rise on the full-voweled *"Enanos."*

The program is completed with sports, girls in blue bloomers and crimson kerchiefs; boys in gym suits—amusing races.

In the evening there is a general dance on the dirt floor of the school house, benches cleared away. The walls are decorated with strikingly talented children's drawings and anti-alcoholic posters:

> "Drink is a curse
> That empties the purse. . . ."

The old musicians are on hand, more full of vim than ever. We wander in and out the open doors, and under a silver chariot moon riding a tropic star-studded path above the restless cocoanut palms. We dance—waltz time and jazz —but always round and round and round in dizzy whirl, a peculiar gyratory step well adapted to unpolished floors and occasional bare feet.

The old musicians, who hark back to the middle of the previous century, saw the reform of Juárez roll over the land and the French invasion place Maximilian on a stolen throne; most of their lives they toiled as peons on the Hacienda Güendulain, for a few centavos a day, bound to eternal servitude under the blazing tropic sun. Nevertheless, now, striking their bizarre music, they seemed the youngest, the most enthusiastic and animated of the crowd.

Valerio Trujano enjoys a spirit of gay enjoyment possessed by few small Mexican towns. Is it the African strain? Or is it that this place is struggling valiantly to redeem itself? Valerio Trujano is a new town. Its independence dates only from 1926. It is affirming its liberty.

A new town, but a very old settlement. Formerly its lands and houses, its people and its time, belonged entirely to the adjacent Hacienda. Hacienda Güendulain, one of the earliest repartimientos of the Spanish Crown, was founded in 1540. Its area extended for eighty-one square miles, from the rolling foothills where the village stands down toward singing Cuicatlán and to far Dominguillo on Thin River. Negroes and Indians were brought in to work the cornfields; and according to a memorial published by the State in 1883, the settlement contained about five hundred people, approximately its present population.

At one time in the Colonial period, imported negroes in Mexico outnumbered the Spanish whites. The negroes, on several occasions, joined hands with the Indians to stir up serious revolts. Alarmed, the Crown henceforth forbade further black immigration. In most places in Mexico, the negro strain has been vanquished, weeded out, assimilated, overwhelmed by brown-skinned Indian. Not so in Valerio Trujano; though the negro blood of this place dates back to the early part of the sixteenth century, it has endured. Why has it remained so dominant? Perhaps because of propitious tropical climate. Perhaps because of the village's long status of isolating servitude. Perhaps because Valerio Trujano was a created settlement while all the towns around were already old and Indian and had their *mores* determined long before the arrival of the Spaniards.

Racially Valerio Trujano is a place apart and the spirit of its life is in many ways unique. But it is thoroughly typical of rural Mexico in the character of its twentieth-century problems. In the earlier days of its history, Valerio Trujano (then known as Güendulain instead of by the Oaxacan Independence hero) had its Mayor, Regidores and Síndico appointed by the owners of the Hacienda. Its inhabitants were serfs, like the old musicians. Now the village, like others in Mexico, is struggling for emancipation.

For the most part, the dwellers in Valerio Trujano held aloof from the bloody national political struggles of the past century which brought about racial leveling. But ill-treatment under Porfirio Díaz caused them to stir and be reaped to violence in the flame of the 1919 revolution. Some of them followed the revolutionary hosts to death and victory.

But it was not until 1926 that the village finally asserted its complete independence and adopted its present name, being then recognized as a free town entitled to manage its own affairs and shape its own fate. It was given a meager slice of land from the Hacienda, including the area occupied by the houses, a few scant acres of bottom land, the rest uncultivated hill slope, in all less than two hundred acres for a population of half a thousand. The cane fields of the Hacienda still come right up to the last houses in the village.

The new town set to work to make the most of its slender possessions. Every inch of cultivable land was set out to sugar cane, beans, corn. Little by little, through simple irrigation works, the village is sowing its hill lands, never cultivated in four centuries and probably never tilled by human hands since this world was peopled.

But in spite of this enthusiasm, the newly attained independence entails bitter sacrifices. The owners of the Hacienda never have reconciled themselves to the new status of the village or the loss of even this insignificant acreage. From the outset, they tried to restore it to its ancient servitude. With the support of a small pro-Hacienda party of about thirty village householders (some of whom were given arms), the proprietors have fought the village every step of the way. Particularly they have opposed the federal school. None of the Hacienda party send their children to be educated. Those belonging to this party get work on the Hacienda, at the minimum wage of seventy-five centavos (thirty-seven and a half cents) daily for twelve hours under the hammering May and June sun; those fighting for the independent status are boycotted in every way and get no work. The Hacienda has a light plant, but refuses to distribute light or power to the town. The owners of the Hacienda lobby incessantly in the state capital and in Mexico City.

A bitter, sometimes deadly feud! Blood has frequently drenched the black soil. The villagers, but yesterday having lost their shackles, wield pitifully limited resources, their obligations are heavy. During the revolution, and the earth-

146

quakes of 1928, the city hall fell into partial ruin. It needs repairing. The school must be supported. To combat the Hacienda's lobbying, the villagers must repeatedly send commissions to the state authorities and to Mexico City; this calls for heavy expenditures at the expense of needed communal improvements.

In spite of the villagers' efforts, the Hacienda gained control of the previous municipal administration. The results were funereal. The Hacienda mayor tried to put the school out of business. School taxes vanished into his personal pocket. He stole materials, bought to improve the school and prevent the caving in of the city hall, to build himself a house. He made utterly no accounting of municipal funds. Confident of being maintained in dictatorial power by the State Government and the Hacienda (which spent over three thousand pesos for this purpose), he was not worried over a four-hundred-peso shortage in the treasury or his other pecadillos. But in spite of all efforts, the Hacienda lost control. The corrupt puppet mayor, now fearing the wrath of the villagers, threw himself under a moving train. Not immediately killed, he died in slow agony.

Four hundred pesos seem a ridiculously small amount, but for these people every centavo is distilled from the blood of toil. A serious loss. Nevertheless, the new popular mayor, square-jawed, determined, passionate, incorporates in his wiry frame the best spirit of the free villagers. Little by little, with his aid, they are straightening out the tangled byways of the town, naming them, numbering the houses. They are putting up orderly fences, draining off the centuries-old pools of stagnant malaria-breeding water, calcimining the adobe walls and improving the school. The city hall still totters.

"It must remain so for the present," declares the mayor. "Other things come first, above all, the school."

Under the slender little teacher, the school has become the material, social, and spiritual center of the courageous town, where no school ever before existed. Its presence is bitterly

147

fought by the Hacienda and the Hacienda Party; but the provisional building is being set in order; the walls are being stuccoed; sacks of cement are ready for paving the floor; work has been begun on an open-air theater; an athletic field —corrals, chicken-coops and a rabbit-run have been built. In this region where traditional sex concubinage prevails and

coeducation is bitterly fought, the parents of Valerio Trujano have made the sacrifice of providing the school girls with bloomers and the boys with gym suits; and (in their own shabby inadequate clothes) they flock to watch the sports. The people of the village have an air of determination, of faith, of joy; they are filled with communal pride. They even dream of forming a cooperative to exploit their fine water-power resources and furnish themselves and the neighboring town of Cuicatlán with the light denied them by the Hacienda.

The night of our arrival, in spite of having spent the previous ten days in the saddle over rough trails, we danced till one-thirty in the morning. To the last moment, the old musicians played and sang with vim.

Towards dawn, we were slowly, sweetly awakened from the deep pool of sleep by the singing of *mañanitas*. Along with a dozen school children, the three old musicians, in spite of their long session the previous afternoon and night, were at our door, singing as lustily as ever. By the time we had saddled and had coffee, day was mantling the lofty purple peaks. The rest of the school children appeared with palm branches to accompany us for several miles out of town, and with them came the indefatigable aged musicians, walking by our stirrups, thumbing and blowing their instruments. . . .

Valerio Trujano is far from the highways of modernity. But its problems are eternally modern: thirst for freedom, for knowledge, for decency. Their spirit of communal freedom is watered by the sweat of the brow, flowering with joy and pain in the heart. But though the problems of the humble village are modern and practical, the people have the grace, the aesthetic appreciation, the hospitality and the refined courtesy of the ancient high-born, which is always and forever startling to the outsider observing their soil-woven, toil-worn lives.

And through their practical world of struggle and their ideal aspirations for freedom, flows the hollow wailing of a black-bellied *cántaro*, swirls the rhythm of dancing *"Enanos,"* echoes the sweet chorus of the *Mañanitas*. In these simple harmonies rises the long ground swell of alien races, of ancient times, of remote struggles, of forgotten sufferings and victories. Here is the flowered pattern of a thought and culture as mysterious as that of any of the unknown continents, doubly mysterious to one like myself bred in a nation doomed to present prosperity. Their problems may seem petty, but they link up with the common struggle of mankind to conquer his environment and to conquer his own soul. And this backstream eddy of a corner of Oaxaca is all the fertile silt of the broader stream of dark-skinned peoples everywhere in Mexico and in many places in the world, flowing inevitably to a destiny unknown, a destiny some day to be linked closely, perhaps fearfully, to our own.

IX   MEXICO: OLD AND NEW

MEXICO CITY is the oldest living metropolis on this continent. It is also one of the largest and most modern cities in Latin America. While most of Mexico drowses in Colonial or pre-Colonial isolation, Mexico City builds and rebuilds and expands. Here converge the tendencies of the modern world. The gulf between Mexico City and the hinterland grows ever wider.

The transformation of Mexico City from a sleepy little world into a busy metropolis has occurred in about a decade. From 1918 to 1930, the area tripled; the population almost doubled. In 1918 horse-drawn *carruajes* far outnumbered the occasional automobiles. Today, for reasons of sanitation and in order to prevent traffic obstruction, horse-drawn vehicles are entirely prohibited. Automobiles have become Mexico's most costly import item. Cobblestones have given way to asphalt. New and luxurious residential suburbs have sprung up like mushrooms. Working-class areas have expanded with equal rapidity.

But in spite of the changes which are overtaking it, the place is still one of vivid contrasts, of sharp sunlight and deep shade, of old and modern, wealth and poverty. Only incidentally is it Mexican, except in its life. Architecturally, it is Spanish, French, American, with a wide band of dislocated Indianism woven in and out and around the periphery. It is not a city of one texture, but a city of wide latitudes—from the hovels of Colonia Vallejo to the Hippodrome subdivision, as modern as Forest Hills; from open air markets, buzzing with Indian chatter, to tall department stores covering city blocks; from the lowly wayside shrine to the enormous cathedral, the largest church in the Western Hemisphere; from the loaded burro to the latest model limousines and the aeroplanes of Valbuena; from medicine women to Doctor Herrero, who has artificially created life in his laboratories; from the curb restaurant with its brick-colored stew to Sanborn's in the Palace of Tiles and the elegant Sylvaine's.

The city grows but things ancient are never quite forgotten. In 1325 a little band of half-famished, half-clothed Aztec refugees fled into the marshes of the Lake of Texcoco to escape extermination. There they discovered an eagle on a cactus, holding a serpent in its beak. Their oracles, early in their migrations, had advised them that this supernatural sign would indicate the proper location for their new abode, the place where they should settle and prosper and become powerful. With the desperation of a defeated people and the faith of religious prophecy, they put up grass-hut shrines to their beloved gods, Tlaloc, God of Rain, and Mexitli, God of War, then set arduously to work to transform the spot into a semi-livable place. By scooping up the mud into miniature islands and driving pales into the water, they succeeded in building their miserable reed hovels. By constructing nets and traps, they caught birds and fish. In spite of endemic fever, brackish water, inadequate food supply and the unflagging animosity of their neighbors in the nearby cities of Atzcapotzalco, Texcoco, and Xochimilco (now suburbs), they survived and multiplied. By cunning and hardiness they made alliances and secured immunity from attack. In time they conquered lands for seeding and finally in 1350 were able to build an aqueduct to the crystal-clear springs of Chapultépec, where later on a lofty eminence was erected the summer palace of the Aztec emperors and where today stands the magnificent presidential castle—the White House of Mexico. From such humble beginnings, by such super-human efforts, grew up the handsome, lake-bound city of Tenochtitlán— Place of the Cactus—the imposing capital of the Aztec empire.

The teaming population, estimated at over 200,000, clustered about a great dragon-adorned teocalli on the summit of which stood the carved chapels of Tlaloc and Mexitli (or Huitzilopochtli), from which four notable causeways led out in the four cardinal directions to the mainland. The city and the empire expanded simultaneously, until the metropolis became mistress over a greater region than that of modern Mexico, from well into Central America up into what is now part of the United States. Tenochtitlán was continuously decorated to match its imperial greatness.

The lofty teocalli was surrounded by a high snake-wall entered by a magnificent carved portico. Around this wall were seventy-two chapels to lesser deities; arsenals, and store-rooms. Other pyramids dotted the city. The Palace of Moctezuma, of red tezontle stone, covered ten modern square blocks. The stone palaces of the nobility rose beside placid canals and gardens. The city was a conglomerate of many units, the smallest being the calpulli, or clan, probably descended from a common leader in the migrations. These inhabited and owned in common their properties and land, and vied with each other in improving their particular portion of the city. Each calpulli, twenty in all, had its own god and teocalli, and was governed by elders similar to the Anglo-Saxon moot. When Cortez entered, his soldiers were dazzled by the magnificence of the metropolis; they marveled at its wealth and beauty, and at its vast market.

But they were also shocked by the native religious practices, which were cruel beyond measure, though the cruelty of the Spaniards was, in its way, no less. The Spaniards were shocked by the accounts they had heard of the inaugural ceremonies of the reconstructed and enlarged central pyramid, just a few years before their arrival.

This was during the reign of Ahuizotl. The first streaks of dawn disclosed, winding up the platform and steep stairs of the temple, a great procession, conducting war-captives to the *piedra de sacrificios*. At this huge block of convex jasper towered six priests with long matted locks, decked with green feathers, flowing in Medusa-like disorder over their black hieroglyphic-covered robes—awaiting their victims who, one by one, were sacrificed before the eyes of the dense, breathless mass below. Five priests would secure the head and limbs, while the sixth, clad in a blood-red cape, slit open the breast with an obsidian razor and thrusting his hand into the open wound tore out the palpitating heart. With a mighty gesture it was held up toward the red sun and then flung smoking at the feet of the terrible snake-sheathed war god, Huitzilopochtli, who reared his grotesque brutal form above the prostrated multitude. Every day for four long days, every day until priests and stones were reeking with blood, the sacrifice continued.

To intimidate the Aztecs and convert them to Christianity, the Conquistadores razed the city, toppling pyramids and buildings into the canals, which were soon filled up, raising the old level. They then rebuilt on the ruins, along Spanish lines. The new city was dedicated to Charles V. But it took more than two centuries for it to regain something of its former dimensions, impressiveness and population. The natives were not easily drawn back to the scene of their death-trap. Not until the viceroyalty of the great Revilla Gigedo (1789-1794)—when the population had climbed to 150,000 —were any extensive improvements, beautifications, building, and street-widening carried out. Revilla Gigedo's methods were drastic. A story is recorded of the street which, to this day, bears his name. Coming upon the spot on horseback, he sat watching a settlement of miserable native shacks along the western walls of a monastery. "I want a street through here by tomorrow morning," he told his attendants. Before the dawn of the next day had broken, the shacks had been cleared away and a beautiful thoroughfare had been laid out.

During the period of independence, because of recurrent revolutions there was little time and little money to develop the capital. Emperor Iturbide did some work but not until the time of Juárez was the city given the opportunity really to expand. The greatest obstacle to this had been the vast monasteries, covering dozens of city blocks right in the heart of the town. The Laws of Reform resulted in the confiscation and cutting up of these properties, through which were run what are now the busiest business streets of the city.

The first real beautification came, however, with Emperor Maximilian. From his time, well past the middle of the nineteenth century, dates the French influence in determining the physiognomy of the city. Maximilian laid out the new wide, beautiful Paseo de la Reforma from the center clear to Chapultepec Castle, replacing the previous fashionable thoroughfare of Bucareli. It is one of the wide and beautiful drives of the world, comparable to some of the Paris boulevards and to the Paseo de Recoletos in Madrid; and it is longer and more artistically laid out than Unter den Linden. At convenient intervals it widens out into glorietas or circular gardens; it is paralleled by walks, gardens, bridle paths, and narrower flanking streets. Too, Maximilian laid out the Alameda, or central park, along its present lines, and amplified and beautified the Chapultepec gardens.

The next significant improvement of the city came toward the end of Porfirio Díaz' rule. Díaz added statues, benches, and gardens to the Paseo. He filled the glorietas with imposing *mementi*, such as the tall Independence Column, and the monuments to Cuatémoc, the martyred Indian emperor, to Columbus, and others. He built that architectural gem, the national postoffice—Venetian, with Florentine bronze work;

other buildings owed to him were the telegraph building, the mining building, many institutes and schools, as well as the massive and ugly National Theatre (of Carrara marble with elaborate stage machinery and a million-dollar Tiffany glass curtain). Too, the rusting steel ribs of the dome of the unfinished Legislative Palace (the beginning of an elaborate civic center plan) poke into the sky to remind the world both of the greatness and the folly of the omnipotent dictator.

Little indeed of the Aztec Tenochtitlán has remained. A few stones were imbedded in the walls of the first Colonial structures. The foundations of the massive cathedral, the National Palace, and other central edifices rest upon the colossal masonry of the old teocalli and other surrounding structures. This is perhaps why they have not tilted during the centuries, for in this filled lake bottom all heavy structures soon sink out of alignment. Most of the old churches are leaning like towers of Pisa. A few stone steps and carved serpents' heads may still be seen by descending the minor excavations of Santa Teresa, back of the cathedral. Every time the soil is turned over, old religious objects are brought to light. In 1926, when sinking a new elevator shaft in the National Palace, a monolith was unearthed. It was a model of the chief Aztec temple, with a symbolic sun carved on its face. (Did this, asked the local savants, fulfill the old prophecy: "When the chief temple of the Aztecs shall appear in the principal plaza of the city of Tenochtitlán, bearing upon it the sun, then shall the ancient people possess their ancient rights"?) The Castle of Chapultepec, the White House of the Mexican Presidents, begun by Cortez, rests upon the foundations of the summer palace of the Aztec rulers. And in the extensive gardens below, one may still walk down lanes between rows of gigantic *ahuehuetl* trees, set out by Moctezuma himself over four centuries ago. Here and there, a *barrio* or ward still retains the name of its ancient *calpulli*; and now and then a street with an Aztec name has survived the revolutionary eagerness to alter all appellations. The avenues that run out toward Xochimilco, toward Guadalupe and Tacuba and Valbuena, are counterparts of the ancient causeways.

But the new Spanish city was rebuilt by the labor of the conquered. Many a church bears Aztec symbols; through many a stone frieze twines the native love of floral emblems. Red tezontle continues to be used, even to this day, giving a roseate loveliness to many quarters. Aztec serpents snarl from the new police and fire quarters. Automobiles roll into garages between the crouched gods of an older day.

If little of the old Tenochtitlán remains, many Aztec customs still rule the lives of the lower classes. Many still bind to their feet the same kind of *guarache* as the forest-treading Toltec. The city Indian flings over his shoulder the end of his scarlet sarape, woven on native handlooms, and if he may not deck himself out as the ancient nobility in the feather work so lauded by Cortez, he may purchase specimens in which the artistic skill matches that of the robes preserved in the Museo Nacional. His wife still amuses herself with beadwork; still fastens about her dusky throat necklaces of brilliant seed-beads; and adorns herself with jewelry as artistic as it is historic. Many still sleep on straw *petates* and eat the flat corn cake, the tortilla, and drink cinnamon flavored *chocolate*.

The older Indian city, typical of most others in Latin America, clustered about the teocalli—pyramid, temple, fort. The new city, the Spanish city, planted its temple on the site of the old pyramid, and in turn the Zócalo or Plaza de la Constitución became the hub. The church, the market, and the plaza—these became the foci of the new city with its low-roofed buildings; its numerous domes and spires and towers; its luxurious tiled palaces; its houses, decorated and carved, built around wide, flower-filled, fountain-splashing patios which exclude the sun and preserve the family intimacy and freedom. The city, in spite of its growing modernity, retains the leisure and beauty of southern lands. Everywhere rise churches, cathedrals and discarded monasteries; and over the low roofs from dawn till dark floats the resonant sound of bells.

The Zócalo or central plaza, one of the largest in the world, is one of the three main foci of modern Mexico, in and out of which flows most of the traffic of the city. On it faces the great cathedral started by Cortez and in later centuries rebuilt on more grandiose scale; the National Palace, of red tezontle (also built by Cortez and recently heightened by a story added by President Calles), the Municipal Palace, with its cool arcades and tiled coats of arms; and a series of early colonial buildings of lovely soft rose texture.

One piece with the Plaza as a center of life, though removed from it by a half a dozen business blocks, is the Alameda, the central park. It is a colonial garden, modified along French lines, filled with tropical vegetation, shade, flowers, birds, fountains, bandstands. The adjacent streets are fringed by impressive soft-toned buildings. Here promenade —properly chaperoned—eligible señoritas, slim ankles displayed by tall French heels, cheek and hair hid by flowing scarves, warm black eyes darting provocative glances at loitering *caballeros*. Here, on Sunday and holidays, play bands and orchestras. The park is an escape from the cloister-like homes; on warm noons, it is a refuge of shade, falling waters and cool air. The trees have a grace and luxuriousness quite different from those in northern climes.

On Sundays the rendezvous becomes Chapultépec park, under the *ahuehetls* of Moctezuma. A formal auto and pedestrian promenade begins at eleven thirty and ends at two. Spanish white and black lace mantillas on high combs drape about olive cheeks. Horsemen, dressed in leather *charro* suits, tight trousers, wide sombreros—all overlaid with gold and silver braid, decorated with silver buttons, cavort on beautiful horses along the bridle paths. A *charro*-costumed orchestra provides music.

The Church is no less a center of social activity. In addition to fulfilling religious needs, it is the Mexican's theatre and parlor. The home is more individualistic. Only the most intimate and trusted friends are ever admitted to the home. But innumerable acquaintances are greeted in church and lovers make them their rendezvous. The poorer churches harbor tawdry gilt and horribly emaciated and blood-drenched Christs to afford appropriate Grand Guinol shivers. The elaborate masses and fiestas provide spectacles, entertainments which feast the senses and supply mystic joy and beauty. The church, in large part, substitutes cabaret and dance hall, operetta and melodramatic stage. Between the church and the saloon or bullfight or cockfight, there is little—at least before the movie came and Hollywood definitely and irrevocably entered the Mexican firmament. But the Church for centuries in Mexico City as elsewhere in the country, has woven the major threads of local life into one pattern. And though its role seems to be diminishing, it still is one of the principal centers of metropolitan activities.

Equally important are the markets. The market is the open air department store. It usually centers in a high, concrete, glass-roofed half-open building, where may be found vegetables, fruits, flowers, wearing apparel, toys, kitchen utensils, old books, rusty hardware, leather goods, carved into Aztec patterns, hand-woven rugs, colored baskets, lacquer ware, beautiful pottery. For blocks around this center, the streets are cluttered with venders under awnings and in wooden shacks, half on the sidewalk, half in the street, the heterogeneous wares stacked into little *montones,* each with its appropriate price. To these markets the peons come early in the dawn, driving their laden mules or burros; or with great loads strapped to back and brow. Beauty and poverty, color and squalor jostle. Meat and flies, soap and beggars, laces and rags cascade in indiscriminate confusion; from the corner

saloons rise the stale nauseating odor of pulque; from open-
air kitchens comes the stench of pork-grease.

And on special holidays, such as All Souls' Day, Easter
week, Christmas and New Years, special markets spread out
along the Alameda.

Thus the market is one piece with the intimacy and leisure-
liness of street-life. And yet street-life in Mexico City gives
the impression of vast animation—not rush, but animation,

a purring peace, a sort of assiduous idleness, pleasing to eye
and ear, not always to the nose. Something is always happening, be it a dog-fight or an accident; an argument or a crowd
about a queer beggar; and every passerby has time to pause
and note and perhaps to participate or to counsel. Street-life
is not glossed over with decorum as with us; nor is it a rush
and speeding up. It is close to the surface; a bit in the raw,
yet at the same time more sophisticated.

Every street is a sort of living key to the complicated

ethnographical chart of Mexico, where the blood of conqueror and conquered have mingled in hybrid offspring—a
new people, obviously in the making. The Spaniards themselves were not one texture. The origin of the Basques is still
one of the ethnic mysteries of Europe. Moor and Goth and
Celt and Iberian contributed. To this day the Catalán proudly
declares that his craneal measurements are different from and
superior to those of the proud Castilians. Mexico, too, was
long the dumping ground of heretical Jews, and many a
modern pious Catholic Mexican has a nose that proves his
family ancestors miraculously escaped the Inquisition. Native
Mexico was no less complex. Eleven distinct languages; sixty
odd dialects. Physically, the Indians varied from the squat
pacific Maya to the tall war-like Yaqui; here an Oriental
caste to the eyes; there a Polynesian physiognomy. And in
every street may be seen the result of this mixing up of
Europe and America.

Perhaps of all the native diversions in Mexico City, not the
cockfight or the *pelota* nor the recently indulged baseball and
football can vie with romantic interest with the bull-fight.
Something more than mere disemboweling of horses or the
killing of a snorting bull—it is a pattern of color and grace
and Southern passion. The ensemble, the crowd and action,
have as definite structural unity as a Gothic cathedral. The
crowd are in the great ring expectant. Vivid Spanish and
oriental shawls are draped over the boxes or cling to soft olive
profiles. The band plays *Toreador*, and the procession of bull-
fighters enters in perukes and bright gold and red and yellow
jackets and tight-fitting breeches. The *toril* opens; the bull
rushes into the yellow arena and the dazzling sunlight. He
charges the red capes of the *capeadores*, who pirouette within
an inch of the angry horns. The *picadores* with their long
lances fare worse. The bull charges, hurls horse and rider
brutally against the stockade—a vivid proof of the power of
the beast, an excitant for the throng, impressing them with
the danger of the play. Come the *banderilleros*, who stamp

and shout taunts, and lift their long be-ribboned darts, which must be deftly planted on the bull's shoulders as he charges at express speed. Enters the *matador*, the most brilliant and braided costume of all, with blood-red cape and deadly sword. He kneels in the very path of the bull, whirls out of the way by a hairsbreadth, his cape describing an arc and draping his poised erect body. The blade is extended, slowly, definitely; the bull is hypnotized, then paws, snorts, lunges. The blade strikes between the horns, down into the heart.

Thus, since the city has become modernized so much more rapidly than the country, which is backward, provincial, and in most places truely primitive, even savage, the contrasts in custom are sharp and wide. Many older customs are rapidly passing away. The old pastime of *corriendo el gallo*, of a group of youths prowling the city at night with guitars, playing tunes under the iron-barred balconies of their sweethearts, with interludes of drinking in the cantinas, still persists, though less frequently. In some circles, the old forms of courtship still survive, though the automobile, the movie, and other innovations tend to break them down.

The ritual of the former middle-class courtship is picturesque. A young man sees a girl who attracts him—in the movies, at church, on the street. Discreetly he flirts with her, follows her to her house. Thereafter, every day at the same hour, he haunts the curb. At first his only reward is a mysterious flutter of the curtains. He bribes the janitor to give him the girl's name and promptly writes her impassioned letters. These are at first returned unopened. Then she answers, ordering him to desist from his molestations. But after a few days the girl shows herself on the balcony, even rewards the swain's persistence with a smile. A missive comes to him, saying that the object of his affections will be in such and such a reunion. The aspirant must use his wits to get invited. If, after talking with her at the little social gathering, he is still impressed, his balcony visits become the established custom. Conversation, interchange of flowers, telephone calls,

162

notes, speed the affair along. All this time the parents presume to be ignorant of what is going on. As a matter of fact, they are busy investigating the family and personal habits of the suitor. After six months of balcony courtship, provided the investigations have proved the boy satisfactory, he is admitted into the house to call, is an accepted *novio*. He is formally engaged, which means that no honorable young man would fail ultimately to go through with the marriage. At these calls, a chaperone is always insistently present. If any kisses are exchanged, they are furtive indeed. If he takes the girl out to a restaurant, to the movies, for an auto ride, he is obliged to invite from one to half a dozen other members of the family. When the day comes for the marriage, the poor bridegroom must provide the wedding gown; the bride is not supposed to bring a stitch of her old clothing to the new home.

But also there are Mexican flappers, who drive their old-fashioned parents half insane. Some of them even insist on earning their living, which in a good family is considered a disgrace.

Mexico is a medley of old and new.

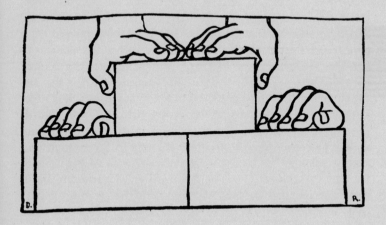

X MULTEERS

"Not the muleteers teach the
mules; the mules teach the muleteers—as happens to every
man who takes upon himself the doubtful task of regenerating the ladies," remarks an unknown Mexican chronicler of
the middle of the past century.

Whether taught by his own mules, or not, the muleteer of
Mexico is sagacious yet naive, courageous and patient, hard-
headed yet romantic. Not so picturesque as the Mexican
rancher, his leather-clad brother of the remote countryside,
the muleteer enjoys greater advantages. Tempered by the
same winds, knowing the same stars, moulded from the same
harsh earth, nevertheless the muleteer's knowledge of places
and of people goes further afield. He is less bound to the soil
by the struggle for a livelihood; he is freer, a readier, more
casual man. He has created his own body of superstitions,
lore, and traditions. "Never let too many asses at the hay," is
one of his pet sayings which perhaps explains why a muleteer
is a muleteer.

His task is rude, but he is master of his days. Though in
part a carrier of other people's goods, usually he is something
of an independent merchant. But a merchant who enjoys
more the doing than the earning. If headed for a given market, likely enough he will refuse to sell his wares, however
great the profit, before reaching his destination; he prefers to

164

gain less and enjoy the trip and market sociability. Thus he has acquired the grace and knowledge that comes from barter, from varied contacts, from many loves—a debonair air born of unexpected situations, sudden risks, and the danger of death at the hands of bandits.

The Mexican muleteer is found on every highway and by-way of the country, though his former indispensable economic importance in life of his country, in many localities, is being destroyed. Trains, autos, aeroplanes, new roads, have cut his role. Yet in an agrarian land, so mountainous, where man-power is still cheaper than the machine, the muleteer persists even along routes covered by buses. On remoter trails he will long remain king of the road.

Always the Mexican muleteer will maintain his romantic dignity. Was not the holy father of the sixteenth century, Fray Sebastián de Aparicio, a muleteer and later an ox-cart driver between Vera Cruz and the capital—out of penance and love of human service? Did not the greatest and truest of the Independence leaders, José María Morelos, begin life as an *arriero* with mules, among the high sierras of Michoacán? And did not a muleteer execute an emperor, for General Mariano Escobedo who set Maximilian before the firing-squad, first learned to use the lash on his long train of mules. To know Mexico, certainly, it is necessary to know muleteers.

My own initiation came years ago when I loaded three burros for a trek across the deserts of Arizona and Sonora. An absolute greenhorn, I soon found myself in a mortifying struggle with beasts who, divining my ignorance, balked, rolled, shook their loads, refused to cross streams, darted under trees when it rained, pretended to be lame, swelled up at the cinching, and resorted to every trick and deceit of their lazy obstinate natures. Undoubtedly they taught me more than I taught them—my regeneration, not the ladies'. They taught me never to lose my temper, to match deceit with intelligent brutality; I learned to twist their tails, to cajole, to reward and to punish. I penetrated the mystery of making a diamond hitch in lieu of a saddle; the art of packing and loading.

It was worth it. Since then, two dozen countries and two score cities have claimed me, often I have felt my throat tighten with the memory of the beauty of the southwest desert—the free open road, the solitude, the vast expanse, the reek of sagebrush and *huizache*; the clump clump of the burros and the rub rub of the loads. And those dawns: the purple sky, the hushed loveliness of the blazing morning star; the cool freshness turning to heat as a red glow stained the horizon and the sun rolled up fat and fierce; and the pulsing sorrow of the mourning doves—a moan and a song tied in the silver knot of an unnamed desire in the aching emptiness of far sands sweeping to horizons of twisted igneous mountains and brittle copper skies.

Here and there in the Sonora and Sinaloa lowlands, I came upon groups of muleteers; some, lugging ore in leather bags from the mines of Caborca to Magdalena; a long dust cloud smudging the horizon. I followed them, toiling under the hammering heat. Now and then a mule laid down on them. He received a few lashes and was left behind. Some times he lay there for three or four days. Each time the train passed, he was given a few more lashes. At last, moved by hunger and thirst, and the inevitable repetition of those daily blows, he would stagger to his feet with a little plaint, a flick of ears and tail, and fall in doggedly behind his fellows.

But not until I ascended the precipitous Tamazula river in the Sierra Madre above Culiacán did I trek with muleteers for any great distance, sharing their food, bivouacking under the stars, listening to their stories. They were four, three mongrel dogs, and about fifteen mules with their trappings and loads. Ricardo was a tall Tepehuane, bronzed and sinewy, high red cheek bones, blazing black eyes. His pink shirt was open at the throat; and a golden brown sash, half a foot wide, held his gray cotton trousers in place. On his rock-

166

scarred feet he wore single-thong *guaraches*. His belongings, he carried in the crown of his black-braided sombrero, or in a fringed leather pouch. Little Pico, his companion, was a thick-lipped, puffy-cheeked mestizo. Diego, a simple Indian, wore white pyjamas rolled to the crotch, the better to cross the winding streams. He carried the food—tortillas and ground roasted corn (*pinole*)—and a few belongings in a sisal bag, on which was painted, with colored native dyes, the form of a deer, forefeet in the air, slim head turned back —like spirited horses hitched to a Russian droshki. A boy of twelve—far more energetic and vociferous than his elders— completed the party.

At every turning, Indian women ran out from little thatched hut settlements, set on high spurs or tucked in snug valleys. They were clad in long dust-dragging skirts, from under which peeked their toes; their black hair, smoothed flat on the crown, hung down their backs in long shiny braids intertwined with red ribbons. The leading demand was salt, which was measured into terra cotta bowls or lacquered gourds. As we pierced higher into the mountains, this commodity increased to the price of caviar.

At some patch of sugar-cane we would halt to cut stalks, which we peeled and chewed, strewing the masticated pulp along the trail. At the streams, I imitated the muleteers' stunt of making a flying leap for the rump of one of the mules, and curling my feet behind me to avoid the splashing. The dogs scurried in and out of the brush, ahead and behind, chasing rabbits, sniffing at lizards, occasionally snapping at the heels of poky mules.

At night, the mountaineers in these parts light watch fires under the front *ramadas*, or thatched porches, of their houses. A picturesque sight, these fires, flaming far up sheer canyon walls; welcome beacons to the late traveler toiling through the enormous ravines and the dark sinister mountains, lifting black into the sky. Higher in the sierras, because of the cold and different building materials, the houses became log-cabin affairs. The undressed logs are halved and jointed; the roofs are made of long home-hewn shingles battened down with stones; usually glowing with rows of ripe calabashes. The doors are of cleated pine slabs swung on leather hinges between thick piles.

Here, beside one of the *ramada* fires, we made ourselves at home, spread out our blankets, cooked our food, prepared coffee, into which we chipped pieces of *pinoche* (an unrefined brown sugar pressed into small cones). This gave the beverage a sort of molasses flavor.

The host (always given some small gift for his pains), squatted on his haunches with us, shared our coffee. We exchanged gossip, news, discussed politics, told stories. Pico drew out a crude home-made guitar and sang songs to the stars—blazing southland stars, big as Christmas tree candles. He sang *"La Llorona"* and *"El Cuco"*; he sang folk songs, wistful, dealing with love, battle, poverty, miraculous cures, the birds, the seasons:

> "When I saw you come,
> To my heart, I said,
> What a pretty little stone,
> To trip one upon his head . . .

> "Fortune is a thorny tree,
> Thorns not fruit I pick;
> When the cactus blooms,
> Comes hope—but not always fruit.

> "Charcoal once lit,
> Lights easier anew;
> Such is love,
> For those on the road."

The river sang its gurgling silver refrain to the guitarist; the flames threw eerie shadows into the bush and fearful fire into dogs' eyes; and fluid gold on bronze faces. Occasionally a mulebell tinkled; dogs barked, or a cow mooed; one night a mountain lion roared down from some far cliff.

Sometimes Ricardo and Pico held long arguments over the proper wording of the songs, and I was reminded of Don Quixote scolding Sancho for mixing his verses, and the simple fellow's reply: "There come so many to my mouth that when I speak they fight with each other to come forth."

In one little town in the river hollow, our rendezvous was one of the village houses. Here on the rear, half-enclosed veranda, facing a wide garden, we toasted our tortillas over the fire. Ricardo that night proved himself not only a prince of the road, a mathematician of weights, measure and routes, and an astronomer to whom the constellations gave the hour, but a homeopathist for my bruised feet. He spent the better part of half an hour grinding nasturtium leaves and herbs to make a paste that would draw the inflammation. Questioning revealed that he was deeply versed in the lore of curative herbs.

The start was made—as usual—long before dawn. By the light of the *ocote* torches—an inflammable species of pine— the mules were rounded up; their *suaderos* were carefully adjusted; they were saddled, and loaded. With fingers stiff with cold, we fumbled at the buckles and the riatas. Ricardo, being a holy man, and doubly so because of his lusty Rabelaisian nature, had to kneel and pray. He took out a sheet of spongy green paper from his wide sombrero; unfolded it; and painfully recited by the light of the torches. Standing around, waiting, shivering, stamping, we tried to get some meager protection from the wind, behind a clump of bamboo, while Ricardo's interminable prayer dragged on. I do not remember his prayer; but I have since come upon a muleteer's oration fifty-two lines long, printed by the famous publishers of popular corridos, Vanegas Arroyo, in Mexico City, which reads:

> Bless me, Divine Father,
> With your charity and love,

169

For today I go forth on the road;
I beg the Holy Apostle
That merely by invoking him,
When he sees me in trouble,
He will always take my part . . .

It goes on to recite the dangers of the trip from which he begs protection: assaults, political persecution, war, sickness, sin.

But, at last, Ricardo's praying was over. The mules clicked over the flaggings through the tunnel arch toward the lofty front *zaguán*, which swung slowly, protesting, on rusty hinges. The dawn was still remote; the night was black as the throat of a wolf. Not a light shone in the village. Dogs barked as the mules stumbled over the cobbles. And so— out to the *camino real*—the royal road—out by countless feet through stoneways, up a high cliff, to face the dawn in the bitter cold glory of rose and purple on far-flung crags.

The road yielded occasional encounters. Always there is the involved courtesy of begging for a light from passersby. This is requested with involved deference; the one asked displays himself overjoyed to be of service. Carefully he shakes off the ashes; but before presenting his cigarette, he lifts his hand to the brim of his sombrero, which he then removes from his head. At this gesture, the other not only removes his hat, but places it on the ground, tilted against his leg. The manner of holding the cigarette, of lighting one from the other, of returning it, are all matters of the strictest etiquette. The one who has bestowed the favor is then begged to accept a cigarette. This is refused, and only after repeated insistence does he finally accept. With another properly modulated gesture, the cigarette is placed behind the ear to be smoked later along the road.

Each populated settlement also calls for etiquette. Stops must be made at the tiny shops along the way. Tobacco and cigarette paper may be purchased. A round of tequila must be drunk to give time to talk over the most recent news.

And there is the etiquette of love; the muleteer must live up to a crude Don Juan tradition. The popular sayings reflect this:

> "The love of a muleteer: 'If I ever saw you, I don't remember it.' "

> "The dirtier the muleteer talks and the wilder he is, the more the Indian girl likes him."

The muleteer is part of the heritage of the Spanish Conquest, though he also harks back to the Aztec traders, who in Tenochtitlán lived apart in a special ward, had their own deities, customs, and dress. Of these, Anita Brenner remarks in her *Idols Behind Altars*: "The trader could hardly be less than a sorcerer to be able to live outside the unit of place and labour. He was a kind of awesome outcast just before he left and on his return. Then, only a very high priest or a king could be friendly with him without a danger to his own soul. It is so much the same now, that a great fair is always coupled with a religious pilgrimage to the shrine of powerful images." The Aztec merchants traveled far into Central America and to the northern desert pueblos and brought back marvellous objects and knowledge and stories. Such travelers, a people so distinct from the ordinary life of the nature world, became akin to the nobility; they were intimate friends of the Emperor himself. The gods of the merchants were considered exceptionally powerful. The modern muleteer is the direct descendant of this select group.

It was the Spaniard who brought in the mule, the burro, and the horse to the New World. The Mexican muleteer is sometimes Indian, but more often mestizan; he has inherited traits both from the pre-Cortez trader, and from the Spanish. The mixture of races seems to have released in him a greater volubility and sociability. He is at once rough, ready and holy.

Throughout Mexico's history, the muleteer has played a role in the great national fairs and pilgrimages—in Chalma, in San Juan de los Lagos, in Guadalupe Hidalgo, in Cholula, in Tlaxcala. In the past, when such pilgrimages were more important than now, over half a million people were wont to visit the miraculous image of San Juan de los Lagos, to pray, to dance in holy and pagan fashion, to gamble, to buy, to enjoy the *carpas* or tent shows. The muleteer became an essential factor in such great *romerías*; he transported goods, religious images and the persons to buy the goods. Indeed, during the fair, fifty thousand mules and burros swelled the local population.

Many of the Mexican churches owe their origin to the miraculous experiences of the muleteers. In the seventeenth century was built the famous shrine on the Sacremonte Hill behind Amecameca, the water-washed town at the foot of the two snow-capped volcanoes southwest of Mexico City.

A train of muleteers, on their way to an important fair, camped on the Sacremonte. Among the objects they were conveying was a beautiful and unusual image of Christ, which, though life-sized, was light as a feather, for it was made out of the porous pith of a local tree. The following morning, after the expedition had set out again, the mule carrying this Christ ran into a cave. After much beating and shouting, she was again started on her proper way; but presently she dashed off and once more was found in the cave. She was lashed back into line, but a third time sought the same refuge. This was considered so miraculous that the muleteers informed the local priest, who at once decided that the Divine Will desired a shrine built on the spot. A *camarín* was hewed out of the living rock for the image of the Christ, and a large and unusually pleasing chapel was built against the side of the hill.

Many such miracles are described in the *Zodíaco Mariano*, written by Father Francisco de Florencia sometime around 1600 and printed in 1755 by the Royal Presses in the ancient San Ildefonso College.

For instance, the nuns of the Convent of the Conception in Mexico were very eager to have a good image of the Virgin,

172

especially made for their congregation, but all the artists asked more money for their work than the prioress felt could be paid. So the nuns resigned themselves to patience and prayer.

One day during the "hour of silence"; between twelve and one, an imperious knock sounded on the portals.

The woman at the gate, alarmed at so sharp a summons at such an unusual hour, called, "Who is there?"

"We hear that the community needs a Virgin, and we bring one to sell," a voice replied.

The door was opened, and two muleteers delivered a sealed box. As it was the "hour of silence," they sat down to wait.

The gatekeeper carried the box into the chapel; opened, it contained a marvellously beautiful image. More marvellous still the image exactly fitted the waiting niche.

The prioress came to look for the muleteers. Neither was to be found. The gates had been locked. There was no way for them to have left. Yet they were gone! Neighbors could throw no light. No one had seen the lost muleteers enter or leave the convent. Not a soul had been seen. So it came to be said that here was a miracle, a sign that Divine Providence had heard the nuns' plaints.

On another occasion, a train of mules was proceeding to Guatemala. In Antequera, Oaxaca, though the mules were still fresh, one lay down on the street. All efforts to make her go along with the others were futile. The muleteers finally removed the box with which she was loaded and lashed it on to another mule. The second mule immediately lay down in the same manner and could not be budged. Opening the box, the muleteers discovered that it contained an image of the Virgen de Soledad. "And they understood, in this wise, that the Virgin wishes to remain in Antequera." The people of the town were overjoyed, and the new Virgin became the favorite of the place, receiving many rich gifts.

The muleteers maintain their homes in special towns, usually prosperous, as a rule, at the beginning or end of their routes. Towns long noted as muleteer centers are Jonacatépec in Morelos, Chamacuero de los Arrieros in Guanajuato, Paso del Macho and Jalapa in Vera Cruz, and Taxco in Guerrero, whence came the first silver shipped from New World mines to Spain.

But every city and town has its muleteer center (corresponding to the Calle de Toledo in Madrid). This center is usually near the main market. Nearby are typical muleteer inns, with large patios or corrals for the animals and upper tiers with rooms—simple whitewashed habitations with a cot, a reed chair or two, a pitcher and washbasin. They are little different from the *Posada de la Sangre* in Toledo made famous by Cervantes. And around about are stores where ropes, saddles, blankets, mecate nets, bags, etc., may be purchased for the road.

Varied indeed are the objects transported by the muleteers. To the highlands are carried tropic vegetables and fruits—avocados, mangos, tomatoes, plums, lemons, oranges. From the highlands: woven goods, cotton bolts wrapped in oil cloth, sarapes and *rebozos* (or shawls). Special tastes must be catered to. The girls of Del Bajío, Tepic and Sinaloa prefer light gray rebozos; those of the Valley of Mexico, Morelos and Hidalgo, black or dark blue; those of Puebla and Oaxaca, prefer broad red and white stripes. The sarapes come principally from Saltillo, from the villages around Texcoco (across the lake from Mexico City), from Tlaxcala, from Santana Chautempán and from Oaxaca. The Saltillo sarapes, largely for tourist consumption, are least typically indigenous; the others are woven with native designs (though with foreign influence): the Chotuteca sarapes, for instance, are usually gray with white wool designs; the Tlaxcalteca sarape is dark brown with white designs, simply done, corresponding to native needs.

Other products frequently carried by the muleteers are sugar, liquors, starch, rice, pepper tree seeds for birds, coffee,

Tabascan coffee, chile, shrimps, beer, herbs, medicines, barley, plaster, cocoa, chocolate, beans, garbanzos or chickpeas, wheat flour, cornmeal, salt, red oxide, gold, silver, mercury, tobacco, peanuts, olives, figs, pineapples, hides, wool, chemicals, light machinery, lard—in fact anything of local demand which can be placed on a mule. Sometimes the mules are piled high with reed-bottom chairs decorated with bright flower designs; or with other furniture; sometimes with rolls of *petates* or straw mats. Often the animals jolt along with towers of bamboo cages full of chirping birds. Other times they carry crates, or *mecate* nets, of large rough woven straw baskets, crammed with pottery; jars of all shapes and sizes; small jars for *atole* (ground roasted corn with milk), chocolate, or coffee; tiny jars in which children may take their milk; water jars; special medicine jars in which to boil herbs; round green glazed jars from Oaxaca; white marble-like jars from Tonalá; red and black jars of ancient form and pattern from Valle de Bravo; bepaunched jars with long thin necks, glassy and olive-colored, manufactured in the historic San Miguel de Allende, cradle of Independence; very perfect jars, well-shaped and well-glazed, from Metépec.

And the muleteer sings:

> "If I die, from my clay,
> Amada, make a jar;
> If you thirst for me, drink;
> And if your lips stick
> To the brim, 'twill be
> Because of the kisses I give."

XI   THE YAQUIS

THE state of Sonora, home of the Yaqui Indians, long ruled Mexico. From 1914, when the victorious army of Obregón swept down from the northwest across Nayarit and Jalisco to the capital, until his death in 1928, the supermen of Sonora dominated national affairs with the help of these fierce northerners. In 1923, the three candidates—Plutarco Elías Calles, Angel Flores (Sinaloa) and Adolfo de la Huerta—were from the Northwest. In 1927-8 the three presidential candidates—Alvaro Obregón, Francisco Serrano and Arnulfo Gómez—were all natives of Sonora. During the later days of Rome, the Cæsars came from north of the Alps at the head of victorious legions, so in modern Mexico the rulers have long hailed from the Northwest—true to the Prætorian Guard tradition. Just as three quarters of a century ago, Benito Juárez roused the fierce Indians from the Oaxacan Sierras to back him in his efforts to break the power of the Church, and Porfirio Díaz rode into thirty years of power on the shoulders of these same Indians, so at the beginning of the present epoch, the leaders of Sonora whirled down the Paseo de la Reforma to the old palace and to victory at the head of serried ranks of tall, war-loving Yaquis, marching to primitive tom-toms.

In a sense, the whole 1910-28 revolution swung on the Yaqui pivot. Those Sonora Indians, harried for twenty-three years by Porfirio Díaz, threw in their lot with Francisco Madero, the first apostle of the revolution, who supplied them with arms. But Obregón was long the real wielder of the Yaquis. The major part of his army that arrived from the northwest coast in Mexico City to oust Huerta and seat Carranza was made up of Yaqui recruits. These same indomitable fighters formed the dependable elements of Obregón's "Revindicating Revolution" against Carranza. Yaqui volunteers saved the Obregón Government at its most difficult time during the De la Huerta trouble in 1923-24.

I saw them enter the capital in 1920 among the forty thousand soldiers of Obregón. They marched down the aristocratic Paseo of the capital, dressed in white cotton "pyjamas," gray sarapes, queer straw hats with red ribbons; on their feet were single-thong *guaraches*. They came beating raw-hide drums with a primitive rhythm that imparted a jerky shuffle to their step. I saw them again at the opening of Congress in 1928, after Obregón's death—these same tall, stern Yaquis. They stood guard lined up for miles along the route taken by Presidente Plutarco Elías Calles. On this second occasion, they were clad in smart gray and black uniforms, disciplined according to the German manual—and with their fierce dark unsmiling faces, they represented the most striking, best-drilled corps of soldiers I recall having seen anywhere in the world. To this day the best rank and file fighters are Yaquis; a goodly portion of the Mexican army is still Yaqui.

Their State, Sonora, is the second largest entity in the Mexican Federal Republic. It is enormously wealthy, agriculturally and minerally. It possesses richer mineral resources than any other state. Most of these have not been exploited because of the harshness of the desert and mountains, lack of communications, and the presence of the Yaquis. Yet many of the mines have already yielded fabulous profits. For years the Cananea copper mines turned out more than three thousand tons daily. Back in colonial times, the old Quintera silver mine in the southern Alamo district enabled the owner, Señor Almada, to line the bridal chamber of his daughter with silver bars and to pave the path from the house to the church with "the same pale chaste material."

In Carranza's time I prospected across the desert and mountains of Sonora. With one companion I crisscrossed the bone-white desert of the Gulf of California coast. And I roughed it on a big rice plantation down near the mouth of the Yaqui River, and I lived in Cajeme, which was later the seat of Obregón's farming operations.

Cajeme is named after the most famous Yaqui chief, who supported the Republicans against Emperor Maximilian, but who was finally shot by Government troops in nearby Cocorit in 1888. The town of Cajeme, on the main-coast highway, was actually held by the Yaquis for more than five years (during the 'eighties) against the most bloody assaults of Díaz' Federal troops.

When I was in Cajeme it consisted of a bizarre yellow station, a handful of adobe huts, a general store, a military warehouse, a barracks, and a number of corrals—all set pitiably in the center of a wide, hot, treeless, yet flower-sprinkled llano. To the east rose the jagged Sierras, to the west—far across the plain the dense tropic vegetation massed on the low banks of the Rio Yaqui. Most of the land about at that time belonged to a large American land company. Now, I believe, it has largely passed into other hands. Much of it was taken over for non-payment of taxes, some distributed to the Yaquis, much of it resold. Obregón was given a concession permitting him to cultivate an enormous tract, and he converted Cajeme into a bustling little town of warehouses, petroleum tanks, and shops. The ex-president made himself the *Garbanza* or Chickpea king of Mexico, growing a large part of this important Sonora product, and controlling the distribution of the remainder.

178

When I was in the Rio Yaqui region in 1918, the Yaquis were on the warpath. We were not particularly alarmed in Cajeme because the town, since the historic battles of the 'eighties, was no longer surrounded by trees, so could not be ambushed. Too, the fat Commandant, who sat in front of the barracks playing cards from dawn to dark and who insistently begged me to marry his anæmic daughter, was a Yaqui himself and more or less openly selling Government guns and ammunition to the rebels in the Sierras. In addition most of our neighbors were Yaquis—industrious, prosperous, upstanding people, but more or less in friendly communication with their unruly brethren. The points of attack were the towns on either side of us, Esperanza, a swarming little village right on the river, and Navajoa, towards Guaymas. While I was in Cajeme the Yaquis attacked Esperanza, drove out the garrison, seized the military supplies, and captured the Commandant and his aide. These two, the Indians tied to their horses' tails and galloped with them heads down, up one street and another until they were dead. In Navajoa the Yaquis found several carloads of rice. Rice evidently is not part of their diet. Corn or *garbanzas* they carry off with them to the mountains, but rice is still a foreign product, grown on large plantations, and connected in their minds with foreign exploitation. On the occasion of this attack they dumped the rice on the ground, slit the sacks, and trampled it into the mud with the hoofs of their cayuses.

In those days we worked in the fields with rifles, and some of our neighbors were frequently sniped at by skulking Indians. Four foreign boys from Cajeme set out one day for Esperanza to buy seed and tools, but were intercepted by some Yaquis burning a railway bridge. They were stripped and the bottoms of their feet sliced off. They were then made to run until they dropped, whereupon their bodies were broken up with clubs. The federal commandant in Esperanza, when informed that the boys had been seized, was too frightened to stir until the following day. The most pathetic of these brutal incidents was in connection with an ex-Bowery bum and evangelist who came to Cajeme intent upon converting the Yaquis. This plump little bald-headed fellow set out alone, deaf to every counter persuasion, with his Bible. He found Yaquis. They stripped him and spanked him out of camp with cactus thorns. He arrived in Cajeme stark naked, blistered by the ferocious sun, swollen up with poison oak.

These anecdotes indicate only the most terrible war-time characteristics of the tribe. They do not indicate the true qualities of the thousands who have entered into the civilized medium to become the most intelligent, hard-working and honest native workers in the country.

The Yaquis are part of the Cahita branch of the Mexican-Opata group, the other two Cahita divisions being the Mayos (not to be confused with the Mayas of Yucatán) and the Tehuecos. The Cahitas have the general physical characteristics of the Nahuatl Indians: large torsos, small legs, small bones, broad faces, straight black hair, piercing black eyes; but they are the tallest, most physically superb Indians in Mexico. The Yaquis are extremely "nationalistic" and look with hatred, fear and contempt upon the whiter outsiders whom they call *Yori*. Their love for their own race and land, the *patria chica*, is intense. When Díaz deported many of them to Yucatán, some walked penniless the whole length of Mexico to regain their native Sierras. And though during the recent revolutionary epoch many of them served in the revolutionary and national armies, and were brought in contact with remote parts of Mexico, they found little enjoyment in the outside world, and waited for the first opportunity to return to Bácum, Pótam, Torín, their beloved home pueblos.

During the four centuries, since Nuñoz de Guzmán, the notorious enemy of Hernando Cortez, penetrated the Yaqui region with an expedition (1533), the race (though knowing but eighty-five years of peace in a stretch of nearly four hundred years) has maintained its original customs, autonomy

and governing habits. The Yaquis have absorbed a few religious notions largely mixed with idolatry, and though calling themselves Catholic, and fanatic in their beliefs, their cult is fundamentally pagan. Even the semi-civilized Yaquis in the lowlands; the peons on the haciendas, the employees in the mines and on the railroads, seem never to quite lose contact with the main race-stock which has been driven into the Sierras. Yaquis continually enlist in the Mexican army, gain equipment, clothing, shoes, ammunition, and a gun, then promptly desert for the Sierras again. The Yaquis are a beautiful, proud, virile, hardship-innured, cruel, war-like people, tenaciously clinging to their independence and the ways of their fathers, only vaguely aware of the terrific force of the march of modern progress which is gradually enveloping them. Yet the Mexican constitution and law—since nearly half the country is pure Indian and eighty-five percent of it within the Indian tradition—make the Yaquis full-fledged Mexican citizens, and, theoretically, an integral part of the Mexican Republic.

The character traits of the Yaquis and the nature of the terrain they inhabit makes any campaign against them comparable to that against the Rifs. The Sierra Madres that run down through Sonora, Chihuahua, Durango and Sinaloa into the Central portion of Mexico are startlingly severe and rugged. Viewed from Cajeme they present a jagged impregnable aspect, jutting up sharply, cruelly, inaccessibly out of the broad lowland llano, their great bare rock-bound flanks purple and reddish and sterile in the blazing sun. I once crossed these mountains south of the Yaqui country with an Indian mail-carrier, from Culiacán, the capital of Sinaloa, through the very tiptop of the Sierras, Topia, Tepehuanes, all the way to Durango; and the great precipices, bottomless barrancas, the sun-seared heights, made them the most consistently difficult climbing I have ever experienced. It was in these Sierras, I think, that I first half sensed, half understood the cruel bravado of the Mexican people; their reckless yet

182

Spartan character, moulded by desert, crag, and drumming southland light, by clear brittle winter cold and remorseless winds ravening over vast valleys. These Sierras have helped to determine the stark impregnable character of the Yaqui Indians.

Another physiographic factor that has contributed to the basic, age-old independence of the Yaquis, but which in more recent times has led to constant bitter warfare with the outside world, is the Yaqui River. This stream starts thousands of feet high in the very crest of the harsh Sierras. Two branches, the Bivaspe and Moctezuma, cut increasingly wide and fertile paths through the very heart of the crags, and, joining near Tonichí, swing down in one broad river through the fertile bottom lands to the Gulf of California. These lower reaches are magnificent—a soil and climate to grow almost anything in the world. Once properly placed under cultivation, they will put California to shame in productivity and beauty. These were the traditional lands of the Yaquis. Gradually pushed back and back into the sterile Sierras, condemned to less valuable areas, the Yaquis nevertheless have conserved their group integrity, but at the same time were forced into a tactic of periodic crop-raiding. The longest intervals of peace with the Yaquis have occurred when, from time to time, they have been restored to some of their ancient heritage and allowed to settle on the old bottom lands.

The Yaquis have had sad experiences with the outside world, but they often managed to hold their own. They wiped out every man of the expedition of Diego Hurtado de Mendoza, the first attacker to reach Yaqui country. Years later the Spaniards were surprised to find their own weapons in the hands of their adversaries—an adaptability to new military devices that still characterizes the tribe. The first real penetration occurred under Nuñoz de Guzmán in 1533, and the first battle occurred on October 5, 1535. Nuñoz de Guzmán represented the most terrible excrescence of Spanish cruelty and greed. He it was who, in Michoacan, vented on the Indian King, Caltzontzín, the most horrible tortures ever devised by the Inquisition itself to make him disclose his treasures. Nuñoz de Guzmán was the most hated of all the Spanish Conquistadores both by his associates and the conquered, and for his cruelties was finally removed from his command and exiled to Torrejon de Velasco in Spain. There is no reason to believe that when he went to the Yaqui country—which he believed to be the storehouse and fountainhead of all the native wealth of Mexico—that he was any less merciful.

Yet, during the Colonial epoch, the Yaquis were not greatly molested and though in almost constant conflict with the vice-royalty, only one really serious rebellion occurred— in 1740. Independence with its factions, its new ideal of Indianism, its granting of political rights to the indigenes, brought the Yaquis, willynilly, in spite of their proud isolation, directly into the national arena as participants. For a hundred years they have been the tools of ambitious politicians, then disillusioned adversaries against their erstwhile protectors. Lured by love of fighting and promise of reward, they have been recruited in various national causes only in the end to be obliged to turn against the central authorities they previously helped to put into power; or they have been weaned over by new rebellious factions to support new unprofitable causes. Thus in 1838 they were recruited by General Urrea and Governor Gándara against the central authorities. In the succeeding two decades they were stirred up successively to further the schemes of Gándara and later his enemy Pesqueira. During the French invasion, they were used by the Clericals in support of Maximilian, though an appreciable group under Chief Cajeme supported the Republicans. And during the more recent revolutionary period, Madero capitalized the Yaqui hatred against Díaz; the Sonora triumvirate, Obregón, De la Huerta, and Calles, found in the Yaquis the nucleus of their military strength. They were given lands, subsidies, and allowed to retain their arms, and

184

with the exception of a short interval during the presidency of Carranza, refrained from any "nationalistic" expression, remaining in concord with the federal authorities they so efficaciously assisted into power. Obregón was the first to betray them and wrench away their valley lands for the "n"th time.

On occasions the Yaquis have had great and fearless leaders who have lived on the slogan of Yaqui freedom and independence. These have been most successful when they have advocated Indianism, and no intercourse with the outside mestizos and whites.

Díaz at the beginning of his first presidency was confronted with the most bitter Yaqui war in Mexico's history. His policy towards them was his traditional policy of *"Pan o palo*—Bread or the club."* In 1882 the Yaquis captured Cajeme and held it against all assaults until 1887, when the Yaqui leader Tetabiate was decorated and lands were given to the Indians. Yet the war continued with short armistices on up until 1900. At times the policy of the central government towards the Yaquis has been liberal and enlightened, but inevitably local officials, greedy militarists, unscrupulous carpet-baggers and land-seekers constantly encroached upon Yaqui rights, defrauded them, and antagonized them into new activities. And so in 1900 Díaz embarked upon his war-to-the-finish policy, sending troops into the very heart of the Yaqui territory, burning their pueblos, deporting them by thousands to the slave-camps of Yucatán. Yet persistently the Yaquis fought off every invasion and returned to the attack. The steady campaigning against the Yaquis cost the Mexican treasury enormous sums and was a contributing cause to the downfall of the Dictator, a most utilizable focus of disaffection for the Maderistas.

With the succeeding years of revolution, the fighting instincts of the Yaquis found outlet in support of the revolutionary movements, particularly in backing Obregón, who may have had some Yaqui blood in his veins.

With the inauguration of a far-sighted policy of land-distribution, the Yaquis until 1926 remained, with the short exception of a part of Carranza's régime, in peace.

After retiring from the presidency, Obregón engaged in growing *garbanzas* on the fertile tract on the lowlands of the Yaqui River, the traditional Yaqui lands. Cajeme, the old objective, was entirely in his hands. In addition he controlled the entire *garbanza* distribution for the Republic of Mexico; and it was freely charged that this monopoly control, the consequent foreclosures of the lands of the settled Yaquis and the antagonizing of the Indians by the local division general, Manzo, a long-standing friend of Obregón, were among the causes when the Yaquis rose up in 1926. The Yaquis also claimed that the Government had been taking away their lands on one pretext or another to bestow them on favorites. The Government, on its side, claimed that the outbreak was but another evidence of the incurable unruliness of the Yaquis. This last revolt was put down after enormous campaign difficulties, a vivid understanding of which can be obtained from such campaigning novels as Heriberto Frías's *Tomochic*. Armed subjection of the Yaqui region can never be expected to provide any final or satisfactory solution.

The Yaquis are part of the Amerind population of Mexico; they represent one of the important "nation" blocs. Any solution of the Yaqui question must be in harmony with a general policy towards all such nation blocs: the Mayas, the Tarascans, the Zapotecs, the Mixtecs, the Nahuas, the Otomies. Theoretically all these people are Mexican citizens; yet many of them—perhaps two million—cannot even speak Spanish. And it is impossible, whatever their attitude toward the Center, to consider them as aliens. The border line between the Indian and the Mestizo with Indian blood is in many cases slight. Probably over half of the people living in the Indian habitat are tinctured with the blood of other races, European or Oriental. As a matter of fact Mexico has never developed a definite Indian policy because the Indian is a Mexican, along with the Mestizo and the Creole. The cultural conflict involved is thus more or less concealed from view. Yet the great popular movements, those of Juárez and Madero, had their roots deep in the Indian consciousness. The revolutionary Mexican Government, on the other hand, is still square within the Roman-Spanish super-state tradition; and the Indian leaders who have risen to power during the past hundred years, establishing themselves by one program of liberation or another, have inevitably, once they gained office, been swept out of the popular current into the closed confines of the super-state, and there developed an arbitrary semi-feudal psychology unrestrained by direct and active public opinion.

Confronted with the difficulty of reconciling the various regional, racial, and cultural tendencies of Mexico, so ramified and complex, the Mexican rulers have ever resorted to the arbitrary methods of militarism. This is a natural short-cut in a country lacking cultural, racial or political cohesion and clamoring for peace, but the circle is vicious. The same old story is being repeated even today. The present governmental tendency towards Boxerism, towards anti-foreignerism, towards the expression of an intense nationalism requires, if it is to succeed, cultural uniformity, and strong political cohesion. Such cohesion, when brought about by pure force, is at once at war with the aspirations of the various *patrias chicas*, or local race cultures. The strong nation-front towards the outside world, the Government fears, may be weakened by a tolerance of internal diversities. Yet, paradoxically, the urge toward nationalism in Mexico is the outgrowth of the autonomous urge of these local cultural and racial entities—if not for political autonomy (as in the case of the Yaquis), then cultural autonomy, by which I mean the recognition the right to cling to the old ceremonies and old habits.

The vital problem of the newer nationalism is its reconciliation with historical local "nationalisms." To destroy the smaller walls may in the long run destroy the best there is in Mexico. The outstanding man in recent times in Mexico to see these difficulties scientifically and clearly has been Doctor Manuel Gamio, former head of the Bureau of Anthropology, who restored the pyramid of Quetzalcoatl and the Ciudadela at San Juan Teotihuacán, one of the most remarkable archaeological efforts ever undertaken by any Government. But in these restorations Doctor Gamio had not merely an archaeological interest. He made them part of a general scheme of reintegrating the culture of the inhabitants of the Valley of Teotihuacán. These restorations went side by side with a social survey of the Valley, a study which aimed to discover what elements of the old culture were worthy of perpetuation, together with some workable methods of perpetuating them. His Bureau was interested in how to arouse group cultural consciousness, how to make the existing handicrafts more economically worth while. This has a value, not only for Mexico but for the world. In other words, Dr. Gamio realized that the problem in Mexico was not merely that of inviting foreign capital, of steam-rolling the people into modern civilization, but of giving to the modern world the valuable elements of ancient cultures which, while not on the modern level, were nevertheless worthy of survival and incorporation into the pattern of contemporary life, and which would tend to strengthen and make more contented the people among whom he was working. He was extending this same program to Oaxaca, and expected ultimately to see similar studies carried on among all the separate race entities of Mexico and thus create an organic cooperative nationalism quite distinct from the Caesarian tactics of merely political and military imposition. Dr. Gamio was shamefully eliminated from the Calles' Government for attempting to suppress graft in his department, and his work, the most impressive and potentially worth while in Mexico, was arbitrarily terminated; a work which had definite constructive bearing upon the Yaqui solution.

The Yaqui problem is not merely one of military subjugation, but of Indian regeneration and reincorporation, comprising what is known as Mexico. The fact that the Yaquis are less amenable to outside discipline and are more war-like, does not alter the fact that they are part of the great Mexican-Opata family of peoples, and that when individually brought into a civilized habitat they prove singularly assimilatable. The ultimate solution of the Yaqui problem depends first upon economic justice, the restoration of stolen valley lands and guarantees of civil rights; and, second, upon constructive efforts like Doctor Gamio's. If the Mexican Governments, during the many years of fighting the Yaquis, had used the millions upon millions of pesos thus wasted, towards developing in the Yaqui nation the traits necessary for any large scheme of national cooperation, conceivably a Yaqui problem might not now exist. Unfortunately every single general in Mexico costs more than a dozen trained experts; generals however are at hand, greedy, reckless, restive from enforced peace; they have to be propitiated. Constructive civil workers are scarce; and so the Government finds, time and again, its readiest solution, military force. Attempts to crush the Yaquis, to exterminate them, can never take the place of a definite constructive policy towards the vast indigenous rural population of which the Yaquis are but one important unit.

r.R.

XII   THE NEW INDIAN

Back in 1918, when travel-
ing far up in the Sierra Madre of Durango, I stayed the night
in the home of a young Tepehuane Indian named Martín.
His house, though better than neighboring thatched *jacales*,
was a humble one-room dirt-floor cabin, containing a table
contrived out of a long home-hewn board on stumps, straw
mats, an adobe brazier, and a flat grinding stone for maize.
A commercial calendar and a cheap print of the Virgin hung
on the walls. His only reading materials, proudly shown me,
were a machinery catalogue, a torn illustrated magazine, and
a small school geography.

Martín, who dreamed some day of going to the United
States, asked me the English names for familiar objects. After
much searching, he unearthed a smudged piece of paper and a
stubby pencil. With labor-gnarled hands, painfully he traced
out the words I spelled for him. Our only light was the glow
from the brazier and one spluttering candle, which Martín's
sister held close to the paper, her free hand ready to catch
the hot falling wax. The rest of the family crowded around
to watch Martín struggle with the stubby pencil—two old
parents, two daughters and a neighbor boy. Their faces,

190

flecked by the gleams from the candle, shone with their awe at the process, for none of them had ever been to school; they beheld the written word as mysterious and magical. The night, strangely forlorn in that lofty remote mountain setting, turned late and cold; but Martín, in spite of a long day's toil in the fields, was insatiable; far into the early hours, while his sister patiently held the candle, he asked me English words and toiled with his stubby pencil; for struggle as he would, his blunt fingers refused to perform the unaccustomed task with any facility. His letters were as huge and scrawling and laughable as those of a child of six.

The next morning, when I left, Martín all but wept. Never have I seen a human being so hungry for the crumbs of knowledge as that Indian boy in the high wind-swept sierras; never have I seen people so awed by the cabalism of mere written words; and ever since that eerie mountain night, the words I have put on paper have seemed more magical and more precious.

Beginning with Obregón's administration in 1920, in spite of repeated unprincipled military revolts and in spite of the unrelieved financial embarrassment of the Government, real efforts were made to carry knowledge to the remotest Indian centers of the country and to incorporate the Indian into the cultural nationality known as Mexico. The work was fragmentary, beset with a thousand obstacles; but it was one of the lode-stars which guided the educational program of the régime which remained in power during 1920-30. More rural schools were established during that decade than ever before existed in the country. Many of the Martíns of Mexico, for the first time, came to have part of their longing for knowledge satisfied. In spite of great gaps in rural Indian education, there was the beginning of a spiritual renascence of the indigenous population. And once there is a new Indian there will be a new Mexico.

For the Indian is the real, the basic Mexican. If actual blood purity is considered, probably there are not much more

191

than four million Indians in Mexico; at least eight and a half million Mestizos, or people of mixed blood; and a scant million whites. But racially the mestizos have been bred closer to the Indian than to the white. The great majority of them are reabsorbed back into the native race-stream. And if the criterion be political, economic, and cultural, a super conservative estimate must characterize two thirds of the country as Indian. At least ten million people in Mexico live in the Indian habitat, have Indian customs, and react according to the Indian mentality. Probably ten million people sleep on *petate* mats or in hammocks. Two million people do not even speak or understand Spanish. Fundamentally Mexico is an Indian country.

Señor Moisés Sáenz, former Sub-Secretary of Education, after a tour of rural Indian school districts, reported, "The traveler on the central plateau feels himself a complete foreigner everywhere. In many villages, only through an interpreter is it possible to obtain a drink of water or the simplest information. . . . Among themselves the children prefer to speak 'Mexicano' (the native Nahuatl tongue). Even in places where the children speak Spanish with a certain fluidity, the adults use their own dialect."

Within a few hours of the capital, in the same Anáhuac Valley, are found villages where no Spanish is spoken or understood.

Mexico harbors at least two score separate Indian peoples; at least four stocks with quite distinct characteristics. Their customs are different; their languages are different; their cultures are different. They are, however, probably of the same race; they live under very similar economic conditions. Their differences however complicate the task of welding them into the Mexican nationality. The four leading stocks are the Nahuatl, on the central plateau and in the western sierras; the Otomies, north of the Nahuatls on the plateau; the Zapotecs and Mixtecs in Oaxaca, Vera Cruz and particularly the Isthmus of Tehuantepec; the Mayas of Yucatán, Quintana

192

Roo, Chiapas, Tabasco, and Campeche—states of the south-east. Besides these major groups, note the Yaquis of Sonora; the Tarascans around the Michoacán lakes (perhaps the oldest peoples of all); the Chamulas in Chiapas, and other important divisions.

What is the rural organization in Mexico? It differs radically from that in the United States. In 1910 (according to the Mexican census of that year), of the rural population (69.3 per cent of the total and overwhelmingly Indian), 9,591,752 persons lived in servitude known as peonage; free souls totalled but 479,074; the semi-rural population (i.e., partially supporting itself with small rural industries and trades) was but 430,896. By the 1921 census the number of persons living on haciendas (though no longer in servitude) was 3,837,800; and the number in free villages, 6,725,600. What a tremendous change in social status!

The free Indian villages have a precarious economic basis. Two types exist—the "scattered" and the "congregated." The scattered communities are those least under the influence of the central government and the national culture. These are found on the highest ranges and in the deepest tropical forests. The inhabitants pay little or no taxes; they retain their own festivals, their own law and its administration. The village is but a casual meeting place; the government center where their officials live for a short portion of the year. It consists of a few houses, sometimes a church, sometimes a school. Occasionally there is a resident bilingual secretary.

The majority of the Indians, however, live in congregated villages. Their lives, though no longer enslaved, are still very uncertain. In spite of the Government agrarian program, the villages for the most part possess insufficient lands; they are still hemmed in by large haciendas; the Indian lands are usually poorer than the adjacent large private holdings. Sometimes the villages war with each other over the boundaries. Youth wars with age in the same village, for the Government program of land distribution failed to foresee population expansion, so that the younger, more vigorous males are disinherited and so must pass back to the hacienda or drift to the cities. In the more truly Indian centers, the village land is owned communally; individually where the Indian tradition has been more broken down. These villages lack tools and work animals; agricultural methods are primitive; often the natives insist upon cultivating corn and beans, whatever the character of the soil, because those products comprise the minimum diet; and because there is no extensive barter, no established system of distribution or exchange with other centers. The villages are isolated; the great majority of them are approached by mule trails, over which no wheeled traffic can pass.

The village sadly lacks professional people. Dr. Manual Gamio but a few years ago noted that in the Valley of Teotihuacán (30 miles from Mexico City), having a population of 8,000 people, there were only 22 professional people; and in this number he included teachers without professional title, native herb doctors, and priests. Probably ninety percent of the villages of Mexico are without any truly professional assistance in the way of engineers, chemists, pharmacists, doctors, lawyers, etc. The houses are one-room shacks, for the most part without furniture, only straw mats, or sisal hammocks. There is little sanitation; though many groups, such as the Maya, are scrupulously clean from the standpoint of bathing and clothing. The food is largely tortillas (corn cakes), beans and chili. Meat is a rare luxury. Milk is almost an unknown treat. The universal tool is the machete, a long curved knife. For the vast majority of these villages to build a school is an impossibility, because, having no hammers, saws, or nails, they cannot construct the necessary tables and chairs. The cooking utensils are a few earthenware pots. The tortilla serves for a spoon. Dress is scanty: white cotton pyjamas for the men; calico skirts and a thin rebozo or scarf for the women; sometimes a sarape serves as a cloak in the day time and a blanket at night. Most of the

Indians go barefoot or wear *guaraches* or sandals. The Mexican Indian is poor.

The revolution has not appreciably elevated rural economic standards; it has merely provided new instruments for bettering them in the future.

For a time the Government made Herculean efforts to make the Indian self-conscious, individually and socially. There have been earlier moments in Mexican history when the Indian became truly self-conscious. During the colonial period there were serious Indian uprisings. In the Independence movement, the Indian was willing cannon fodder. Later, he found leadership in the reform movement under the pureblooded Zapotec Indian from Oaxaca, Benito Juárez. But at no time, during the 1910-30 revolution, was any serious effort made by him or his leaders to create the basic economic independence which would lead to permanent social, political and cultural expression.

By the end of the Díaz period, the Indian was in an infamous position of servitude, more terrible than any known since the conquest. In the Dictator's day, the Indian could not stroll down the main avenue of the capital. He could not loiter in the public gardens. Most towns had two promenades, one for the well-dressed, another for the Indian. Class distinctions and race distinctions were sharply drawn. The Indian was in serfdom. He was subject to arbitrary conscription. He could be rounded up, at will, and set to forced public labors without compensation. He could be beaten and killed by his employers with impunity. Yaquis were sold into slavery in the sweltering henequen fields of Yucatán at $65 a head; some of them walked the whole length of Mexico to regain their *patria chica*. The hacendados often took first night privilege with the serf's daughters. Thus the Conquest was not really completed until the reign of Porfirio Díaz. By 1910 the Indian could be no more brutally enchained.

In 1910, Hope girded herself in bullets. The Indian piled pell mell into the revolution. Little wonder he committed acts of brutality. The story is told of enslaved Yaquis on an hacienda in Oaxaca, who at night were locked in a narrow barred room, so small they had to sleep with their legs across each other. At the call of the revolution, these Yaquis burst loose, seized the Spanish proprietor and nailed him alive to his own housedoor. The Indian, in the revolution secured arms, which he has never completely relinquished. In 1928, the Governor of Morelos invited me to attend the anniversary of the death of Emiliano Zapata, the Indian peasant leader of south Mexico. From the state palace, I watched ten thousand agrarians in tall peaked sombreros ride by on their cayuses; sarapes and guns strapped to their saddlebows. The Indians, in many places, are organized into corps of social defense, and retain a loose military hierarchy. Such peasant volunteers in 1923 undermined the De la Huerta revolt in Vera Cruz and Oaxaca; and during the revolt of the early part of 1929 thousands of them swarmed from nowhere, across the arid deserts of the north, to offer their services to Calles at Jiménez when he was facing the rebel General Escobar.

After the rifle, the peasant next learned to use the assembly hall. He proceeded to organize—a thing unpermitted, undreamed of during the Díaz epoch. The Leagues of the Tillers of Common Lands, the National Agrarian Party, the National Peasants League, have been partial expressions of this new Indian consciousness, transcending primitive and ancient tribal units and hurtling itself into the arena of national politics. To attend any gathering where the Indian peasants gather in their regional dress, is a colorful experience. Here mingle tall Zapatistas in black silver braided sombreros, so wide they scarcely pass through the doors; short, stocky, broad-faced Mayas from the Leagues of Resistance; leather-clad rancheros from the Sierras; "pyjama"-clad Huachinangos from Puebla; slender Huastecans from Vera Cruz, their shirt-tails out, knotted over wide cartridge belts.

Originally the agrarian ideal of the Government was to see that each village had its communal lands, the necessary implements to exploit them, a cooperative organization, a cooperative store and distribution mechanism, and a school. This effort was to be coordinated with a system of rural credits, based upon the cooperatives and cooperative banks affiliated with the central National Agricultural Bank established in 1926. The states where most progress has been made along these various lines are probably Tamaulipas, Morelos, and Hidalgo. The cooperative groups are known as Local Societies for Agricultural Credit; the basis for loans being collective responsibility, since the communal lands cannot be mortgaged; and these societies must acquire shares in the bank before they can receive loans. At present there are four such state farmer banks in Mexico: in Durango, Hidalgo, Guanajuato, Michoacán.

Such efforts have been only sporadic. The technical equipment of the free village is still inadequate. But the distribution of lands (nearly thirteen million acres provisionally; and nearly eight million acres definitely); the creation of the free village; efforts to organize the peasants and to facilitate them with rural credits, irrigation, and implements—all this has permanently and profoundly altered the economic, political and psychological map of Mexico.

This partial emancipation created the immediate necessity for educating and directing the rural masses. A purely village system of agriculture, with its production restricted to beans, corn, and chili, stands in open contradiction with modern industry, with the needs of urban life and the creation of a unified national consciousness. The self-sufficient village creates a limited and ingrowing mentality, which cannot be successfully utilized for founding a national state. The government, under such conditions, would soon revert to a parasitical institution controlled by the army and upper-class cliques, without cultural or racial roots.

The educational problem was approached from both the technical and the cultural side. The Department of Agriculture originally hoped to plant agricultural schools in each of the states and territories. Five such modern institutions were created. The pupils live at the school in model dormitories. These are planted on large haciendas, big enough to permit diversified crops, so that the schools may ultimately become self-supporting. Those already founded are rapidly approaching that status. Half the time is given to school room instruction, the rest to work in the fields. Special night courses are given to adults. The instruction includes, not merely the practical aspects of farming, but instruction in native handicrafts and rural industries, also physical education and sports. Unfortunately these schools are almost too good and pretentious. A peasant student accustomed to a model swimming pool, to clean beds, to advanced civilized habits is in a predicament when he returns to his village, where he must revert to a more primitive life. He is too apt to drift to the cities instead.

Under José Vasconcelos, Obregón's Minister of Education, an effort was to send out "missionary" teachers. Though called "missionary," their work was non-religious.

Once on a high sierra in the tropical state of Guerrero, I watched a long cavalcade wind along the brow of a ravine and vanish from a sheer skyline that sent the eye hurtling down over a vast empire to the Pacific. The queer, slow-moving file brought to mind those Aztec processions in which the priests wound up to their star-pointing teocallis, to tear out the hearts of their human sacrifices. It revived the gold days in California when long mule teams struck through the mountain wilds to find fortune. But this train of people was not going to place a heathen god, nor was it seeking the gold that glitters. It was made up of Indian Mexicans going to greet the visiting Government missionary teacher and open a People's House (Casa del Pueblo) where they and their children might congregate and study to add a broader cultural unity to their racial unity.

Under the Bureau of Indigenous Culture in the Department of Education was built up a special corps of these native rural teachers, who went out to teach the more isolated racial elements. In 1924, there were about one hundred and ten so-called missionary teachers, ten "cultural missionaries," and six hundred special rural teachers. In the six years that followed, instead of single teachers, small corps of specialists were sent out, a director, teacher, nurse or social service worker, physical culture director, an instructor for small industries, an agrarian expert, music teacher and art instructor. Such units train the local teachers and give special courses to the adults. They are provided, each with a model exhibit house, made of the same materials as those in local use, but constructed in accordance with the minimum needs of comfort, hygiene, and ventilation.

These missionary teachers often suffer real hardships. Frequently they must sleep on the ground, eat the scant beans and tortillas that comprise the native diet. A missionary teacher from Chiapas once sent me the following:

> "San Pablo . . . the municipal center, is composed of a palace for the Ayuntamiento and a badly roofed retreat (called a church) in which may be found half a dozen images of such antiquity that they have completely lost the character the artist originally sought to give them; while scattered here and there may be counted some twenty houses—empty. Their owners occupy them only when they come down from the mountains to consider some government order. These conferences are usually celebrated when they wish to elude or make difficult the enforcement of some law or regulation. In general, the only permanent dwellers in the place are the municipal agent, the school teacher, his family and about a dozen pupils."

This missionary then went into the mountains to the tinier villages, the very names of which betray the problem involved: Pat-Pom, Blancol, Tzalatón, Huaquileim, Toxho, Canteal, Pakanán, Cachuit, Potzacoalc, Maenlum, Temanil, Chichinsulum, Saclum, Jolyulantic, Hachochén, Itzalachón, Juagulatón, Yaxhaljeml. . . .

Mere schooling alone, however, cannot alone overcome the traditions of village isolation. Thus Xochiapulco, a town in the state of Puebla, has had a government school since 1870; yet to this day three fourths of the adult population does not speak Spanish. It is not enough merely to teach the children to read and write the national tongue, but common interests must be created which tie up permanently with the nation at large.

Under Díaz, rural education was woefully neglected. Madero conserved the remnants of the Dictator's rural system. Carranza was harried by military problems so severe that even urban education almost ceased to exist. The last year of his administration, only a little over six million pesos were spent; and most of the schools, even in the Federal District, were closed. Obregón immediately pegged the budget for education up to fifty million pesos. Rural education came to life again. By 1924, 1,044 rural schools had been founded with a personnel cost of $1,540,128 (pesos); by the end of 1928 the number had increased to 3,392 with a personnel cost of $4,296,810 (pesos). By 1930 the number had been brought up to nearly five thousand. Yet in that year in the rich, populous state of Querétaro but four children in a hundred went to school!

In some places the Government encounters obstinate Indian resistance to its educational program. Schools among the Chamula Indians in Chiapas frequently have been attacked and the lives of teachers endangered. When the Yaquis signed their last pact of peace with the central authorities, they demanded that no Government schools be established. But for the most part, the educational department has met with enthusiastic cooperation. Hundreds of villages have built their own schools—invariably the most imposing building in any village,—and have begged the central authorities to send them teachers. Often they guarantee the salary of the teacher. Early in 1929, President Portes Gil showed me numerous photographs of imposing school buildings erected in his state,

Tamaulipas, by the local cooperatives. Once I accompanied Moisés Sáenz on a trip to the schools of Puebla and Tlaxcala. The Indians from villages for miles around heard of the expedition, and appeared at the schools we were visiting with banners heralding education or their desire for a school, and bringing gifts of flowers. I have seen little children carrying stones to help build schools being erected with voluntary labor.

In order to foment interest in schools, the Department of Education has promoted the organization of local school committees composed of a government official and leading local citizens, in order to gain support for the school already existing, or to create sentiment for the establishing of a school, to secure donations and consolidate the public interest. Such efforts were of untold democratic importance in a country where popular organization is a new and thrilling undertaking, where for more than four centuries any popular initiative in any public matters was severely discouraged. It is indicative of the new Indian's consciousness that such groups could be organized.

In 1925, the Mexican Government opened the "House of the Indian" in Mexico City for the purpose of training Indian boys from all over the country. This institution has by no means brought the desired results, since the gulf between Mexico City, its civilization and its vices, and the local village habitat is still too enormous. But President Calles, on opening the school, stated what may be considered an epitome of the policy of the régime at that time toward the Indian:

> "My purpose is to convert each one of you into a leader, an apostle, an instigator among your people, there where your brothers are; that you preach to them the light, and free them from their vices, and that you defend them. . . . You should struggle to better the lives of your kind, to elevate them spiritually, and see that they are no longer exploited . . . that their moral level be above that of the privileged classes . . . that they may thus cooperate for

202

the welfare, the prosperity, and the greatness of the father-land."

And Señor Ramón Beteta, formerly of the Department of Education, in his address to the Inter America Institute at Claremont, California, summed up this effort which has "taken away from the Indian his feeling of inferiority . . . which has given to thousands and thousands a chance in life and an opportunity to educate themselves . . . which is endeavoring to integrate the Indian in our civilization . . . which is determined to make a nation out of a starving country." He declared:

"For you of the United States, for whom the only good Indian was the dead Indian; for you, the descendants of the Englishmen who advanced like a wall on this continent, pushing in front of them the buffalo, the Indians, and the wild beasts alike; for you, with your Indian reservations and those theatrical degenerate Indians of Yuma; for you, my attitude must seem foolish. But for anyone in whose veins Spanish and Indian blood mingle, for anyone who has not regarded the negro as a domestic animal and the Indian as a wild animal, for anyone who understands Christianity as meaning *treat your fellow-man as thyself*, and as commanding *never treat your neighbor as a means, but always as an end*, for that person, my opinion must seem just and reasonable."

All Mexico in a way has adventured on rediscovering the soul and the capacities of the Indian; his poetical imaginings, his fine sensibility, his remarkably plastic fingers, his craftsmanship as displayed in his weaving, his pottery; his communal democratic spirit; his grotesque humor as revealed in his toys and art products; his power of directness and simplification. The rediscovery of the ancient Indian and his powers, is shaping a new Indian who will be brought into relationship with the country and the modern world.

To summarize: Since 1910 the Indian population has been

taken out of serfdom and restored to status as a free Mexican citizen; two thirds of the Indians of Mexico now live in free villages. Probably 800,000 heads of families have received land; this means that over half the Indian population of Mexico has a new and free economic hold upon life. A very small minority has also been helped by rural credits. Probably a fourth of the Indian population is in touch with some autonomous peasant organization. Probably between a fourth and a fifth of the Indian school population has access to educational opportunities. Educational contacts of one sort and another probably influence many more.

This means greatly altered the outlook for the mass of the Mexican population. On the other hand, the Indian, if present tendencies are aborted, can fall into an even worse state as a free man than as a serf. The new free villages, still lacking sufficient good land, lacking technique, tools, equipment, knowledge, power, remain in a twilight period. If the promises of this freedom are not fulfilled and recent reactionary developments make it very improbable that the agrarian gains will be properly consolidated, a free Indian can become more dangerous than an Indian in serfdom. But if an organic peace ever is achieved in Mexico, it will be because the new freedom is being systematically utilized and directed.

XIII   DON MELCHOR:
FLESH OF THE REVOLUTION

1

We HAD ridden northeast from Uruápam—the end of the railroad line—into the very heart of the Tarascan region, up toward what are known as the eleven pueblos. The serpent road wound through ascending pine-clad ridges, thrust itself through the primitive villages of San Lorenzo and Apácuaro, gay with tissue paper and bright costumes for festivals in honor of the Assumption of Mary, then uncoiled across a fertile meadow to Paracho, nestling against remote hills. In San Lorenzo and Apácuaro, the natives had crowded around us with gaping mouths, black tangled hair clouding their animal-like eyes, so fierce and yet liquid; or they had fled with chirps of fright into the depths of their corn fields. But in Paracho, a much larger center of four thousand inhabitants, we found a hum, throbbing through its sleepy provincialism. Remote though it is, the place is stirred with some purpose not quite discernible. There is an air of change, of the subtle passing of an epoch. Actually, Paracho is a town twice reborn. It is in the throes of its second rebirth.

We arrived in the plaza in the midst of squealing uproar. A *topil*, one of the town constables, an ancient rifle slung over the shoulder of his tattered jacket, was busy dragging pigs off the central bandstand plaza to the municipal corral, where they languished unfed until the owner redeemed them for a silver *tostón* (twenty-five cents) fine. Two bulls had their horns tied close against the trunks of the plaza willows, near which a dozen Tarascan Indians lounged in black sarapes and white trousers, stroking guitars. The bulls had broken into a neighboring corn *milpas* and were now redeemable for two and a half dollars. The *topil*, a boy of eighteen, first cousin of the mayor, boasted to us that he made five pesos a day commission off the animals he impounded. The pigs of too influential villagers, members of the National Revolutionary Party, the official ruling group, were shooed away; but less favored owners had to trudge over to the town hall and pay their fines with wry faces. Paracho—the *topil* informed us proudly—was determined to be clean and sanitary and up-to-date. It was a disgrace to use the plaza for a pigpen. Besides, he was saving money to go to the United States.

Over in the dilapidated one-story, flat-roofed adobe town hall, the town judge, an old man with steel-rim spectacles, sat laboriously writing about these and other matters in longhand, lengthy documents gummed with long ladders of bright-colored revenue stamps. After completing each page, the judge would waddle out the door, across the sidewalk to the center of the street, where he would stand blinking and groaning in the sun to wait for the ink to dry.

Beside the main plaza rises a mountain of tumbled round stones, a crumbling wall and a bell tower—all that is left of the once lofty church. During the early days of the revolution, Paracho was razed to the ground; its people scattered to the four winds. Many went to the United States; others lurked nearby in the high timbered sierras, living on roots and berries, clothes reduced to rags. Slowly the place rebuilt itself. In 1928, the Cristero rebels swept into the plaza and once more made a clean sweep of everything. They fired their rifles into the town clock: the hands still stand at six thirty-two, the hour of the attack. We wandered through the stone lava lanes—in places gray, crumbling and cactus-grown, in others new and trim—between fields of magnificent red-stalked corn, twelve feet high. Everywhere were shattered blackened walls, sprouting weeds and lizards; but beside them are newly built houses.

Before the revolution, Paracho was typically Tarascan, with few outside influences. It lived from agriculture and handicrafts. The fame of its hand-made guitars, banjos and violins had spread throughout Mexico. The best carved, inlaid *molinillos*—chocolate beaters—came from here. Its workmen made carved furniture—which like the Tarascan houses had no nails—carefully jointed and fitted, sturdy as any machine-made product. The town had many primitive looms for weaving sarapes and *rebozos*. It was known for its religious masks and idols, the first remarkable for their ferocious and weird aspect, the second for their meekness and adoring humility. The tradition of masks and saints is now largely kept alive by Doña Lolita, a haughty Tarascan dame, who, where nosey infidels are concerned, will display no politeness and will sell nothing, pagan or Christian.

The town still makes some of the old products, but much of the traditional handicraft skill has been forever destroyed. There is only one loom in the town, which somehow miraculously escaped the general smashup. Some crafts, more fortunate, such as that of the ringed, inlaid chocolate beaters, survive. The wood for the beaters is turned by the most primitive lathe in the world. The motor power is an ancient flexible bow with the string passing about a spool. This is drawn with the right hand. The wood revolves against a chisel held by the feet. The left hand remains free for a cigarette.

Pre-revolutionary and even pre-conquest habits, a few still prevail. As of old, the women with red glazed Patamban jars, decorated with white birds, drift down to the deep wells on the outer edge of the town. They go chattering, mantled in their blue rebozos, the ends of the hundred pleats of the skirts of their *guari* costumes stick up behind their buttocks like the fan of some tropic bird. They haul up the water by buckets and ropes that swish through the ferns of the well-walls, in long swinging right-armed work rhythms, quite distinct from any of our Anglo-Saxon gesture. At dawn venders drive burros through the streets, each animal laden with four Patamban *ollas* swung dripping in sisal nets, and sell the precious fluid at house doors.

But in spite of these ancient patterns, Paracho is more and more another uprooted non-descript mestizo Mexican town, one foot in the primitive world, one foot in the mobile modern world, neither one thing nor the other, largely lacking the technique of the far-off civilized centers towards which the community unconsciously and inevitably is gravitating. Though many of the former residents have come back with a faint nostalgia, hoping to recover the old life, many newcomers have come, seeking a bustling center to settle in after the destructive decades of the revolution. New businesses have been started, alien habits and ways of thought follow in their wake. Emigrants to America have also come back with an outlook which prevents a revival of the old Tarascan isolation. Most Parachans now find it disgusting that the town has no modern plumbing, no electric lights, no adequate communication with the outside world.

What is amazing is how little, really, the emigrants to America brought back with them, beside a spirit of order and enterprise. Most of them, when in the States, worked as menial laborers on plantations, in the cotton fields, factories, steel-mills, packing houses. Their American world and their provincial Mexican world are so utterly distinct that little carries over. The women settle back to the laborious kitchen methods of past centuries, the back-breaking grinding of corn on prehistoric stone *metates,* cooking over pine-fed braziers. Their men now want to return to the United States. They work hard to get the money for the trip; and though they cannot be said to have acquired any American efficiency, still some special briskness they make show of gives the town an air of notable busyness.

2

Don Melchor swaggered down the sandy street. A blazing bandanna was knotted under his dusky bony chin; his black broad felt hat was drawn low upon his forehead; his puttees, encasing the pantaloons of his new khaki clothes, were highly polished. He sported an enormous repeating Mauser pistol, which we learned later had spit deadly fire into the face of an enemy not long before our arrival. With a sinister tilt of his head, he stared at us with a sharp squint from his one good, but slightly crooked eye. That investigatory optic and his insolent stare, as he paused in the shade of one of the gabled, jointed, wooden houses, so typical of Michoacán, seemed to symbolize the entire reckless menace of rural Mexico.

Don Melchor, of the wicked eye, lived in the United States seven years. His first job was on a Louisiana slave plantation, contract labor. After four months working sixteen hours a day, with scarcely enough food to keep alive, he escaped. A half dozen such experiences taught him how to look out for more regulated, less exploited employment. His last job was in a Carnegie rolling mill. Back in Paracho, in spite of being looked up to in the village, he longs to return to the United States.

"One can even die happily there," he announced. One of his four children, three of whom were born in America, died in Philadelphia. "It was taken to the grave in nice clothes and a pretty hearse. Today, when they carted Don Antonio off to the cemetery, I said to myself, 'Don Antonio is a wealthy Indian, yet he has never had shoes on his feet.

He was buried in *guaraches*, leather sandals. Is that a proper way for a human being to be buried?' "

"At any rate Don Antonio will not march to heaven with corns on his toes," I suggested.

Don Melchor did not rise to the line. He is a retired captain of the Mexican army and a deserter from the American army, the hero of eighteen battles. His horse was once shot from under him. He was wounded in the leg. He participated in the earlier revolutionary struggles in this region, galloping over the pine-clad ridges in a fever of courage and death. After his return from the United States, he promptly reenlisted with the Federal forces, this time against the Cristeros. Now, he is alienated from all his relatives, who are staunch Catholics.

Don Melchor as town constable nets about three pesos a day. Moreover he is chief of the local Social Defense Corps, a body welded out of voluntary revolutionary elements, mostly armed peasants, who alone of all civic organizations are permitted by the army to carry weapons. Don Melchor as local chief of Social Defense, while responsible to the army authorities, carries much of local justice in his hands. For political dissidents, bandits and personal enemies, that justice is peremptory—the justice of the firing squad, without trial, no questions answered, for that matter, none asked. Not all the forces in Paracho look on the Social Defense Corps with favor; but Don Melchor remains a man to be feared, a man to whom it is unwise to deny a favor.

He has, certainly, utilized his position and his guns to his personal economic advantage. He runs one of the smaller stores, the only place where liquor may be legally sold. His shop consequently has become an instrument of political control. Arms and booze, restricted to government favorites, explain the new rural dictatorship throughout all Mexico. Not merely in Paracho, but in many other places, the right to bear arms and the right to dispense booze are in the hands of the National Revolutionary Party, the official ruling party of the régime.

210

Land-distribution has been another political vote-getting instrument of the controlling party. Paracho is no exception. The lands seized by the government from haciendas adjacent to Paracho have been distributed with an eye to perpetuating political controls. Don Melchor, with capital, a store, and a town job, legally should not participate in land-distribution. As a matter of fact, he has three of the largest and best plots of the *ejidos* or so-called common lands, which he hires tilled, paying wages lower than the miserable doles of the old haciendas, again using his official position, his Mauser, and his prestige to secure results.

When we tried to find horses for a further ride into the Tarascan country, all threads led to Melchor. The five animals we needed could not be secured—until Melchor got on the job. At eight o'clock in the evening, he confidently assured us that we would have our mounts early the following morning, that he himself would accompany us wherever we wanted to go for as long a time as we wished—*"palabra de inglés."* His word was sterling. The horses were on hand—borrowed. No one cared to refuse him, except his own relatives. He charged full tariff on the borrowed animals and whangled three dollars a day out of us for his personal services, a sum which we paid with some amusement, for not to everyone is it granted to travel with the local political boss armed to the teeth with pistol, rifle and poniard. An economy, in the end, for he opened official buildings to us in which to sleep free of cost; and in Indian villages, suspicious of outsiders and averse to being photographed, he achieved results by arbitrary command, which would have cost us long delay and infinite tact and persuasion.

Don Melchor, with his wicked eye, his swagger, his heavy Mauser, his rifles, his long poniard, his right to dispense liquor, his participation in the spoils of the revolution, his status as a land-holder and an employer and a granter of favors, with one foot planted on good economic self-interest, the other on the good-will of federal higher-ups, bearing aloft and unsullied the ideal banner of the revolution, in addition to his ready weapons, is typical of the new ruler in rural Mexico. Don Melchor can almost say—"I am the Revolution." As a matter of fact, he is the latest variety of the pre-Cortesian Indian *cacique*, who after the Conquest became the hireling of the creoles; who after Independence reorganized the armed *ventenas* of the villages, and who in Díaz' day played with the large landholders instead of with the slogans of liberty.

Everywhere, the new Cæsar of the pueblos is the ex-militarist, the man with the gun on his hip, experienced in the use of it. The man with the gun on the hip first monopolizes drink. He sees that the proper people receive the lands distributed by the agrarian commissions. This cuts the roots of the budding peasant organizations, which for a time promised to provide a more democratic government in the autonomous villages. "The Free Village" was one of the great cries of the revolution. But in freeing itself from the *padre* and the landholder, it has fallen more than ever before in Mexico's history into the hands of the Melchors, the traditional *caciques*. Guns, booze, and land—this is the holy trinity on which has been founded the new universal political church of Mexico, a dictatorial National Revolutionary Party, sustained by forced collections from all government employees—a one-party system, more bare-faced than the Communists in Russia, or the Fascisti in Italy, hence now worthy of the plaudits of all those who value success more than liberty or honesty.

The system is practical, in that, for a time at least, it is likely to work. Yet it is threatened. Discontent in local communities will even again be surging up. More blood will ultimately be spilled, either by rivals of the actual Melchors or by the villagers as a mass asserting themselves anew. And the system is also exposed to the personal ambitions of the leaders at the top of the heap, the revolutionaries in Morelia, the state capital, or in far-off Mexico City—bigger and more prosperous Melchors. Cabinet ministers and generals—one and all are potential presidents; one and all are incessantly patching their personal political fences. One and all they ferret around for local support, out in the Parachos, the pueblos in the far Sierras. They prefer to utilize the established *caciques* like Melchor, or often they prod other aspirants to shoot the Melchors from behind adobe walls. More bloodshed. A transfer of Mausers, booze-permits and land.

Don Melchor senses something of this. He is not easy. He rides, singing *Adelita* and *Una Noche* and *Cuatro Milpas*, laughing, but ever his crooked peering eye searches the wayside walls, and scrutinizes the approaching traveler. He is ever examining and readjusting his weapons. The scurry of a lizard on the stones is enough to make him to rein his horse to its haunches.

Suddenly, as we were riding into Zacapu, end of our expedition, Melchor sang a *corrido* about a Mexican emigrant to the States, a song dealing with tribulations, and the joys of the traveler, each verse ending with the refrain:

> And of the money I make,
> The dollars I earn,
> Half go to a friend,
> And half are for my family.

"I shall go back to the United States as soon as I can," he announced for the tenth time, "for there they bury a man with shoes on his feet."

He rode down the chalky main street of dirty Zacapu with more than usual bravado, for he had many political enemies in that place. But scarcely had he said goodby to us and collected his money, than he swung from the hotel steps on to his prancing black horse and scurried away in a cloud of whirling dust.

XIV   THE UNBURIED PATRIOT

1

At Zeli's, in the Montmartre above Rue Pigale—the only hill street in the world where men roll up and walk down—I ran into my friend, Don José Avellaneda, gloriously drunk. Disengaging himself from two dazzling cocottes, he lurched from behind the cigarette strewn table with its three dead champagne bottles. Slightly swaying as in a slow wind, he gave me an affectionate *abrazo*, with gentle thumps on the shoulder.

"A seat, dear friend!" He ordered a glass for me, then sank back grunting to the soft breasts of his white-skinned, half-naked companions. Don José, himself, was a radiant chocolate color, the peculiar mahogany brown of alligator-skin bags. His sooty hair swept stiff and straight, back from a low corrugated slanting brow, above the black blaze of his large long-lashed eyes. His pink lips blurred sensuously.

"Of all things—you in Paris!" I began. I repictured him in Mexico: once in khaki with the staff of General Obregón on the Ocotlán front, a squat, cursing, spitting fury of a man. Now a purr had crept into his voice.

Before his Paris exile, in the former days when he became

Secretary of Current Affairs, I interviewed him. The bang of his energetic fist had made the terra cotta caricature of a bloated priest dance on his desk—that was during one of the numerous religious controversies. Now, his face sagged a bit. The table edge creased a sizeable paunch.

In tropic Córdoba, I had seen him orating from an improvised platform, overshadowed by a tangle of vines and mango trees, to a massed crowd of hoipoloi. Brown faces of unbearded peasant men in faultlessly clean white "pyjamas" shone up at him; brown moon-caressed faces of peasant women in blue *rebozos* shone up at him. Brown glazed terra cotta jars in crooks of polished arms, matched the brown of skin. Intoxicated with words, he was shouting, "We revolutionaries . . . the rights of the proletariat . . . land for the peasants . . . down with the landlords . . . never give up your rifles . . . the cursed Yankee imperialism. . . ."

Now he was spending thousands of dollars a night on the Montmartre; the sweet snarl of a greedy foreign tongue in his ears, kneading the white flesh of poison-sweet breasts with his heavy, brown fingers. Paris. Champagne.

This was not, however, the first time I had seen him thus. Just three days before his Córdoba speech, I ran into him in the Quixote salón of the Hotel Regis in Mexico City, dancing under rose lights with his notorious paramour, the long-bodied sultry actress. He had loaded her with jewels. She blazed across the floor.

Two days later, I saw him roll down the Paseo de la Reforma and around the garden glorietas in a French limousine with his wife—a beautiful sweet woman from the ranks of the old aristocracy—and his three children. . . .

"I heard you had left Mexico——" I began.

"Yes, the game went against me. The assassination of Obregón—well you know the story. Lucky to slip out with my life!"

Don José drained his champagne glass, ordered another bottle. He motioned to the automatic telephone on the table.

"Call yourself over a couple of girls," he suggested. "Each table, you notice, is numbered. Why not that girl over there, the fluffy blonde in the red sinful dress. What women, what women!"

"And Celestina?" I ventured, the first time I had ever dared touch upon his intimacy with the actress.

He scowled. "She chucked me when I fell. The Minister of Finance took her on. I'll get back one of these days, and if it's the last thing I ever do, I'll heave her where the *perros* can nose her." He laughed morosely. "Anyway, he was a fool, let her get him into a jam—that scandal when he took her to New York in his private car and was raided. Great stuff for a cabinet minister!"

Sour grapes, I thought, remembering his own arrogant, public display of his former mistress.

2

Don José's rise to power had been phenomenal. Some incidents he told me himself. Others I collected from the mouth of public gossip. Others from the press. I did not, for instance, see him shoot the tiles off one of the Quixote panels of the Hotel Regis, but the following day I did see the havoc his bullets had wrought. He had grown morose in his cups,

over some flippant remark of Celestina's. Brooding at his table a while, suddenly he rose, drew his gun and announced to the dance floor that he would shoot anybody who laughed at him—dead. Sweeping the room slowly with his gun, he watched everyone freeze in fear. Then he wrenched Celestina brutally to the entrance, where he calmly peppered the tiles off a section of the wall. Elegantly gowned ladies shrieked.

The stocky, but small-boned body of Don José betokened him largely Indian, though he had a sprinkling of Spanish. Once I asked him, "What does your Spanish blood give you?" "Headaches!" was his lightning reply. An illuminating description of the spiritual dilemma of the Mexican mestizo, torn between the brooding canniness of the native race and the civilized greed of the white, a cultural and racial conflict within the very breast that issues forth in vagaries of desperate conduct defying rational explanation.

He was a son of the Tepehuanes, a mountain race living in log-cabin huts battened down with stones, high in the Sierra Madre of Durango. When a child, his ears had been pierced; even at sixteen he still wore red crescents dangling down his dusky cheeks and never had had shoes on his feet. His parents drifted to the town of Tepehuanes, then to Durango, finally to the desert city of Chihuahua. A few years of rural schooling saved him from being quite illiterate. His parents died. Raking up a dilapidated pair of shoes, he got a chore job in a dance cantina, La Gloria. Because of his sturdy young body, his fierce black eyes, and occasional streaks of thrilling brutality, the girls—when the boss was out and there were no clients with pesos jingling in the pocket—inveigled him into the cushioned *reservados*. Drinking cognac, screened from public gaze, they had sport with him, teaching him gratis, vices other men had paid them to learn.

He became a bull-fight fan. Every free moment, he hung around the ring. In the cantina, he met many of the professional players. On rare occasions, they even treated him

to drinks. He listened eagerly to their technical arguments
about the sport. This acquaintanceship gave him entree behind the scenes. He sniffed the acrid bull odor from the
black-walled *toril* and watched the *capeadores* twirling their
scarlet capes, practicing graceful poses; he practiced himself.

He fell in love with Esperanza, one of the dance girls.
Her white skin drove him mad. She was a lithe dare-devil
girl, with firm pointed breasts faintly visible beneath black
lace. But she spurned José time and again.

Furious, disgruntled, he disappeared. Some said he had
ridden off with the Madero revolution which was stalking
in from the north. As a matter of fact, he had gone to a
cattle ranch, to be near his beloved bulls. He learned to ride
like a dervish and to shoot the spots of rattlesnakes.

Madero was successful. Shortly after Madero's War Minister, Victoriano Huerta, had smashed the revolt of Orozco,
Don José returned to Chihuahua. Soon he blossomed as the
leading local bull-fighter. He haunted the cantinas and the
poolrooms; money jingled in his pockets. Esperanza tried to
make up to him then, but he ignored her, insulted her, once
even struck her. When she was not aware of it, though, he
watched her with sultry, mad eyes. All the other girls ran
after him, more than ever. He had his fill, but he cared for
none of them.

Huerta butchered his way into the Presidency. Again, revolution stalked and hammered and rattled across the sun-
burnt plains. Carranza marched through on his way to
Sonora. For a few days, the plaza was buzzing with bivouaced
Indians, rifles in tepees, long-skirted women fanning charcoal braziers. The cantinas were rollicking full of officers.
Don José met them all. He was popular. He got girls for
them. The girls pretended love, well knowing that instead
of money they would receive stolen finery. José staged a
special bull-fight and was well paid for his pains—in paper
money worthless the day after the brummagem crew pulled
out.

Later, Villa banged down out of the Durango crags. The
story was repeated. Chihuahua was a whirlpool of cavalry,
gun-carriages, motor-trucks; Don José became the crony of
the highest officers. From their talk, José learned many
things. This was not mere fighting, but a social revolution.
The peasants would receive lands. The country was being
saved. His best friend, a Villa colonel, told him confiden-
tially that the real military chief was Alvaro Obregón. Villa's
history was more romantic, but Villa's squat Indian body no
more convinced Don José than did his own. By another filip
of the wheel, Don José could himself have been a Villa,
could have loved and shot with just as much brutal ac-
curacy. Obregón, the colonel insisted, was more of a genius.

Sure enough, Obregón marched into Mexico City ahead
of any other constitutionalist chief. Then came the bitter
split between Carranza and Villa. Obregón, loyal to Carranza, was massing troops against Villa in Celaya. The colonel
decided to desert Villa and invited José to go with him.
Before leaving, José gave Esperanza a glittering bracelet
bought for a song from the loot of a soldier. But he laughed
at her crudely when she then wanted to sleep with him.

José and the Colonel arrived in Celaya with fifteen men.
Don José immediately staged a bull-fight for Obregón. Six
of the best blooded bulls were looted from a neighboring
hacienda. Obregón came in person. He invited Don José to
call on him. They became jovial friends. Don José was added
to Obregón's staff.

Villa was smashed in Celaya. He was smashed at Aguascali-
entes. He was driven in wild galloping rout into the
Durango cactus belt. Obregón entered Chihuahua in triumph.

A great moment! Whooping men, shooting at the stars,
caroused down the streets. They smashed doors. They looted.
They raped. They guzzled. They killed. The cantinas overflowed. A prostitute was knifed in the belly.

In all this mêlée of saving the country, Don José was in

his glory. Again he secured girls for the high chiefs of staff. One night, in a high fettle of intoxication, he led a group of officers into Cantina Gloria, tore Esperanza from the lap of a mere citizen of the Republic and stripped her where she stood in the center of the floor, among guffaws and mad huzzahs.

José was the hero of the city. He had learned the revolutionary lingo. He discoursed to the Indian folk in the markets: Obregón was a friend of the people. When peace came, he would give everybody work and lands. And so simple folk ran after José, hoping to receive favors. He righted

several petty injustices done by officers, and everyone immediately had boundless faith in his great influence with the big Jefe. He was fast becoming a political boss.

Unnecessary, here, to recount his election as member of the State legislature or his subsequent election to Congress, or his duel with an opposition colleague in the marble corridor of the Chamber. Avellaneda was shot through the belly and for two weeks hovered between life and death. More important was his success in organizing the National Agrarian Association. The Government helped him. It paid the train fares and hotel expenses of the delegates—a picturesque motley of Indian and mestizo types, for the most

221

part dressed in white "pyjamas," sandals and huge sombreros
—a sansculotte army if ever there was one. This conglomera-
tion did not seem likely stuff out of which to build a political
machine. Yet these bizarre, dark-skinned men, with a non-
European odor, each in his own way, were powers in their
local communities. At this first convention, Avellaneda made
a typical address regarding "we revolutionaries" and promised
"land to the peasants."

The new Association brought about a union of certain
Villa and Zapata elements, thus cutting the ground from
under the rebel chieftain of the north. He had to make his
peace with the government. Some time later he rode into a
death-trap. Zapata also rode into a death-trap. Avellaneda,
rumored to be behind these two assassinations, emerged as
the leader of the peasant movement of the country—a national political power.

Our hero was duly rewarded. He was given charge of
the Army Supply Department with an annual budget of
thirty million pesos. He set to work to improve himself. He
hired teachers and polished off the knots in his grammar.
He read the revolutionary literature of Europe—Marx,
Grave, Bakunin, Kropotkin, Sorel. Some of it stuck. His
mind became a patchwork quilt of odd radical theories, political cunning, vainglorious pride.

Contracting for army supplies brought him into close
touch with the Spaniards—the Gachupines—who were always hanging around the banquets of power in Latin American countries, picking up fat, golden crumbs, which soon
make quite a loaf. The Gachupines also are always connected
with the so-called reactionary aristocracy. And as business
is stronger than the *mores* of cast, Avellaneda was dragged
into exclusive society. He climbed socially. He knew that
people sneeringly remarked that his ears were pierced, but
doggedly he persevered in his purposes. At one dinner party,
he put his cake into his finger-bowl, but soon learned to

avoid such faux pas. He hired a private barber to keep himself trim, and a valet to coach him on clothes.

In the gatherings of this wastrel but cultured set, he met and wooed one of the finest flowers of wealth—Josefina Blanca Espinosa del Valle, a nineteen-year-old beauty, pure and unspoiled. Don José was thirty-six. Remembering his humble beginnings in Cantina Gloria, he must have been duly proud of his new conquest. The papers gave lengthy accounts of the elaborate and costly wedding. It was stated he gave his young bride a diamond collar costing fifty-four thousand pesos.

The following day, he attended the Hidalgo State Peasants' Convention and delivered a flaming revolutionary speech. Undoubtedly he was doubly inspired by the inner knowledge of the marvelous things the revolution could do for the poor.

From a wife, he moved on to costly mistresses. His first was Consuelo, a slim, dark-eyed girl, daughter of a wealthy family gone to pot in the revolution. She came to ask him for employment—he made her—as they say in the best sellers—his tearful sweetheart.

He built up a palatial retreat in a Tacubaya suburb. It must have cost well up toward the million mark. He installed a luxurious Turkish bath such as the Caesars never knew; also a beautiful tiled swimming pool, with submerged color lights, and inverted light around the edges. There, Don José, Consuelo, and a group of intimate political friends and their mistresses, disported themselves in communal bathing.

Carousal did not cause Avellaneda to neglect his political fences. With the National Agrarian Association as a basis, he boosted his adherents into political jobs. An inner ruling clique of the Association was created, known as the "Grupo Machete," the *machete* being the curved scythe used by the peasants. This group, possessing fat government jobs, soon came to have strong ramifications in the bureaucracy. They could dispense favors and so built up a machine. To hold a job from the Grupo, a man must belong to or immediately join the newly formed National Workers' Revolutionary Party. A percentage of his wages automatically went into the treasury of the party. Actually it passed into the hands of the Grupo Machete, which made no accounting of the funds thus collected.

Avellaneda also organized his famous crowbar gangs, made up of thug men, hard-boiled angels employed in the munition works. Their duty was to perpetrate any violence demanded by the needs of the proletarian movement. They killed strike-breakers—"squirrels" as they are called in Mexico. They smashed up newspapers which criticized Avellaneda. They beat up or assassinated opponents in the elections. They stole ballot boxes.

For the head of one of the crowbar gangs, I once bought drinks in a dingy little saloon on Calle de Aquiles Serdán. "I have fifteen men in my gang," he declared, "three too many, for three of them still have a little pity in their hearts." He went on to describe the Querétaro elections. He and two other gang units hurtled through the streets in trucks, shooting with machine guns into knots of bystanders. Just before poll closing time, they raided the booths, stealing the ballot boxes. Naturally a worker-peasant governor was seated.

Came then one of the periodic revolts against the Government. A flame of war sprang up, ringing the capital around with steel. At the most crucial moment, I was invited to a barbecue by the Grupo Machete at an Atzcapotzalco hacienda. There, though the fate of the Government hung in the balance, Avellaneda sat all afternoon with his cronies, unconcernedly drinking cured pulque and playing poker.

But the following day, he showed his hand. At the San Diego Theater, he delivered his famous address: "Shall we stand idle while our comrades are dying at the front? There are traitors in the government itself. But be they cabinet ministers or members of the Senate or the Chamber, the direct action of the workers shall know how to deal with them.

Disloyalty shall not be allowed to crouch in safety behind the trenches of a government job. Wherever treachery raises its head we shall stamp upon it as upon the head of a venomous snake."

The following day, one of the crowbar gangs, stationed in the patio of the Secretariat of Education, menaced the Minister, who sympathized with the rebels. He resigned, fearing for his life.

That afternoon, I called upon Don José for news. A telegram came. Avellaneda opened it. His jaws clicked, then a satisfied smile curled up his brown cheeks. The telegram was from Pedro Hill Ramírez, opposition Senator from Oaxaca, head of the august upper chamber. Avellaneda read it aloud.

"Sir: It requires no imagination to know to whom your threats in the Theatre San Diego referred. Your loud talk does not frighten me. I shall remain at my post in the Senate undaunted, until the victorious armies of the true revolution, now advancing upon the abusers of power, enter triumphantly into the capital. As usual, I shall enter the Senate hall tomorrow afternoon at four o'clock.
                                   "Senator Pedro Hill Ramírez."

Avellaneda rang a bell. "Send in Cárdenas and Martínez."

Two squat brutal armed men entered. They were killers. They were hairy apes. They were drinkers of blood. Their walk, their bearing, showed they had no pity in their hearts. Avellaneda handed them the telegram.

"Read this. You will know what to do. Go do it."

He turned to me again, calmly chortling over a recent undress comedy at the Lirico Theatre.

I left, nervous, excited. I knew Senator Hill Ramírez personally. I did not laud him for skulking in a government job immune from punishment. Yet I could not see him shot down like a dog.

I phoned his home. "A friend is speaking. Don't enter the Senate Chamber tomorrow at four."

225

He did not. I scanned the papers two days later with great relief. That evening at nine o'clock, I was again with Avellaneda. The two gunmen entered.

"Done!" the bulkier of the two men lifted his lips above his rat teeth. With flat pudgy hands, he lifted his cartridge belt a little higher on his paunch.

Just half an hour before, the two gunmen, with their respective gangs, had driven up in autos along the curb and shot Senator Hill Ramírez down on his own doorstep. Twenty-two bullets riddled his body.

Avellaneda calmly discussed where the two gunmen should hide out until the scandal blew over.

The following day, the papers announced six Congressmen (unfriendly to the régime) had disappeared. They were sequestered for a week. When finally released, their terror was so great they gave only reluctant vague answers as to what had happened to them.

By that time, the revolt had been downed. Investigation of the assassination of Senator Hill Ramírez was instituted. Avellaneda was called to the witness stand.

"Direct action," he informed his hearers solemnly, "is a sacred weapon used by the workers only in strikes, when traitorous 'squirrels' are employed. It is a sacred weapon to protect the legitimate rights of the workers, but it never goes to the length of assassination."

Again Avellaneda was rewarded, made Secretary of Current Affairs, a key cabinet post, usually considered the stepping stone for the Presidency itself. He conducted one of the perennial fights with the church, of which he was an arch enemy, though he had been married to Josefina Blanca by a priest. I called on him. With a hand, blazing diamond rings, he lifted the carved cocoanut lid of a little oval lacquered box. I espied a terra cotta monk and nun in an erotic posture that would have been considered a bit modern, even by the decorators of those red and black friezes in the homes of the heterae of Pompeii. Avellaneda laughed heavily.

226

He became enamored of the visiting Spanish actress
Celestina Campoamor, a luscious prize for any man. Her
body was sculptured by Phideas himself. She was tall, dazzlingly white. Dark-skinned Don José went mad over her.
He spent his nights drinking and dancing with her in the
Café Regis until four every morning. He loaded her with
jewels and Parisian costumes. Twice in the same gown she
was never seen. Every night in the week, a different fur coat
swathed that precious glowing form of hers, on whose semi-
nudity, earlier in the evening, a thousand men had gazed
with lustful eyes.

Avellaneda rarely appeared in his office, and then not before seven in the evening. He saw nobody, hurriedly signed
the papers his secretary put before him and rushed off. Part
of Sunday, only, did he devote to his young and beautiful
wife, Josefina Blanca. Mortified, heart-broken, she had tolerated his Tacubaya orgies and other infidelities, now she
was crushed to earth by this public ostentation of the actress.
Josefina Blanca, in spite of her beauty, could not compete
with the unscorched vanity of the bull-fighter and his perennial desire for exhibitionism.

Finally she told the President her sad tale. The President
personally warned Avellaneda that he must drop Celestina.
For a time Avellaneda and his mistress dined quietly in back
avenue restaurants. But soon they again reappeared in the
full public gaze. At last, in spite of his great influence, Don
José was dismissed from office.

To show his power, he forced all the members of the
Grupo Machete to withdraw from the Government. Grandil-
oquently he announced before a specially called convention
of the National Agrarian Association: "They may strip us of
our offices; they may take away our motor cars in which we
have speeded to do the work of the peasants; they may
snatch away our diamonds, which in time of need we might
have pawned to provide necessary money for our comrades;
but they can never take away our rights. Let them never

dare touch the organizations of the workers and peasants. In the last resort, we know how to defend our sacred cause, with barricades if necessary."

Did he feel himself so powerful? Or was this more bombast, just the bull-fighter's self-vanity and love of exhibitionism?

A new presidential election was coming on. Don José found himself at outs with the official candidate, General Obregón. A bitter feud developed. Pitched battles occurred, precipitated by Avellaneda's crowbar gangs. Bullets hailed near the candidate. But assassination is a dangerous two-edged game.

One morning, speeding in from his sumptuous Tacubaya palace, Avellaneda's auto was riddled with bullets. He escaped unhurt. The police discovered his machine was triple-steel lined, equipped with bullet-proof glass, and carried a machine-gun stand.

Obregón was elected. A few weeks later, at a banquet, he was assassinated, shot through the back. The supporters of Obregón, cheated out of prospective jobs, swore vengeance on Avellaneda. They swarmed over the city, guns in hand, looking for him.

For several weeks, Avellaneda skulked in his Tacubaya palace, surrounded by Crowbar brigades, every entrance bristling with machine guns. At an opportune moment, he issued a ringing statement to the workers and peasants, skulked low again, then slipped off to Paris, his political career apparently broken. His wife divorced him. Celestina abandoned him.

3

Not until two weeks ago was I able to complete the story of this amazing character. Quite by chance, I met one of five men who fled with him to the Guatemalan border.

For some time after my encounter with him in glittering

Zeli's, he lived on in Paris, provided with enough of this world's goods to finish out his span, even with the wildest extravagances. Wealth, easy living, hypocrisy continued to deplete him. Already, when I saw him, these had eaten deep into his fibre.

But he was still relatively young. In spite of the safety of Paris, Mexican politics was in his blood. The bull-fighter needed a stage. And he was no coward. So he went back to his patria, into the whirlpool, boldly to face death, to tempt fate. For revolution again had broken out. The fight called. Dreams of grandeur called. He would recoup power, fortune, glory. A wild gamble. But other men had staged daring comebacks. Don José was so sure of his own superior qualities. Deep in his heart, he was determined to become President, even if he had to butcher his way into power.

He preceded his return with another ringing manifesto to the workers and peasants, then landed from a private boat on the azure coast of Campeche, where he took charge of rebel forces and marched triumphantly into Mérida, the capital of Yucatán.

But elsewhere the new revolution went from bad to worse. Desertions occurred on every hand. Don José finally evacuated Mérida. Before he pulled out, he executed a fellow peasant leader and lifted the bank reserves. The remnants of his forces were hacked to pieces near Uxmal.

With a handful of followers and a Maya guide, he fled past the ruins of earlier centuries, across the flat limestone peninsula, on into the swamps and jungles. What finally happened to him, no one knew. We all conjectured. Did he escape into Guatemala and there hide his ignominy incognito? Did he drift back to the Montmartre? Or did he perish?

Two weeks ago I learned all the gruesome details—from one of the survivors of his final tragic flight. The fugitives, now reduced to five besides Avellaneda, when within a day of the frontier, bivouaced as best they could on a jungle-ringed trail.

A pleasant Dantesque region! No longer in any immediate danger from the federals, but the tropics themselves lowered deadly menace. The fleeing group was not properly prepared to withstand the jungle ravages. Mosquitoes might bring malaria, even yellow fever. The chiclero fly might deposit its larvae in the nasal membrane, whereupon nose and cheek would rot away. Other insects pierced near the temple, devouring the optic nerve; others in the hip or beneath the toe nails. If you put your hand on some innocent tree, it might come away with a viscous substance that shrivelled the skin. The brackish water reeked typhoid. Deadly snakes lay among the leaves. There were wild animals, too.

But none of these dangers overcame Don José. That last night when he lay asleep in slumber before the frontier and safety, two of his subordinates conversed in low whispers: "This is the end. We are fleeing in exile into Guatemala. We have nothing. But General Avellaneda's saddle-bags are stuffed full of American bills. He will forget us as soon as he crosses the border. We need money to get from Guatemala to the United States or Paris."

There lay Don José sleeping. He lay on his back, his saddle for a pillow and under it the leather bags stuffed with wealth. He lay on his back, his round brown face to the tropic stars.

Knives in their teeth, the two conspirators crept stealthily towards him, inch by inch, so as not to awaken him or the others. They reached his side. At that moment they had no pity in their hearts. They stuck the knife between his ribs, once, twice, thrice, again and again.

They pawed at the saddle-bags.

The other three awoke. Alarmed, they sprang to their feet.

A fight ensued. One of the assassins was shot. The other scuttled off into the jungle.

The three survivors stood astounded over the two dead

bodies. Blood was seeping into the black humid earth. They shrugged—nothing to do but divide the spoils.

They set about it in business-like fashion. They even pulled the diamond rings off Don José's pudgy hand—difficult, for it was badly swollen from a chance infection.

They talked little. Their breath came heavily. They were suspicious of each other. Each prayed that soon he might be far out of sight of the other two.

They did not even stop to bury Avellaneda. In a few days, the jungle, the flooding tropic rains, the insects and the vultures would wipe away all trace.

XV   CARICATURE

MEXICAN caricature begins
with the landscape. The deserts, the mountains, the vegetation seem eternally knotted in the travail of new birth—and
procreation is a kind of caricature of both life and death.
In the northern deserts, the mountains rarely run in orderly
chains, but poke up in isolated buttes, like jagged red tongues.
. They are purple and ochre pimples that have burst the cutis
of the fevered sands. They are caricatures of mountains.
Nearly everywhere in Mexico, the mountains are igneous and
volcanic, with outlandish profiles, jagged, unsmoothed by ero-
sion, uncovered by the blanket of vegetation necessary to
hide their bony ungainliness. They are double-jointed, knock-
kneed, pigeon-toed, hump-back mountains. There is a cruel
quality to Mexican landscapes; the twisted rocks and saw-
tooth crags are filed to sharp edges and points by the cruel
southland sun; the landscape is a slashing blade that cuts
deep with its grandeur and absurdity. Rarely can one be at
peace with the Mexican horizon. It provokes silent, nameless
mirth.

The vegetation twists into the grotesque. The maguey
plants writhe against tilted gray brown hills. The Jordan
palms thrust bunglesome tridents into brittle copper skies.

The cactus growths reach out flabby spined hands, or tower like fluted columns of fantastic ruined cities, or squat in fat barrel obscenity, barbed with death. The mountain flora is often scraggly and tattered and tufted, like the rags of a haystack beggar. Ever a suggestion of demoniacal lascivity in Mexican vegetation, be it desert or jungle. The jungle lianas, cord and loop in white nudity over majestic leonine trees in lustful embrace. The trees seem to caricature contortions of the human torso. Always there broods over the Mexican landscape the quivering hint of divine laughter, eternally repressed but potentially capable of shaking and shattering, ever threatening abrupt return to primordial chaos.

Mexico has long had original sources like these for satire and caricature. It has also had the inherent technique of caricature. But caricature itself is recent, born of the national independence birth-travail. Does not caricature come of sophistication, civilization, conscious utilization of mediums? Mexican caricature is one result of the definite release into expression—through political independence—of the ludicrous struggle between races and cultures; European and native, Spanish and Indian. It is a mestizo product, a hybrid growth. It is the *vacilada* of the man of mixed blood.

He has long had sources and methods of caricature, without developing them into a conscious art form. He has beheld his native landscape; he has possessed the symbolism and the grim grotesques and distortions of the native pre-Cortesian art; he has long enjoyed a bizarre intimacy with Death; sex with him has always been a monstrous, serious joke, where passion and ridiculous laughter twine in scarlet and gold thread. He has been exposed to the Baroque in its most extravagant form—the Churrigueresque. Góngora, the most involved theoretician of Spain, was the most potent literary father of Colonial Mexico. And lastly the Mexican has the *vacilada*—cactus growth of a hybrid racial expression, a philosophy and conduct of aesthetic irresponsibility, of egocentric hedonism buffeted between extreme extravagances.

233

So woven is caricature into the texture by the Mexican loom of life, of sex, of death, that one is always in doubt whether the artistic formulation (which is a popular as well as a refined pastime), is but a spontaneous outgrowth of the inner reaction or is consciously built into divine blasphemy and lampoon.

The native art—Maya, Aztec, Tarascan, Zapotecan—undoubtedly possessed some of the best tools of caricature, and in highly developed form. Formerly, I believed the native pre-Cortesian art consciously practiced caricature; but more extensive contact with surviving artefacts, has permitted me to gather a subtler comprehension of the spirit and system which actuated them, with the result that I have completely discarded this belief. The religious *mores*, as we know from Sahagún, and other early observers, were fixed and immutable; no man violated them unless prompted by spirits and deities. There was, apparently, no consciousness of a division between sane and insane except from this standpoint. The half-wit and the insane person were more than likely to be identified with some godhead and to be scrutinized and venerated with awe. Hence all manifestations of human conduct, however distorted, were normal until they definitely violated the religious *mores*, but such aberrations were of divine inspiration (either good or evil), and so by this circuitous route, the abnormal returned to the level of the normal, the explicable. The absurd immediately became an object of veneration, not for being absurd, but because it contained the spirit of the eternal mystery. Hence the normal and the normal divine-abnormal usurped the world. Neither could be caricatured. There was, in short, no place for caricature in the native philosophical comprehension. But the native artists had an uncanny power of exaggerating and fixing for all time, individual idiosyncrasies. They had a keen eye for the grotesque. It invades all their art forms. But this was far from being caricature; it was, rather, serious and intensely truth-loving.

234

Yet what superb instruments of the art of caricature the earlier peoples developed! To this day, some of the tiny clay portrait heads, some of the reproductions of animals, strike to the marrow with their quite unconscious mirth, with their truthful discernment. They contain a shafted laughter of which the original artist was, in all probability, entirely unconscious. He was naïvely expressing artistic truth. Yet artistic truth can, on occasion, be the sublimest caricature.

The native craftsman was trained in symbolism, which is an exaggeration of type characteristics and the forerunner of written hieroglyphics and language. He was thereby obliged, constantly, to use exaggeration and distortion in all his art forms. It was an economy born of economical necessity—an elimination of the superfluous to concentrate on type forms. But on many occasions the early art-craftsman transcended the limits of his technique and pierced to the gripping individualized conception. It was an intuitive combining of impressionism (on rare occasions, futurism) with the accented symbolic. And what is this but the sharpest instrument for modern caricature!

The major Old World cultural influences to which the Mexican was exposed possessed much unconscious exaggeration and distortion. In architecture, Mexico borrowed the extravagant Baroque phase—the Churrigueresque. Gold piled on gold; great scrolls of gold; cubes of gold; angles and triangles and rhomboids of gold; involved surfaces suggesting gold depths; a chiaroscuro of gold; spirals and circles and loops of gold, suggesting graphs of infinity. A nation swathed and chained in gold. Heaps and gobs of gold, almost suggesting human excrement. The sublime turning back upon itself scorpion-wise and stinging itself to the agonies of vulgarity. A caricature of decorative æsthetic. Most Mexican architecture, as a result of this and the blend of native and Spanish forms, is bastard architecture. The symmetry is there, subtler because of the exaggeration of parts, because of the irregularity of columns and buttresses and windows. The unexpected buffets one; really, it conceals a frozen torture of spirit.

In literature, the dean of the Spanish world was Luis de Góngora y Argote, the involved rhetorician and poet, who heaped up his phrases in Churrigueresque circles and loops and iterations; who gave to the Spanish language two new words: *gongorino* and *gongorismo*. Known as the "Angel of Darkness," because of the frequent inscrutability of his meanings, Góngora practiced the most daring inversions, the most extravagant neologisms,—and far more than his Italian contemporary Mariani (who founded the obscure tendency of *Marianismo*) Góngora was a trapeze artist of style, a verbal acrobat. Sor Juana Inez de la Cruz, the leading writer of the Colonial period, a poetess far too little known in the Anglo-Saxon world, shows Góngora's influence in every turn of her verse. Góngora ruled the contemporary Spanish literary world as completely as did Nicolás Boileau Despreaux or Samuel Johnson in their respective *ambientes*. This has given an abiding flamboyance to Mexican prose and poetry, a quality of sophisticated involution, which has left a lamentable impress upon its literary history—save in the realm of satire and caricature. It is a further instrument contributing to the genre we are considering.

The brutal mixture of two or more races, of two cultures, has created the mestizo and the mestizan culture. Neither Indian nor Spanish, sporadically it is one or the other. It has been set adrift—without imperative traditions, without an organized social system, without a definite life philosophy—to work its untutored will upon the Mexican plateaus. The mestizo is distinctly an individualist. He is undisciplined; his group is undisciplined. Lacking texture and continuity in his psychic and will processes, he reaches out to France, to the United States; or deep into the unknown depths of his own petty cosmos, for guidance. The result is almost pathological, a series of disjointed distortions of conduct, unpredictable, beyond the realm of the logical European mind to fathom.

This mode of conduct and of living is aptly described as the *vacilada*. The major portion of the Mexican world is subject to the *vacilada*, which is characterized by irresponsibility, recklessness, whimsicality, irrationality, passion, daring, Cæsarian ambition. The Mexican is the Machiavelian par excellence. He is the Nietzchian par excellence—except that he has no imperious destiny, either of power-lust or culture-lust. He is a creature of unbridled desires with often the cunning and courage to seek fulfillment. The opinion of his fellows does not carry weight. There is little social will to restrain—only individual wills, conflicts of desires within the breast and without. Luis Urbina describes the Mexican and his mixture of Spanish and Indian in his *Vida Literaria de México*:

> "Physiologically we (Mexicans) are neither the one nor the other; rather we are a well differentiated ethic type, partaking of the characteristics of both progenitor races. Both strive to coëxist, even strive against each other in our organisms for survival. To the Sancho Panzan jollity and the Quixotic delirium are united in our hearts the sadness of the Indian, the ancestral submissiveness of a subject race, and the gentleness of the aborigine. And if we are Mexicans in life, we are Mexicans in speech, in dreams, and in song."

The *vacilada* is a combination of the ridiculous and the sublime, of vulgarity and purity, of beauty and ugliness, of spirituality and animality, disconcertingly tripping over each other, showering the world with passing glory, like the spray of a rocket flame.

The Mexican's approach to life, death and sex, an approach dominated by the *vacilada*, is shot through with poetic irresponsibility, it defies direct logic; takes serious things lightly, and insignificant things with great gravity. This is a gracious and self-protective distortion, a creative destruction of values cherished by the European mind.

The Mexican, for time immemorial, has had the caricaturist's approach to death. The Spanish-Catholic intrusion

Diego Rivera

heightened this attitude because Catholicism, promising life hereafter, draws the pus out of man's ulcerous fear of death. The Mexican has a jocular camaraderie with the major mysteries, be they death or God. He does not set too great store on his life. He wears life like a flower behind the ear, to be tossed to the seductive siren, Adventure, the stately dame known as Pride, to winged Victory, or the debonair Goddess, Courage.

He caricatures life with death and death with life. He peoples his beloved scenes of native life with skeletons. On the Day of the Dead, he buys skeleton jumping jacks; the dusky sweetheart buys her lover a skull stickpin with gleaming ruby eyes; the children munch candy purple funerals; and the whole family picnics on the graves of their ancestors, carousing and getting drunk. It is holy joy, bathed in sinful abandon. They believe the dead ones to be present, in the same hilarious circle, drinking pulque from the same terra cotta jar. The living wish ever to be joyously near to death. Who can fear the thing he knows well? Recently I read a volume of tales entitled "Tropic Death"—stories of the untimely ending of negroes. These negro deaths portray brutality, fear, horror, terror, brutal fury. The Mexican's death may be brutal, but there is no brutality in Death or in his feeling for Death. Dying is not important; the gesture at killing and dying is supremely important. The Mexican must distort the process. He is interested, not in the fact of death, but in the number of knife wounds, the calibre of the pistol that caused the fatal wound. Death itself he converts into the grotesque, into gaiety, into luxurious satisfaction. However generous with his pity he may on occasions be, the Mexican is covertly amused by the most tragic catastrophes. He is rarely tense, but rather good-humored and mentally stimulated to irrevelant absurdities in the presence of extreme danger. The mockery of satire is always gleaming, a deep-set fire, in his fixed regard of sacred things.

No one knows better than the Mexican, in spite of his

reputed romanticism (which is doubtful) that sex is the greatest joke ever played on human beings. This, perhaps, is his only balance to retain some sanity in his majestic and terrific passions. Knowing sex to be a humorous inevitability, he feels no need for joking about it in the dull, sordid fashion of the corner grocery store spittoon gang or the Pullman smoker. The Mexican's conversation regarding sex, turns upon subtle repartee, double plays of words; it deals with absurd intersex nuances, physical and spiritual; with the frailties of woman's resistance or the discomfitures of rejection or betrayal. Even when in the throes of the most terrific passion, the Mexican remains debonair, clever, grandiloquent. He is never brutal until conquest; then brutality alone can make tolerable the tenderest and most delicious of human experiences. He will caricature his weakness with strength and pride—once more it is the gesture, not the deed, that is important; and what are the gestures of the grand passion, the illimitable sacrifice, revenge, conciliation, but a reckless caricature of his inner tough cynicism, his ruthless realism, his predatory desire to tame and subject the object of his affections—an inverse caricature if you please.

Mexico has had a few master caricaturists. Guadalupe Posada, in his illustrations of popular *corridos* (songs of the illiterate populace of Mexico) has embodied some of the rarest art—unpretentious, fantastic, imaginative. Had he lived anywhere but in Mexico he would have been recognized long since as one of the world's significant artists. In him, however, caricature did not reach its full maturity. One is never quite certain whether his distortions are naïve or conscious. Does his work flow calmly in the full stream of Mexican life apperception? Or did he more consciously shape his art? It is difficult to know. Certainly, at times he seems closer to those native retablos, hung in the churches the length and breadth of Mexico, with their naïve exaggerated portrayal of miracles and divine dispensation. A miracle is essentially a thing without chronology—caricature has definite

241

chronology, however much its intrinsic value may surpass this limitation.

Posada in 1888 left his clambering cactus grey-green state of Guanajuato to come to Mexico, where he secured employment with the famous house of Dr. Antonio Vanegas Arroyo, which specialized in the printing of popular ballads, scenarios for puppet and miracle shows, and other bits of popular literature. The ballads were printed on spongey colored paper and were invariably illustrated. They were then peddled on the street corners and sung from Sonora to Yucatán by itinerant troubadours. They were taken up by the little *carpas* or street-shows and carried by rude guitarists to the remotest sierra hamlets, where they rang forth in the mountain-shadowed plazas and leaped in rhythm to leaping mountain fires under cabin *ramadas*.

Posada established his studio in a carriage entrance beside the church of Santa Inez and the San Carlos museum, and from 1888 until his death, he toiled on these illustrations producing more than fifteen thousand engravings, most of which are lost. He drew his compositions in black and white directly with acid on zinc plates—revolutionary episodes, adventures of Villa and Zapata, scandals, accidents. Often he lampooned the mighty, telling in picture what the verses contained; stories of earthquakes and floods and untimely deaths; of train-wrecks and hold-ups; sometimes just simple bucolic portrayals of native life. They were drawn in acid not only on zinc but on the souls of men.

Posada loved to use skeletons for living humans. In his "Return of the Dead," he pictures a barrel of tequila (of which he was inordinately and disastrously fond) around which are skeletons dancing. These rattle-bones are topped by ridiculous sombreros; they wear Indian skirts bunched into clumsy folds. He will depict Díaz or Madero or any of the high and mighty in skull and skeleton guise. He brings them down from their lofty niches into the beauties and pains of the commonplace, making them carouse in the festivals of everyday folk. He makes skull-grinning Death live, quarrel, booze, dance, weep, love—an orchestration of clean white bones, shaded off into the dark cosmos, into the sinister murkiness of things living. What is powerful is made effeminate. What is wicked is stung by jovial fiends more fiendish than fiends ever imagined. He depicts miracles, racy and exaggerated. A soul is snatched to hell by a devil with a gruesomely long tail. On the ground lies the dead woman in black: the soul is a doll-like figure wearing a dowdy white dress and square shoes—preciously proper and stupid and middle-class—ready for the celestial transmigration.

Thus Posada interpreted the sorrows, the happiness, the anguished aspirations of the people. He fought for the people in contemporary political sheets. He integrated in his art the race-soul of flippant tragic Mexico, so typically that few even bothered to ask the name of the humble illustrator, especially in that pompous, aristocratic, European-minded era of the Dictator Díaz. Most of his work has vanished.

Of contemporary professional caricaturists should be mentioned Miguel Covarrubias, García Cabral, Erasto Cortés, Matías Santoyo, and the worker in wax, Luis Hidalgo.

The genial Miguel Covarrubias, having made his habitat the United States and Vanity Fair, has had his native propensities altered and smoothed out considerably by the northern environment, removing much of the inherent bitter cruelty. But his keen vision of types, of absurdities, of human frailties remains undimmed.

García Cabral, most of his life-time collaborator on the "Excelsior," Mexico's leading daily, has remained more typical. His sharp insight into native idiosyncrasies from ragged *pelados* to aristocrats never fails. He picks up the quaintness of saloon types, sierra Indians, politicians, the shoddy bad taste of the middle-class; he knifes the gunmen both of the *ranchos* and of the national Chamber of Deputies. His range is Balzacian, and anyone who reviews his work can gain deep insight into the local shindigs.

Erasto Cortés is a master of technique. With a broadening smudge, as in his caricature of Señorita Bringas, he can fling a whole assumption of lascivity, which coupled with a cold slitting of the eyes gives a typical suggestion of the mysterious "x" quantity of his subject. This "x" quantity, different for each type, ever arrests in his caricatures. In his depiction of General Calles, one senses again the terrific will, drive and physique of the man, made fearsome by combination with the unknown inexplicable element in his character which has made him the Sonoran master of Mexico.

Santoyo is always clever, with a much keener eye for details, but much less depth of penetration. His caricature is nearly always subtly metaphoric. His treatment of Will Rogers is based on the theme of a parrot, with the wrinkled eyes and curving beak and a little tufted detail of hair. Thus he has captured our rare bird of humor.

Carlos Orozco, again, is more ferocious and savage. He has caricatured his namesake José Clemente Orozco, the painter, with a sombreness of spirit that matches the bitter agonies of that one-armed artist. A dark funeral drawn-out figure with bulging antagonistic eyes and thin-set mouth, his shoulders drawn up as though poised for a remorseless spiritual fray, yet his feet crossed and his free arm drooping in eternal spiritual perplexity. He has caricatured a Jewess with a maximum of cruel physical incisiveness, beady-eyed, thin-lipped irony, and passionless lubricity. His portrayal of Lupe Marin in a demoniacal treatment of a demoniacal, untamed fury of energy and aggressiveness, stepping forth to pounce in greed. He is undoubtedly one of the most resourceful of Mexico's younger artists.

In Luis Hidalgo's wax figurines, already well known to the American public, cruelty links hands with the ultimate of absurdity. The dimensions, the material, the artist's love of awkwardness suggesting grace, strip human dignity to a pathetic and helpless laughter.

Caricature has been one of the main props of the local

painters. The Mexican school of modern painting, as forceful
and interesting as any in the world today, constantly resorts
to caricature. Particularly the painters have utilized it to
propagate their revolutionary faiths. The true caricaturists
like Posada, Covarrubias, or Cabral, have been more iconoclas-
tic than the painters, more realistic, as cruel with the revolutionary gods as with the gods of the old régime. Yet, in some
ways, the painters, in spite of their philosophic limitations,
and their major interest in a different genre, have been more
powerful caricaturists.

The most effective user of caricature in paint has undoubtedly been José Clemente Orozco. There is no pity in his
representations. They are brutal, almost fantastically brutal,
in their annihilation of local types, be they priests, elegantly
gowned women, politicians, or generals. Brutally true is his
portrayal of the violences of the recent upheavals; the ring of
pitiless revolutionary soldiers making a nude aristocrat in a
silk hat dance to the tune of bullets peppering about his bare
ankles. Orozco is even more brutal and less amused than
those who perpetrate the prank. There is a desperate, glaring
sort of laughter in his portrayals; the *vacilada* is lifted to
frightful Promethean hilarity, not quite sane, and therefore
as illuminating as Dostoievskian pathological insight into
human depravity. A tormented soul! Orozco's satires have a
passion and hate utterly devoid of the geniality lurking in
caprichos of Goya, a painter to whom he is in many ways
comparable. Orozco's laughter, his cruelty, is harsher than
any European satire. It is Hogarthian and Swiftian, plus the
Mexican irresponsible maliciousness; and it is far more dramatic than the work of Goya or Daumier. Even Orozco's
rare moments of compassion possess a brutal torment. He
will rip the universe open with both satire and compassion;
until even his compassion becomes mocking satire.

Diego Rivera is the greatest painter of the epoch. His vast
frescoes sweep across the walls of the Chapingo Agricultural
School, the three-tier double-patio of the Secretariat of Edu-

cation, the Secretariat of Public Health; the flame of whose color mounts the main staircase of the National Palace. But his caricature lacks the emotional vigor of Orozco. His Judas kiss of satire is like the osculation described by Baudelaire, "a pensive and passionate kiss." All of his painting has a poster-like quality; a decorative and pictorial announcement of events. It is closer to the Mexican *corrido*, or story song, by which news is propagated throughout Mexico. Many of his frescoes illustrate such story songs. There is narrative in his painting. He has something to tell and to teach, something simple men can understand. His caricature is handmaiden to his communist philosophy; it is found in the brutality of mine-bosses, in the greedy cupidity of government market inspectors, in the bloated importance of Wall Street magnates; in the elegant but crass aristocracy guzzling food, wine, and gold; in his portrayal of Croesus-like cabinet ministers; in his sharp thrusts at pallid and degenerate literati. He loves the common crowds; his paintings reflect the white "pyjamas" of masses of peasants; the blue overalls of factory hands. He caricatures the types of this crowd also, but it is a friendly caricature, genial where the former is brutal, heavy, lumbering, without the lightning stroke of Orozco.

But caricature is no monopoly of the major painters. Part and parcel of the *vacilada*, it pervades every Mexican aesthetic concept, from that of the most humble peon to the most powerful politician. It is found, as I have suggested, in the popular *corridos*; it is found in the native exaggerations of the *retablos* hung as offerings in the churches; it is found in the toys—the terra cotta and straw replicas of muleteers, peasants, workmen, horsemen and animals, which are found in every market place; a mocking exaggeration, a playful whimsicality woven around realism.

It invades the petty burlesque theatres, where not only everyday life is lampooned, vulgarly and deliciously, but also the ways of politicians. Nowhere have I see such devastating political satires as in the cheap theatres of Mexico. Political leaflets and pasquinades carry double weight because of their mordant caricature. The last campaign saw two such colored sheets: "Flit" and "*No importa a nadie*." The letters of "Flit" were alternately composed of grinning skeletons and obscene nuns, the latter a hint at the opponents' clerical support. Needless to say each candidate: Ortiz Rubio and Vasconcelos, was stripped bare. The Mexican, so polite in personal contact, has no innate respect for personal dignity, however important his nibs. If the Mexican can perpetrate familiarities on God and Death, how can mere man, be he the King of the Loaves and Fishes, expect to escape lampooning?

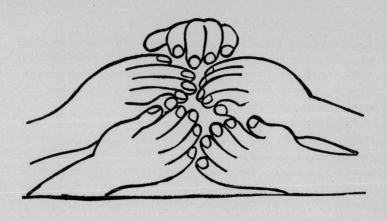

XVI   STREET THEATRES:
LAS CARPAS

Old Clown (spying a passing girl): Ain't she a peach! Ah, if I only had thirty years on my head! Say ——

Young Clown: You've a good eye yet, Dad. Ah! If I only had thirty pesos in my pocket! Say ——

Both (in chorus): Step up! Step up! Five cents to see a whole *tanda*. Four numbers. See the beautiful blonde sisters dance the Charleston!

T<small>HIS</small> by-play takes place in front of one of the itinerant tent-shows of Mexico. Patched and weatherbeaten, this spring holiday, they have been set up side by side, half in the parking, half in the street, along the Alameda gardens. The blare of music and trumpets and drums rattles up and down the avenue. The bawl of the barkers through the megaphones smashes in with the roar of tramways and traffic; gigantic pinwheels shower sparks over the crowds. High overhead revolves the enormous Ferris-wheel, a moving many-headed snake with a series of gaping mouths. . . . Pick your way along the paths lined with Spanish tiled fountains and graceful southern shrubbery, and view the whole ensemble of tent-shows, venders, *puestos*, eating-booths and crowds—the soaring National Theatre as a background, its marble massiveness and unfinished steel ribs breaking the texture of the city's glow.

Pleasure seekers slump down on narrow benches before oil-cloth tables lit by gasoline torches and are served brick-colored stews with crisp tortillas to shovel them into their mouths—or chicken with *mole*, a sauce of twenty odd spices, or *enchiladas*, chile con carne, tamales, milk-white pulque, or pineapple *tepache*, or beer.

In the nearby *puestos* are food, pottery, toys, sarapes, candy, jewelry, handiwork of every variety. Golden dried fruit from California cascades alongside of *cajetas* from Celaya filled with milky caramel; *camotes de Puebla*, candied sweet-potatoes; red, yellow and green gelatines in inverted tumblers lit to transparency by candles; golden wedges of fresh pineapples, mangos, plums; on a woven straw *petate*, a heap of peanuts—five centavos a wooden measure-ful dumped into your side pocket. A blind man wails out a *corrido* to the accompaniment of a broken-stringed armadillo guitar. A vender holds out a flowering cornucopia of rose-colored mamey ice-cream. A ragged barefoot Indian sells imported fluffy powder-puffs from a long string draped about his dirty neck; another dandles kewpie dolls. The pottery booths are a melange of delicate tints: blue and gold Talavera ware from Puebla, ruddy *ollas* from Oaxaca; brown and blue vases from Guadalajara; clay and wax figurines of the rural life of Mexico: men drawing pulque from the Maguey, Indian women selling vegetables, charcoal venders, tortilleras, venders of ducks, fruitmen, woodmen, flower-sellers, the gaily-dressed ranchero, horsemen, soldiers. In the toy booths: German automobiles and dolls alongside of tiny replicas of native household goods, miniature grinding stones for the maize, strings of seed-beads from Cuernavaca, straw-woven horses and riders, stuffed dolls of corn husks, bright-feathered cocks on wires—a twist brings their spurs and bills striking viciously, feathers flying. The vivid red and yellow sarapes and hangings come from Texcoco or Oaxaca or Saltillo. The central design of one carries a humorously dwarfed Tlaloc or rain-god; some are reminiscent of the inlaid stone motifs on the ruins of Mitla. From Michoacán and Tehuantepec come lacquer ware—broad *jícaras* from painted gourds, little boxes made of sapote and rosewood for My Lady's jewels; painted plates, bowls, trays—portraying flowers, wedding and church scenes, combats, horsemen, bull-fights, landscapes, birds, animals. In among these booths are the *carpas* or shows —rough wooden frame-work covered with rain-stained patched canvas, often sewed with gaudy red and white stripes. Inside are crude board benches, tiny stages, and tattered and faded drops painted with gay butterflies or wondrous scenery.

These shows are the delight of the lower classes. For ten centavos one may sit through a *tanda* of four numbers: song and dance, burlesque, dialogue, puppet-shows, and other forms of amusement. The audience is a rough and ready, slam-bang sort, ranging from the barefoot tatterdemalion Indian to the mestizo and the lower middle-class—the better-dressed are rare, occasionally some roué interested in one of the dancing girls. Among the onlookers are most of the prototypes of the wax figurines in the *puestos*: *camión* drivers in overalls, charcoal venders, faces smeared black; a candy salesman, glass case and wares on his knees; Indian girls in bright silk beaded dresses, vivid combs sparkling in their glistening black hair, long blood-red pendents dangling against their swarthy cheeks. Beads glow against necks daubed to a marvelous purple with cheap powder. Everybody freely shouts boisterous witticisms; the actors and actresses chaff the too rowdy. The facetiæ are keen, ribald, but always laughable. An actress may call up a fellow from the audience with whom to dance or on whom to bestow a lip-stick kiss—whoops of delight from the audience which fairly bashes the victim with jocose banter.

"Oh, this young man," sings the actress, pointing her beringed finger:

> "Oh this young man—you there, yes you—
> Whom the girls make such a fuss over;
> If they only knew you're too poor, too poor,
> To buy vaseline, so you slick your hair with your tongue."

A roar greets this crude sally; the singer dances around the stage, pleased at the discomfiture of her victim, then returns to attack someone else, in a series of limericks, bawdy and various, on to songs about "the young man who fell through the hole" . . . to "that son of a Guadalajara moustache." . . .

The dances themselves rarely consist of more than a few weaving Indian-like steps; the gestures are not unlike Lesson I in the old-fashioned elocution books; the music is produced by the usual jazz combination: piano (lacking in some cases), a banjo-mandolin, a C or B saxophone, a fiddle, a drum, sometimes a trombone or cornet; but the result is always tom-tom and Indian. The main ingredients of the dance are a girl with good legs (risquely dressed in short skirts, suggestive drawers or tights) and the popular melodies dealing with ranch life or love: *"La Borrachita"*—"The Little Drunk Girl," *"Que risa me da"*—"What laughter it gives me." A tandem of mestizan beauties prances out with a parody of the religious chant *"Ora pro nobis"* concerning a Virgin interestingly absurd. There is a humorous ballad about a sweetheart with a baby, deserted by her lover, who meets another girl in the same predicament, and because of the same scoundrel. They console each other very well, and in many verses. The songs are alive with hate and love, separation, and reconciliations, seduction, betrayal, disillusionment. The subjects vary. A millionaire takes the actress to New York, or a gray-haired *viejo* should know better than to "pussyfoot after

251

chickens. . . ." One girl is no good for love because she sleeps too soundly to hear her sweetheart hammer on the door. . . . A monk and a nun do not leave each other "from fear of the dark." Sometimes the song is a simple love melody old in the hearts of the people—"*Te mandé por correo cuatro suspiros de mi alma*"—"I sent you by mail four sighs from my soul."

Often these simpler melodies are sung by a rancher in a *charro* costume, to the accompaniment of a guitar—those beautiful melodies of love and jealousy, of affection for horses and dogs, for flowers and storms and moonlight, which are the heritage of Mexican rural life. The *charro* outfit consists of a broad-brimmed peaked sombrero of fine-woven straw or embroidered leather, of black felt and silver work, or of brown felt and woven pearls and beads; of a leather jacket, embroidered, or covered with silver or gold ornaments; of trousers, skin-tight clear to the instep, opening at the sides with silver buttons. Many of the songs are wistful memories of the "*rancho donde yo nací*—the ranch where I was born." Better, declares the singer, than the city pin-stripe trousers and spats are the tough country "*pantalones de cuero*"; better than tight shoes are the comfortable sandals (*guaraches*); better than autos are the slow-moving ox-carts creaking along with unhurried dreams under the lazy sun; better than new-fangled brilliantine to make the beloved's hair glisten is the dear smell of country grease.

This contrast between city and urban life is always to the fore. For instance, the clever but shallow city fifi. His nimble tongue and sophistication are set over against the simple, credulous countryside Indian, who, though easily duped, proves at bottom, much to the delight of the audience, far wiser than his city-baiter. A city-worker of the middle-class, the office-clerk type, tries to describe to a peon, dressed half clown, half Indian, all the wonders of a motorcycle, a machine the latter has never seen. The rube's enthusiasm mounts: he offers to trade for it his cow.

City-worker: Why, I'd look like a boob riding down
Francisco Madero Avenue on a cow. I'd never get my
errands done. You are a goof.

Peon: Quite so. I never thought of that. Come to do so, I'd
be even more funny.

City-worker: How come?

Peon: Wouldn't I be a popinjay trying to milk a motorcycle?

The burlesque hits off the politician. A youngster in a tall
gray stove-pipe hat and a check suit with a frock tail sallies
out and half in song, half in patter, asks does he not look
exactly like a Congressman. He recites the various high public
posts he has occupied, including one in the city jail (Belén)
from which place he was promoted to the penitentiary, finally
gaining his release because he was such a good poet—and gives
a sample, his new opera "Teresa."

> Teresita, vamos a casa,
> Ya hace una hora que estamos aquí,
> Y la luna está clara, clara, clara . . .
> Que ya parece de día.

Other favorite jests of burlesque are the foreigner, the
American and the Spaniard—the Gringo and the Gachupin—
nor do they get off more lightly than the burlesqued foreigner
with us. The American's weak points are his love of money-
making, his lack of romanticism and imagination, his fear
of discomfort and death, his fondness for order. The Spaniard
is laughed at for his aggressiveness, his dialect, his boasting,
his volubility, his penny-wise pettiness.

A few street-shows attempt more serious drama. Often
the play is medieval and Spanish, with great ladies and
grandees in swords, courtly attire, cock hats, gowns and
jewels. The patent dilapidation of their costumes cannot destroy the illusion. There are duels and betrayals and delightful

provincial moralizing. One play, I remember, dealt with the return of a bullfighter to his home after a tour. His wife informs him of a forthcoming child, the yearned-for outcome of three years. They fall into each other's arms and begin to plan for the event—the name, the baptism, the education, the marriage, the future—and end by quarreling whether the boy (the sex is taken for granted) shall be a bull-fighter or something less dangerous. The wife falls into tears and tantrums, bitterly arguing her own frequent loneliness and fears of possible death. At the same time she warns her husband of the terrible effect of unpleasant prenatal episodes such as the very quarrel they are having on the son! Or the play shows a boarding-house scene, with a burlesque on Spaniards, on the arrogance of a youthful bull-fighter, on the apparent submissiveness yet dominating character of the Mexican mistress on a penniless wretch half-clown, half-vagabond, and on a most credulous, warm-hearted landlady who would prove a wonderful find for any struggling artist—the whole rich in vulgarities, slap-stick, and singing.

There are, of course, among the *carpas*, the customary fire-eaters—wild ring-nosed Tarahumare Indians who have loaned their religious rites to the eyes of the vulgar; there are bodyless heads, the abortion monstrosities, the houses of mystery and all well-known side-show stunts. Unique are the *fantoches*. Derived though they are from the Italian *fantocci*, they have become indistinguishably Mexican. These puppet-dwarfs with their human heads—they seem like Cretins—perform their antics on a miniature stage with a black drop, usually a peon and his wife or sweetheart. The former is dressed in white "pyjamas," *guaraches*, or sandals, and a battered straw-hat, half concealing a big shock of uncombed black hair and shading a red bulbous nose. His companion uses the typical colored skirt, embroidered *huipil*, or waist, and wears her hair in pig-tail braids over her bosom. These two *fantoches* sing native songs; they dance and talk, their drawling Indian-Spanish slum dialect—garbled "g" for "d" and harsh "j's"—is supremely racy, much about sex with pretended coyness on the part of the woman. Slap-stick episodes occur where the two kick and bite each other with right good will. The peon makes gestures with his toe. The whole is rich with the flavor of the Mexican countryside and the lower-class slums; of the *milpas* of growing corn and flowers, the markets of humming camaraderie. Sometimes the *fantoche* is a *charro* or rancher, who has seen the United States and tells his mirthful experience and botched impressions, making great fun of American prosperity, smugness, and policemen. Behind his rube talk always glisten the wistful tears of the outlander, the Mexican in exile, bewildered by foreign ways, obviously glad to be back among his own kind; yet with all the pride of having traveled far and seen many strange sights.

The *Titeres* and *Titiritipis*, or marionettes proper, are as good as anything in the old world. These string puppets, accompanied by clever behind-stage ventriloquists, perform dances, hold witty dialogue, do acrobatic stunts, play buffoon. A common combination is a Mexican clown whose foil is a sedate "Meester X" in a Prince Albert—the repartee hitting off both native and foreign failings. The clown plays excellent music (thanks to the orchestra) on a coffee-pot and dances native dances, the *jarabe* and the *jota*, with verve and personality. The crossbar and ladder acrobats, tumblers and trapeze artists, perform so realistically that each hazard steals the breath. Often the ensemble is more elaborate. A bull-fight, quite as thrilling yet far more laughable than the original. The tiny bull charges in shaking his horns furiously; richly dressed *capeadores* flaunt their scarlet capes and side-step cleverly. The *picadores* come prancing in on their extravagantly-caparisoned horses, lances set; the bull flings horse and rider down, gores them. The *banderilleros* in braid and gold, stamp their high-heeled shoes and plant their sharp darts into the bull's shoulders as he charges. The various episodes are dramatic, flavored with quaint humorous mishaps. A peon in "pyjamas" blunders into the ring, followed by an irate policeman. The peon is attacked by the bull and thrown on the runway fence. He loses his trousers. When he tumbles back into the ring, he uses them one moment as a modest shield against the audience, the next as a cape to fend off the bull. Both he and the policeman are finally flung high and clear of the ring on the bull's horns. The *matador* in queue and golden jacket and breeches enters with his red flag and sword, and makes his killing with the aplomb of a real star to the fanfare of the customary trumpets. Attendants race in with a brace of most unruly horses and drag out the dead bull with an expeditious flourish.

The Indian marriage as portrayed by the puppets is humorous folklore. A most delightfully belaced, black-skirted, pot-bellied priest enters followed by three candle-bearing acolytes in red and white. The *compadres* and *comadres*, who sponsor the wedding, drop on their knees. The bride wears a red, white and green bespangled *China poblana* costume; the groom, a *charro* outfit, with a brilliant red sombrero and flowing red tie. They end the ceremony by dancing the *jarabe*, with wild excellence. During the affair the imaginary crowd from behind scenes recklessly throws in fire-crackers; at each explosion, priest, acolytes and beneficiaries jump startlingly. The finale is the lighting by one of the marionettes of a beautiful set-piece which showers its sparks over stage, puppets, audience and the tent walls with pleasurable disregard for any possible conflagration.

In the puppet-shows, there lingers the stuff of the old miracle play—the Apparition of the Virgin of Guadalupe, whose likeness appears in every home and store, on the auto busses and in a hundred wayside shrines. The puppets reproduce the age-old beloved story of how the Virgin Mary first set foot on the Western mainland, appearing to the poor Indian, Juan Diego.

Juan Diego, befittingly "pyjama"-clad, comes into the scene at the base of Tepeyac, with his gourd and stick, his sarape, and his fibre-woven knapsack, on his way to tend to his maguey plants and to visit his sick uncle, Bernardino. Juan lies down to rest under a false-pepper tree, and a most pathetic angel flutters down from Heaven to inform him of the proximate apparition. An image of light shines through the drop amidst the choir-singing of invisible cherubim and angels. The dazed Juan is informed he must go immediately to the Archbishop. Juan, after lengthily arguing the urgency of his own private business, with all the hard-headed, humorous realism of the Mexican Indian peasant, is finally persuaded by the angel to perform his nobler duty. But at the Palace in Mexico City he is charged with being drunk and is thrown out by the ear.

The hill of Tepeyac again. Uncle Bernardino more dangerously ill than before. Again the angel and the apparition —a similar argument. Juan, in view of his previous experience, this time asks for a sign to take back to the Archbishop. He is told to pick roses from the garden on the other side of the sterile hill. Juan tragically insists that he will find only rocks, lizards, cactus, and false-pepper trees, but at last consents to have a look, and finds not merely a garden but a miraculous fountain, to this day as curative as the waters of Jordan. And so—with roses—Juan Diego convinced the Archbishop of the necessity of building a Cathedral on the spot which in earlier days had been the site of the holy *cu* of another Virgin, the Indian Virgin of Tonantzín, protectress of the Tononqui Indians, a spot for untold ages revered as miraculous in the imagination of the Indians.

Juan Diego, successful in his mission, returns to his beloved harsh Tepeyac, and the Virgin reappears again, with the same singing of the invisible choir; but this time she springs from out the very heart of the hill; a great gilded star unfolds and from the center of it shines forth the Virgin with overpowering radiance; from behind her an enormous pinwheel showers living flames which remind one for all the world of that Baroque sun-rayed window behind the apse of St. Peter's itself. The play is reverent, humorous and wise. Vividly it renews the dearest legend of the humble Mexican people.

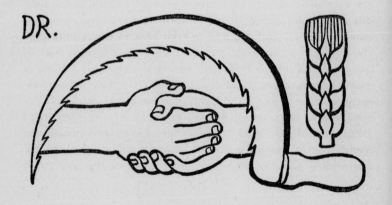

XVII   THE NOISEMAKERS: *LOS ESTRIDENTISTAS*

1

REVOLUTIONS come and go. But Porfiriata, the Indian, remains. He remains to dance the rumba in convulsive distortions under the open portals of the Hotel Diligencies in Vera Cruz. He dances madly, endlessly, in patterned black and white, tropic sun and shade, before the centuries-old Spanish plaza.

Revolutions come and go. Winds blow in and out—acrid spirals off the Chihuahua desert; icy northers of Tamaulipas; trade hurricanes of Sinaloa. Voices lift in high babble— revolutionaries, reactionaries, Students of America, antiimperialists, Mussolini, Lenin, the Unknown Soldier, Generals, bull-fighters, buzzards—all thunder from Sinai. To the queries of his would-be benefactors the phlegmatic Indian replies ever the same, "*Quién sabe?*—Who knows?" The Army sings its slave songs—*Adelita, Valentina, Cucaracha*—"*no longer can I march . . .*" Shout the Liberals: "We must forge the Fatherland." From under a roadside cross, set among cactus, comes the hoarse voice of the executed: "The Fatherland, the Fatherland. . . . What Fatherland?"

Revolutions come and go. But Porfiriata remains.

He bursts on the throng of arcade idlers, who are sipping beer, mint julep, lemonade and cocoanut juice—an old crazy man, selling newspapers and lottery tickets, wearing a sailor's *boina*, using a thick carved cane.

"Gentlemen, here is Porfiriata."

He offers lottery ticket No. 9669.

"It has its mystery, this little number!"
"Heads or tails, heads or tails!"

Porfiriata dances the rumba shouting:

"This ticket will win—
  Heads or tails, heads or tails,
  This ticket gives
      96, ay 96!
      ay, 69, 69, 69 . . ."

"Doesn't it make your mouth water, little one!"

"This ticket will win,
  This ticket will win ——"

Revolutions come and go. Mexico is whirled into changed life. The Gringoes descend upon the oil lands. John Bull arrives. They come in cavalcades. They come on horses, with guards and officials—"only a priest is lacking to have the whole country represented"—*tlac, tloc, tlac, tloc, tlac, tloc* . . . they come and go, buying oil lands—

"Gringoes with their cursed big hoofs,
  abortions of hell itself,
  mules, vile blond ones,
  hating our government . . ."

Come the Gringoes:

"*Yes. No. All right. Very well. No. Jesus Christ!*"
"Shut up, damn Gringo!"

260

"You stupid fool, you Greaser."
"Shut your trap, damn Gringo!"
"You Greaser!"
"Your mother you goat of a Gringo ———"
Pam! Pam! Pam!

One Yankee less and one passenger more for old
Charon . . .
Uncle Sam presents his bill to Mexico, very seriously, with
great solemnity.

"Fifty thousand dollars please!"
"Ujule, Gringo, at the frontier we'll give ———"
"Fifty thousand dollars, please!"
"In Arizona, we'll give; at the frontier, we'll give ———"

Reclamations commission. Notes, notes, discussions. Uncle
insists. Mexico shrugs. Nothing is settled. Inertia.
"Ujule Gringo! Ujule Gringo!"
And so a thumbing of the nose ("the Government of Don
Porfirio looked out for the Gringo. It feared something might
happen to the old duffer hunting oil. For Díaz, Uncle Sam
was an insect to be cared for. . . . Many years had to pass,
much blood had to run, before Mexico learned to laugh at
him.")

Revolutions come and go. *The Buzzard Chorus cries*:

"Cannon fodder, cannon fodder, we wish to grow fat!"

Cry the troops:

"Viva the chief? Viva the Chief of the Revolution! Viva
the Savior of the Country."

The upstart leader:

"Fellow citizens! The Mexican people! Tyrants! The Vote.
The violation of the vote! The tyrants! The people!
Suffrage. Imposition. I go to save the Fatherland! The

261

people call me. I sacrifice myself for the Fatherland. The vote, the tyrants . . ."

That Which Seems the People:

"Bring on another bull-fight! Another bull-fight! Another bull! Another record! Something new!"

The General of Division:

"Long live the Chief of the Revolution! He comes to save the Fatherland!"

Cry the Crowd:

"Viva! Viva! Viva!"

"Bread and bull-fights. Bread and bull-fights."

But Porfiriata still sells lottery tickets and dances under the Vera Cruz portals.

Now the revolution is settled nicely for everybody. Everything is lovely. The radio stations are calling CHAPULTE-PEC—Mexico's White House.

Chapultepec listens:

"Chapultepec ready!"

Radio 1. Washington talking:

"Coolidge at the instrument. Coolidge congratulating the President."

Radio 2. New York talking:

"The stock-exchange at the instrument. Wall Street congratulates the Government."

Radio 3. Europe speaking:

"Europe congratulates the President."

Radio 4. Radio 5. Radio 6.

"Congratulations, congratulations, congratulations."

Revolutions come and go. But the lottery-ticket vender leaps through the archway to dance his rumba.

"Here is Porfiriata!"
"When would he fail ——"
"What wind does he bring!"

"Why always, as long as the *mitote* is, he'll be here to dance it . . ."

"Porfiriata, listen to Porfiriata!"

"Here, Gentlemen, is Porfiriata,
Gentlemen, here he is!
I am your Porfiriata,
Viva the rumba; viva good-times,
Viva the Government,
Viva your mother—
Viva Porfiriata,
For I am Porfiriata, Gentlemen,
And I'm agoin' to dance the rumba,
I'm agoin' to dance the rumba,
Because I'm Porfiriata!"

And he makes grotesque contortions. He dances the rumba violently. He dances the rumba with ardor.

"Turn, turn little nigger!"
"Little nigger, turn, turn!"

The revolution is crude, the revolution is loud: it is battle and cannon fire and stentorian hopes, futility and false creeds, landseizures and strikes, bastard ambitions and strutting generals. It is all in the mill, and much of what was good has gone down before greedy militarists, grafting politicians, and bondholders. A Renaissance aborted. A people hauled here, hauled there. Many voices, little knowledge.

And no two parts of the country singing the same song. The Vortex.

To keep pace with this turmoil, literature has had to slug hard quick. No Alfonso Reyes of the milder diplomatic traditions, no Justo Sierra, or Amado Nervo, uttering from ivory towers to the revolution: "Don't forget to be intelligent." No time for sweetness and light.

And so expressionism—in poetry and in the novel. The theatre just isn't save for a back-stairs effort called Ulysses on Mesones Street. But in the novel, and to some extent in poetry, there have stepped forward the Noisemakers—the Estridentistas! They have to shout to be heard. They have shouted. Hence *Estridentismo*. Noisy-ism! They have shouted. Arqueles Vela has shouted. And Kin Taniya. And List Arzubide. And Salvador Gallardo. And Gutiérrez Cruz, Elena Alvarez, Mariano Azuela, and Xavier Icaza.

Xavier Icaza, in his shouting, chanting novel *Panchito Chapopote*, from which the foregoing extracts were taken, has told a tale in the French *sur realiste* style, with the punch of an engine piston. No time for leisurely characterization or plot complications; the colors are slammed on, the colors of Vera Cruz, sharp, overpowering: the dense vegetation, palm-trees, gibbering parrots, gyring buzzards, the dance, the song, the odors of the oil revolution. The village Tepetate is turned overnight into a buzzing city. The officials who formerly walked barefoot in the dust—"their rapid and martial advance lacked the merited effect"—now wear shoes that click over pavements.

No longer is it the ancient picturesque and drowsy Tepetate. It is traversed by a wide asphalt street. No more palm-thatched houses, but large dwellings with wooden galleries. Bad hotels, dearer than the Ritz: twenty dollars a bed. Yankee food. Costumes Yankeeized. Lunches. Quick lunch. Free lunch. Banana lunch. No more white blouses of women who lean out to gaze at the newcomer. There is

264

continuous intense traffic. Heavy trucks with hardware
and machinery intercept. Tank cars. Sprinkling carts.
Freight trucks. Trucks jammed with workers . . . Automobiles with magnates from New York: from New York,
from California, from No Man's Land.

The story of Icaza's novel is simple. The humble clerk of
the Alcalde of Tepetate has been spurned by two of the local
belles. Suddenly he is able to sell out a piece of property
(which up to this time would grow nothing because of the
"cursed" oil in the soil) for a fabulous sum, and so he clears
out for Vera Cruz where he goes to the dogs. He sleeps with
a flamboyant mulatta prostitute and between rounds of *zotol*
and *tequila* tells her his story. Then, in a fit of maudlin senti-
mentalism and consciousness of lost tranquillity, he deter-
mines to return to simple Tepetate and get married. But there
all has been revolutionized. His wealth, however, enables him
to force Amalia María Dolores, his former sweetheart, to
abandon the man she loves and marry him. Panchito's joy is
short-lived. He is caught in the toils of the mad-house revolution; he is held for ransom, gets released, but when the
storm of cavalry sweeps away from the place he is shot
through the head by a stray bullet in a moment of too idle
curiosity; and the author brutally announces to his hero, he
has no more use for him anyhow.

The story is hairy-chested, slam-bang, half chanted, half
shouted, attuned to the revolutionary uproar. It has none of
the leisurely artistic calm of Hergesheimer's *Tampico*. It is
more akin, in the crude strength of its treatment to *Proces-
sional*. Here in *Panchito Chapopote* is the whole wild whirl
of Mexico told in a few swift pages. Feudal slavery has been
wiped away not for the sake of freedom but that the American invasion can proceed more smoothly than before. Con-
gratulate the government everybody. But Panchito is dead.
Only Porfiriata dances on. This is the dreary finale. It is
savage satire; fierce, bitter disillusionment, bitterly vital

disillusionment. This is the paradoxical Estridentista combination.

The Estridentista movement—which embraces more artists than those willing to accept the tag, and among them the leading painters who are the real expression of the period —was definitely launched in Carranza's time in Mexico City, but the most sustained group has centered in Jalapa, the small, picturesque, tropical capital of Vera Cruz. Here, under the aegis of Governor Jara, the Estridentistas published their *portavoz, El Horizonte,* one of the most original and stimulating magazines in Latin America, now, unfortunately, defunct. And so, just as the cradle of a new tendency in painting was the stately Guadalajara of Jalisco (the true region of the *paesista,* the land of beautiful traditions and beautiful women) so the center of Estridentismo became Vera Cruz.

Vera Cruz, that does not merely listen to the revolution. It does not know how to do so. It does not meditate. Through its veins runs the fire of the tropics. Vera Cruz translates everything into action. It invents laws, laws, laws. Vera Cruz is the legislator of Mexico: Labor law, Renter's law; Projects of petroleum laws; distribution of land; obligatory land rental; Sunday rest; Profit sharing, Padlock law, Hunger law, and agitation, revolution, agitation.

The leading poet of the group is Maples Arce. His *Urbe* is a political harangue to the strong men of the new cities. Rebellion filters it. Not until *Andamios Interiores* (Interior Scaffolding) is written, and he sets forth on *Interdicted Poems,* is he swimming full in the revolutionary stream, yet ever haunted with disillusion, a consciousness of misspent effort in all this social upheaval. Quieter, daring, more lovely and more human, is Kin Taniya in *Aeroplano* and *Radio* and a number of other slim volumes. Arequelas Vela, most careless of the Academy, the freest prose-writer, strikes the customary pessimistic note. He refuses to recognize the Mexican revolution as a motivation of art, but rather a subject—for humor, for ignoring logic, for fantasy and sarcasm. Most of the Mexico City bureaucrats look askance at this group. Strangely enough, though on the left in technique, it remains on the right because of its hard-headed refusal to romantize the revolution. It has had no need for revolutionary rhetoric and sophistry as have the politicians, though it includes a number of valiant propagandists, whose work is not entirely without merit. List Arzubide in *El Horizonte* definitely harped upon revolutionary ideology. In his books of verse, *Voyager in the Vertex* and *Corner*, he is out and out Estridentista; in his *Exaltation of Emiliano Zapata* he is Revolutionary; and his *Plebe* is definitely directed to the masses. In Gutiérrez Cruz' *Red Blood* literary experiment has turned into direct Communist propaganda in clod-hopper but interesting verse.

Came the Villa hordes down from the north. The break-up, a nation harried by steel and fire. The iron heel. The upsurge. Madero had lifted the lid. Hate met hate. Pandora's box. Huerta tried to clap the lid on again. But he had his own Pandora box. Assassination. Civil war. More hate versus hate. The deluge.

Swarming down from the heights over plain and valley, came the Villa *dorados*. Came the hordes of "the Under Dogs —*Los de Abajo*." Nicklemen croaking up from the slimy depths. Demetro Macías, the hero of *The Under Dogs* came croaking up. Illiterate rancher, saloon brawler, assassin of unjust officials, outlaw—with nerves of iron, sure-footed, lover of battle and cold steel, madly brave, cruel but filled with a measure of fair-play, a man who never forgets a kindness and never forgets an injury—he leads his host like a swarm of hungry locusts through the states of Zacatecas and Jalisco. And with him goes Mariano Azuela, the novelist, and military doctor. Fortunately he lives to write the tale.

The Under Dogs gives none of the broader outlines of the

Mexican revolution; it is close-up photography of day-by-day struggle. Some unseen giant, named Monsieur Destiny, has lifted the nation by the scruff of the neck and is shaking everything loose. The cynical Solís is speaking: "The revolution is the hurricane; and the man who gives himself to it is no longer a man; he is a miserable withered leaf whipped by the gale." Even the leader Demetrio is a bewildered actor in a vast scheme of which he has faint conception. He is thinking all the time of his little ranch, his yoke of oxen, his wife, of the fields to be planted—a feeling so strong that on one occasion, he almost sets out on a terrific three days' journey to see his wife and his old haunts. It is Luis Cervantes, the turncoat of many parties, the leech-like secretary, who gives Demetrio a reason, a mission, a goal, an ideal; and at the same time tries to corrupt him with gold, for which Demetrio, trader in kind, has not the slightest use. Why worry about gold when there are plazas to be stormed; if need be, when guns and ammunitions are gone, with daggers in the hand? What is the need of gold when there are wealthy houses to be looted, saloons stored with mescal and habanero, and women for the taking? The scenes have the brutality of Gorki. Azuela is the Mexican Tchekov only in so much as he is a doctor; in all else he is close to Gorki, with a touch of Gorki's terrific pessimism and none of Gorki's revolutionary optimism. The style is crisp; it burns like the flash of a gunmuzzle close to the skin. Azuela knows the Under Dogs. He has seen the revolution; he has smelled it; he has felt it. His language is the language of reality, the patois of the Nicklemen, crude, often vile, truculent, fiendish. Prostitutes, La Pintada, and others, come and go. One is shot through the belly. Women are taken on and cast off, like old trappings. A country girl, kind to Demetrio, is sent for. The leech Luis, whom she loves, tricks her into the arms of his chief. The saloon talk is of killings: "In Parral I killed . . . In Chihuahua I killed . . ." The theme is inexhaustible. Now the topic is stealing. "In such and such a place I stole . . ." Old scores are settled, savagely, murderously, two eyes for one, two teeth for one . . . And orgies, vivid as Carlyle and the French Revolution. Broken wine-casks. People licking up aged wine from the gutters. Abysmal violence. "If I could catch Pascual Orozco alive, I'd yank off the soles of his feet and make him walk twenty miles through the mountains." And if there is gold and jewels stored in the houses of the prelates, why not steal them, especially as there are armed reactionary bands abroad equally cloven-footed, fighting for the Prince of Peace, led by priests, and shouting medieval slogans, *"Religión y Fueras."* When the grabbing is good, grab, for "If there are days when the duck swims, other days there is not even water to drink." It is a great release. An eruption of submerged passions, the explosion of sealed-up desires, lusts, rapacities. Now every under dog can roar out his mind, "without hairs on the tongue," if necessary even if not necessary, just for sport's sake, he draws quick and shoots quick. It is enough for these *de abajo* to feel life, to let their repressions loose, to follow the gust of desire wherever it leads.

Here again in Azuela, is the terrible disillusion, the *Götter-dammerung*: "What a farce, my friend, if those to whom we offer all our enthusiasm, life itself, to overthrow a miserable assassin (Huerta) turn out to be the makers of a monstrous pedestal on which a hundred or two hundred men of the same kind can mount! . . . People without ideals! People of Tyrannies. . . . Sorrows of the blood! . . . The psychology of our race condensed into two words . . . ! Rob! Kill!"

It is a very dark corner of the revolution. Over and beyond are the vague outlines of the Aguas Calientes convention, of the struggle against Carranza and Obregón, of the defeat of Villa at Celaya, but of these things the bewildered though brave Demetrio knows nothing. He is a blind agent. He is the withered leaf. And his story is the story of his kind, of those who because of ruthlessness of the Díaz régime were tossed into the arms of rebellion, forced to fight, without ever really knowing why they were there, yet swept on and on in ever faster rhythm, lifted up on a sea of conscious freedom as they swung over ridge and valley tasting the glories of clean hot skies and the scent of mesquit and sage-brush, and the camaraderie of marching feet and clicking guns. Ever faster the rhythm. Cold steel in the hands, new cheap joys to be seized, yet all the time the sad nostalgia of the tranquil ranch-life throwing a lurking wistfulness over their Tamerlanian enjoyments. The cycle of Demetrio, who dies alone, firing his last shot from behind a mountain rock, is the cycle of his kind in an hour of terrible birth throes for Mexico.

Demetrio is a humbler, less grandiose type than Sarmiento's *Facundo*. Nevertheless, in some ways this novel surpasses the masterpiece of the Argentinian. All in all Azuela bids fair to become the novelist of the Mexican revolution. His books mount up, and they form a broad canvas of the dark events of the past eighteen years. The author was born in 1879 in Lagos de Moreno, Jalisco, a small provincial town, on the banks of a forgotten river. He studied medicine in Guadala-jara. He returned to Lagos and wrote novels. *María Luisa, Los Fracasados (The Failures)*—intimate pictures of the Díaz régime, soon to crumble. He feels the quickening of the pulse, the stirring of the masses, the Gringos smelling out the petroleum. *Mala Yerba* (Evil Weed) tells the story. The Madero revolution begins, conquers, fails: *Andrés Pérez*. But through Madero's rise, Azuela becomes a local political figure. He writes *Sin Amor* (Without Love). Comes then his career as a doctor in the field with the blind hosts of Villa. He ab-sorbs first-hand the material for his best novel *Los de Abajo*, which though printed ten years ago in exile in El Paso, went unheeded until the last year and a half. Now its fame is sweeping the Spanish-speaking literary world. Azuela comes to Mexico City, settles as a poor physician in the poor *barrio* of Santiago Tlalteloco, and in silence and obscurity he paints the rest of the canvas of the revolution: *The Caciques*

(Bosses), *The Tribulations of a Respectable Family*—the middle class in the revolution, a pitiful tale. He steps fully into the modern current and style, approaches the Estridentistas with other recenter books: *La Malhora* (Evil Hour), *El Desquite* (Recompense for Injury).

2

Put beside Azuela *El Feroz Cabecilla* (The Ferocious Little Chief), stories of the revolution by Rafael Muñoz, and *La Sombra del Caudillo* and *El Aguila y la Serpiente* (The Eagle and the Serpent) by Martín Luis Guzmán, the latter for anecdotal background, and you have the best of the "literature of the Revolution," all told in striking narrative form. Some of the stories of Muñoz, especially *El Feroz Cabecilla* which is of another Demetrio hoisted into power beyond his capacity, are fully the equal of Georges D'Esparves tales of the Napoleonic period. Muñoz paints with lightning strokes; he gives us the cruelty, the heroism, the ferocity, the pathos of the times. The descriptions are memorable—the reckless barehanded charges upon machine guns, the constant uncertainty for the immediate future, the reaction when opportunity presents towards any sort of excess, the terrible physical ordeals, the suffering from the frightful heat across that sink of death, the Bolsón de Mapimí.

Strangely enough it is the revolution of the North and not of the South, the revolution of Villa and not of Zapata, that has had its story-tellers and chroniclers. The South has merely felt and hated and died; the North has ruled—especially, the states of Sonora and Coahuila—hence has been articulate. The most articulate book is *The Eagle and the Serpent* by Guzmán, the perfect companion piece of Azuela and Muñoz. It is a book of personal reminiscences, of adventure, of brilliant character etching, of dramatic episodes. More prolix, less incisive, written with that mixture of good-humor and farce and devil-may-care attitude which never deserts the Mexican even in the moments of grimmest difficulty, of gravest danger, of most serious responsibility. The book also embraces the political and social ramifications of the upheaval of which the heroes of Azuela and Muñoz are ignorant. It explains the gale as well as the leaves in the gale. Though prolix the story is told simply in a delightful and vivid prose style, without the slightest affectation. There are pages of quick tempo drama, of executions, of pursuits, of assassinations, of spies, a vivid episode when, during a flight of Villa, sleep became a more terrible pursuer than the Federals with Mausers in their hands. Guzmán has his prejudices; he is rabidly anti-Carranza; he loves Villa, and never deserted him in his darkest hour. Yet he is truthful. The worst of Villa becomes admirable in Guzmán's eyes, even his cruel, fanatic, ruthless and irresponsible characteristics, even his babyish sentimentalities, his infantile pomposity, shine in Guzmán's eyes; all is worth the telling, and so the caudillo stands out stark and clear. Guzmán's attitude is Boswellian. But above all his book gives an adequate frame in interesting narrative form for the etchings of Azuela and Muñoz and other isolated tales of the period.

The novel, *La Sombra del Caudillo*, from the standpoint of objectivity, literary construction, and conciseness, is far superior to *The Eagle and the Serpent*. Don Martín's present book is a synthetic, swiftly moving description of a futile Mexican revolt, probably that of Serrano in 1927. Guzmán's own revolutionary experiences, his activities as a member of the agitated national Chamber of Deputies, have been tempered by his quiet methodical life in Madrid, where he frequents the memorable *tertulia* of Valle Inclán in the Hotel Regina. His new work has unbroken texture, sureness of touch. In relentless, sculptured Mexican prose, he throws the cruel spotlight on all the treachery, the sycophancy, and corruption of generals, politicians, and labor leaders; here is oil graft, murder, plotting, and vileness of the local political and military scenes pinned down by the dagger of truth. He takes the wheels out of the clock; he passes from the façade gilded with fine words regarding the freeing of the peasants to the grimy back stairs of Mexico's political edifice.

Across his pages stride Olivier, leader of the euphoniously but inconsistently named Radical Progressive Party, an oratorical demagogue ever ready to double-cross his best friends; Axkaná, the devoted confidant of the Secretary of War, capable of superior and objective understanding, but obliged, because of the revolutionary turmoil, to drift like jetsam on the fast torrent of greedy politics; Jiménez, the tricky, cold-blooded official candidate, who "no one knew how, and in spite of his terrific indictments of the landed proprietors, had just acquired the largest hacienda in the north of the Republic,"—a paradox that might be laid at the door of almost any of the actual revolutionary leaders; Protasio Leyva, the murderous Commandant of the Valley of Mexico, who gloats in killing; the puffy assassin labor leader, Ricarde, with his sumptuous residence and scandalous orgies; La Mora, the prostitute whose fierce loyalty toward the group by which she is favored shames loftier treacheries.

The power of Guzmán's delineation lies in its complete lack of moralizing. Here is a simple narration of a relentless chain of circumstances. The characters, on the whole so despicable, are illuminated with occasional searching gleams, into their recondite nobler possibilities, choked from ordinary sight by their helpless enslavement to their sordid environment. Some of them are powerful men, clever men, fearless men, yet they never overleap the wall of treacherous Mexican politics. They are puppets of their debased theatre. "Mexican politics is conjugated with only one verb," declares the cynical Olivier, "rise early." Get the drop on the other fellow, be your weapon a Colt '48, a regiment of troops, or a political convention.

Ever in the background of this ignoble picture towers the majestic yet caressing landscape of Mexico, brooding sadly, wistfully, over the debasement of the children of sin who tread the land so haughtily and so stupidly. Every once in a while the glory of the gigantic volcanic setting impinges upon the blurred consciousness of the protagonists, imparting to them a fleeting, lost-soul stirring, some weak, distant beauty, harshly thrust aside from lives ill-spent.

Thus Guzmán has quite passed beyond the romanticism of the earlier raconteurs of banditry, such as Manuel Payno in his *Los Bandidos del Río Frio*. *La Sombra* is charged with a grieving consciousness of some lost, yet potential, Mexican greatness, some tremendous hope undivined, a realization of social forces twisting out of mire into light. The book will easily hold its own with Valle Inclan's *Tirano Banderas*, with *Facundo*, and several other type novels in Latin America. Cruel as *El Militarismo Mexicano*, by Blasco Ibañez, it is free from the flamboyance and maliciousness of the Spaniard, and is better written. I doubt if Guzmán achieves the classic simplicity of *Los de Abajo*, but he is more sophisticated, more conscious of the entire range of contemporary Mexico. His canvas is broader. The gang-war scene in the Chamber of Deputies, the final execution of Aguirre, and the fantastic tragic escape of Axkaná, are unforgettably vivid, palpitating with suspense, touched with the sanguinary majesty of d'Annunzio.

What is the intrinsic significance of the "literature of the revolution"? Icaza is a spectacular *tour de force*, a projection of the French *sur realiste*. He is interesting as phenomenon and as a state of mind; but Azuela, Muñoz, and Guzmán have carried over into more durable literature. The significance of most of this writing is that it definitely tears lose from the European current. It is national literature. It begins at home with things intimately known. It is that much stronger. It becomes a point of new departure. Mexico has become important enough, dramatic enough, terrible enough, for its writers to seek native themes, native characters, native style, and tell the story in a native way. This presents difficulties, first of all because the Mexican language is not yet shaped, the Indian dialects, the foreign intrusion, the Castilian, have not been fused into a workable amalgam.

The first burst of Mexican freedom, the wars of independence, resulted in realism and naturalism in the novel. It saw the production of the most powerful piece of fiction yet written in Mexico, perhaps in all Latin America—*Periquillo Sarniento*, by Joaquin Fernández de Lizardi, "the Mexican Thinker." Though this takes as its prototype the Spanish picaresque novel—seventy-five years after the European models had reached maturity—it comes to grips with the Mexican scene. No referee could break that clinch. *Periquillo Sarniento*, for me, is one of the world's greatest books, and perhaps the greatest book that has come out of Latin America. It has a super-Johnson screed against literary patrons. It even has a glossary of Mexicanisms, much as certain present-day American novels must have a glossary of Americanisms when making their bow to the English elite. With pitiless insight and tremendous humor, with Dickensonian flare, *Periquillo Sarniento* investigates every Mexican institution. Added to this, harsh caricature—the art in which the Mexican is always supreme—gives the work a flare of Smollet and Fielding. And so far as the social scope is concerned the sweep is Balzacian. It examines every angle, every level, every profession, every institution. Azuela probably does not tie the

shoe laces of El Pensador, but he and other contemporaries
I have mentioned are interesting, certainly, for the possibilities they open up. They are free from all maudlinism, and
they twist the current of Mexican literature back into the
sunlight of things Mexican—and it is a pitiless sunlight.

Azuela, it is true, consciously or unconsciously borrows
from his predecessor, Heriberto Frías. This writer's *Tomochic*,
if it lacks the cruel incisiveness of Azuela, has similar subject
matter, and though it deals with the Díaz period, similar
treatment. *Tomochic* reveals that the forefathers of the
Villa hordes were the lawmaking and terror inspiring Federals of Díaz, with just as little respect for justice, for decency, for the law they enforced, as the upstarts of the
revolution. In *Tomochic* are depicted the same orgies, the
same brutalities, the same loot spirit, save that the perpetrators wore the uniform of the great dictator and hence
could do no wrong. *Tomochic*, in its entirety, is sufficiently
stupid, nigh worthless; characterization is inferior to Azuela;
but it deals with the same under dogs, save that they have
the suave majesty of the State behind them. In one or two
passages, however, Frías rises close to genius. In describing
the taking of Tomochic, no more terrible, more skin-crawling
description of human warfare and military depravity has ever
been written. Henri Barbusse and Latzko are tame beside a
certain chapter of Frías. And what is more frightful, more
majestic, more purging to the soul, than the camp saturnalia
after the victory? An unforgettable picture of Díaz army
life!

In any case, the Mexican novel has established a tradition
in the realm of realism, in its exploitation of themes of rural
militarism, revolution, and banditry, be it Lizardi, Frías,
Azuela, *Astucia* by Luis G. Inclán, or that interesting picture
of southern Mexico of an earlier epoch, Payno's *Los Bandidos
del Rio Frío*.

Yet when all is said and done, this is the "ten-twenty-and-
thirty" thriller of our post-Civil War period raised to a lit-

erary category—for the authors sure know their stuff. There
is yet to be established the tradition of a novel which embraces Mexican life as broadly as did El Pensador, and at the
same time penetrates the depths of the Mexican mind, setting
forth Mexican characters in the light of modern Mexican life
comprehensively understood. The psychological trend of the
modern novel will not be found in Mexico, save in Torres
Bodet's efforts à la Paul Morand and Gide. Yet the writings
we are considering have much of the physical aspect of
Russian realism plus a pessimism peculiarly Mexican, not the
Mencken pessimism of gusto and ideas, but rather a shovel-
ful of that earthy fatalism which nourishes a race in sorrow
and leaves all graver issues to the gods, or at least to the sun,
the winds and the rain.

3

The City of the Gods—Teotihuacán. On the summit of
the Pyramid of the Sun. The valley, a checkerboard of brown
and green, dotted with maguey plants, stretches to the gray-
blue mountains. A train, reduced by distance to toy dimensions, slips through the gap, leaving a trail of motionless
black smoke. The sun is hot; the sky is blue silk. Diego
Rivera, the painter, strikes the ground with his Apizaco
cane. Sparks fly.

Winds of the Revolution. Voices of the Revolution. Turmoil and battle. Declares Don Diego: "The Indian is right.
There are too many words. The Indian pays no attention
because he is too intelligent and realizes that there are too
many words. It is necessary to do things. It is necessary to
create. It is necessary to be Mexican. Death to Paris! Down
with the French-ized who have lost caste! They should be
deported! Let us learn from the builders of the pyramids. We
shall continue their work uninterrupted. We shall realize a
Mexican labor: It is necessary to be of the country. It is necessary to express Mexico."

And so Don Diego has painted. And the real spot-light of present-day creative expression in Mexico hits painting. Here Estridentismo strikes its stride. No understanding of Mexico is complete without approaching its painting. Here are the real *primitivi*, and the High Mogul is Diego Rivera.

Don Diego is a huge man, with a Pilsner paunch, a frog-like baby face, and short chubby arms. He exudes from his clothes. He cannot fit into bath tubs. He paints enormous frescoes furiously for thirty-six hours at a stretch without food. Once he became so dizzy he fell off a thirty-foot scaffolding and lived to laugh about it. He involves every utterance in gargantuan fantasy; he is a legend-maker and a Munchausen liar; yet at the heart of his fables, in the pith of their meaning, lurks absolute truth—for those wise enough to comprehend. In short, he has all the earmarks of a genius; and his painting and that of those who revolve around him is as significant an experiment in the way of art as is to be found anywhere in the world today.

The group of modern Mexican painters came out of Guadalajara, that great seat of Colonial culture and last bulwark of medieval Catholicism, and landlordism, the city of beautiful women and beautiful traditions. In their way, these young artists came like Villa hordes, breaking traditions, smashing idols. Many names graced the group; Clemente Orozco, Xavier Guerrero, Jorge Enciso, Adolfo Best-Magaud, J. Guadalupe Zuno, D. Siqueiros, Roberto Montenegro, de la Cueva—but to mention a few. With the group was also associated Carlos Mérida, the original and interesting Guatemalan painter; several Spanish painters; the Frenchman, Jean Charlot; and the photographers Edward Weston (American) and Tina Modotti (Italian). Many of these have jumped up to their necks in politics or have discovered a new creed, or a new technique, and have gone their separate ways. Guerrero and Siqueiros for a time turned active Communists and only lifted the pencil or brush to turn out propaganda posters.

Zuno has become the political boss of Jalisco. Modotti has been deported.

Rivera and Orozco have emerged as two outstanding figures. The one-armed Orozco is Rivera's nearest competitor. His interpretation of the revolution is explosive, terrifying, grotesquely powerful. His work has a Hogarthian, a Swiftian satire, cruel and derisive. He has something in common with that remarkable Mexican caricaturist of the last century, Posada; something decidedly in common with the Caprichos of Goya. There is a Grecco-like abnormality to his painting, a constant straining at the leash, as of a desire to leap over and beyond the possibilities of all artistic expression. Hence his work is more erratic. It is as erratic as the revolutionary hosts he depicts on the march, whirling over the harsh deserts with gun and Juana, battling, looting, burning, fornicating, boozing, shouting freedom.

Rivera's work has less of this emotional urge; it is more rationalistic; his mind is ever at work on gigantic conceptions. His painting has a plastic calm even in its greatest moments of hate or adoration. It is the Byronic rainbow in the storm. And hence, because of his scope, his statuesque massiveness, his persistence, his unrelenting vitality, Don Diego is superior to Orozco. His endeavors, aside from his easel paintings, are largely to be found in the two three-tiered patios of the Secretariat of Education, in the Chapingo Agricultural School, the National Palace, the Public Health building, and the Palace of Cortez in Cuernavaca. Here he depicts *Mexico*, not of the Conquest, save by historical reference, but the teeming Mexico of today. Here is Indian Mexico. Here is life in the raw. And here is propaganda of the revolution. Hence his frescoes have a theatrical poster-like quality; hence satire. Hence the grim tale of the revolution—a fist in the face. Yet, unlike Orozco, he sees the revolution as a whole, not in patches.

All Mexico is at work here, just as Renaissance Florence was at work in the open-air frescoes of Benozzo Gozzoli in the Campo Santo in Pisa. Here are the gala-clad workers of Tehuantepec, the weavers of Orizaba, the half-naked iron-workers of Torreón, the bronze sugar-workers of Morelos and Vera Cruz, the runty miners of Pachuca, emerging from yawning shafts. White-pyjamaed peasants embrace—brothers in sorrow—in the brown sweep of mesas rising up to ribbed mountains that strike against blazing skies. Here are burning haciendas and the rattle of the revolution. Here, tans and reds, quick-growth green, the yellow of corn leaves and ripe wheat, find burnished repose in the festivals: the corn festival, the hunting dances, the war dances, the religious festivals, the Day of the Dead, the burning of the Judases, flower-decked Santa Anita; and the great social festivals: the Sunday markets *(tianguis)* heaving up a scramble of raw-hide bound crates and petate baskets and surging people to the nigger-blue portals of a beggar-littered church; the return of the *ejidos* or communal lands, and a mass of eager white-clothed dark-skinned peasants; and lastly a great May Day labor festival with a bloody surf of red banners carried by blue-overalled workers and pyjama-clad peasants.

Ascend the stair-case from the sea of Antilles, through the Vera Cruz tropics and jungles where the writhing carnal vegetation overhangs, teeming and hot; where people loll in sisal hammocks in the heat and a beautiful nude woman pays obeisance to the obscene god Xochipilli, Lord of Flowers. Go on up to the Mesa Central, the high-lands, where the lightning of a whirling Almighty strikes the sword from the hands of fratricidal brethren; where worker, peasant, and soldier clasp hands for a new conquest of the soil, that tractors may hum, and aeroplanes glide through turquoise sky, and the fields overflow with wheat and corn, and men exploit the earth instead of other men. Here are nude cloud figures—the tropic storm—in spots as powerful as anything of Michael Angelo. Here is the great sweep of the Valley of Mexico—the fabled Anáhuac, its lakes glistening in the shimmering sun.

In the second gallery are the symbols and personalities of mathematics, philosophy, architecture—made over for the benefit of mankind. Martyred Felipe Carillo of Yucatán, the blood gushing from stigmatae, as from saints of old, stares down with sad kind eyes; the martyred Emiliano Zapata and Montaño of the agrarian upheaval, stand guard.

The paintings of the topmost gallery are woven about a popular agrarian *corrido*, or song, which recounts the episodes of the revolution, the freeing of the peasants, the achievement of peace through common effort. Here are some of the freshest notes—beautiful pastoral themes, great surging bundles of wheat flowing from ample arms beneath bronze chins, naïve and happy. Also the cruelty of the revolution in the making—the American intervention, the murder of priests, landlords, and bankers. If in the work-scenes of the ground floor the worker paid tribute to hard-faced thin-lipped blue-eyed Gringo foremen, in the top gallery, the propaganda note becomes, at times, bitter, mordant. Ford and Morgan, fingering the tape, Rockefeller fingering his glass of milk—all guarded by a miniature statue of liberty—are set off against the local accomplices, the debauched and drunken aristocrats, the pig-like officials, guzzlers all, eating gold from a foodless table: priests with their skulls crushed in by sickle and hammer.

But though Rivera is a proletarian watch-dog, communist dogma is not the real secret of his art. The secret is Mexico in revolution, in turmoil; tortuously discovering itself at the cost of brutality and bloodshed and thwarted ideals. Rivera has had his foreign influences, chiefly the Italian *primitivi*—for he himself is a *primitivi*. Rivera is the Giotto of Mexican painting; he has broken the Byzantine tradition, which in Mexico is French, not the French of Manet and Degas, but of Corot and Rousseau, the seventeenth century paesistas, the court shin-diggers, the painters of flowers and fish for dining rooms. Rivera, on the other hand, has known something of post impressionism, and above all he knows Picasso, under whom he studied. For fourteen years he roamed Europe. Then he came back to Mexico and found himself with a bang. He found himself because he found Mexico.

Rivera's communism merely provides the emotional fuel for a genius fundamentally rationalistic, intellectual; just as religion provided emotional fuel for the Renaissance artists. But the Renaissance artists were both pagan and Gothic, clear-sighted, too; and the models for their Madonnas were frequently mistresses and cocottes. As in all ages, the most acceptable cocotte has a soft oval face, gracious tender curves, finely penciled eyebrows and perfectly harmonious features devoid of intelligence, arranged in holy inexpressiveness quite suitable for the best Madonnas. Rivera, for his part, is also pagan—and Mexican. Communism, as a motive force, has given Rivera an interest in the submerged racial elements of his country and their struggles, a sympathy for the poverty and misery, but his interpretation is fundamentally quite native, neo-Aztecan. He is planting his feet in the tracks of the pyramid-builders. He belongs to that Mexico, *mas allá,* that vast uncharted sea upon which the modern capital of the country drifts like a lost ship without a port—that Mexico of unknown semi-oriental mystery, where the gods are more ancient than Cortez, and the first cause moves through men more intimately than through the modern slaves of the machine.

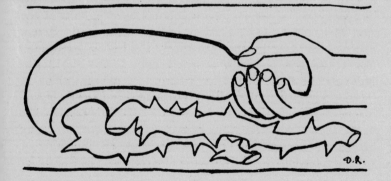

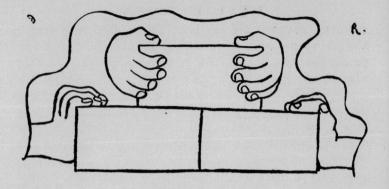

XVIII   CHURCH AND STATE

1

BACKGROUND

THE *chalupa* drifted under a stone arch past wide patches of bright blue water-lilies. The Indian, paddling at the bow, quickened his strokes. The boat shot between islands of shining sword-leaved corn and floating gardens of carnations and golden poppies. My companion was a barefoot, bow-legged Indian in white "pyjamas" and thong-bound *guaraches*. A great cone of sombrero shaded his broad brown face and scraggly beard. And here, in this Venice of the West, Xochimilco, just a dozen miles from Mexico City, he told me an outlandish tale of mythical battles between his town and Tepoztlán; of the birth of the perfect race from flowers strewn by the old gods; legends of Moctezuma and Cuauhtémoc; the magical placement of the heavy bells in the lofty Xochimilco cathedral tower by a forgotten wizard; and into his hodgepodge he mixed the story of Sodom and Lot's wife turned to salt, quoting verbatim thousands of words from the Bible.

Down in Tepoztlán, the week previous, an Indian boy, while we were sitting in a cave waiting for the passing of a

mountain shower, told me Brer Rabbit done over into a
Mexican version with cactus and coyotes and native gods and
quaint Christian turns. And in the same pueblo, old Don
Vicente, one of the patriarchs, described to me a pagan procession in which the villagers had climbed lofty El Cerro to
the temple of the old god of the town, one Tepozteco, beating
their *teponastles* as in the old pre-Cortez days to pray for
rain; and how, at the behest of this same god, they had also
bought a new jeweled robe for the Virgin.

In a certain church on the outskirts of Oaxaca, where I
spent two days with the golden-faced Cura, the Indians had
long worshipped a saint whose image had been carved out
of the stone of an older god. Some years ago the priest de-
ciding the old image was too dilapidated, substituted a modern carving. The Indians no longer brought their offerings of
flowers and fruit; and when the De La Huerta revolt broke
across the land, the local troops bee-lined for the church and
emptied their rifles into the new saint.

A few miles north of Mexico City, around the base of the
Hill of Tepeyac, where rises the chapel dedicated to the
Virgin of Guadalupe, the national patroness of Mexico, the
Indians, every December twelfth, still perform their old
religious dances in the churches—as they do in hundreds of
others.

Manuel Gamio in his *Forjando Patria* describes a ceremony
he witnessed in the Sierra of Zongolica, in the state of Vera
Cruz, performed by Indians professing Catholicism:

> When their maze-fields begin to sprout and give forth
> young shoots, they consider it indispensable for some aged
> Indian, possessor of mysterious incantations, to protect the
> crop from destructive animals, especially the deer, which in
> the silent, moon-lit nights come down from the mountain.
> . . . The lowly native, true priest of his race, hums in
> the Aztec tongue and in tearful and supplicant tone en-
> treats the Deer God not to graze his children—the deer of
> the forest—in the sacred corn-field. A little later under a

great silk-cotton tree which interrupts the light of the moon, among the red coals of a fire, are burned sacrificed birds, scrapings from the horns and hoofs of deer, strips from the plantain trees, and amber grains of copal which the black hand of the sacerdote throws upon the flame, enveloping himself in fleeting white smoke clouds. This, at bottom, is nothing more than the old prayer to the God of the Chase, "the heart of the mountain," as the Aztecs called him.

Incidents such as these remind one that the Catholic Church—the Roman-Spanish-Aztec Church—in Mexico is a maelstrom of conflicting tendencies. They also remind one that the Church from an historical and administrative standpoint is an alien institution, imposed upon the country in large part by force of arms, by the brutal overturn of the older temples, and the cruel torture and assassination of the older sacerdotes. And although the first Christian priests strove to enlighten the people and better their lot, the Spanish church, because of its form of organization and institutional control, has for the most part conserved the traditions and psychology of the Conquest. Even more than any other Catholic organization in the world, it keeps a feudal and superstate outlook. A large portion of the clergy—and that portion the most prosperous—until the conflict with the Calles Government, were foreign. The Church, except where it bent itself to local rites, never truly represented the spontaneous religious sentiments of the mass of the Mexican people. Its mold only partially contained and directed the older religious afflatus.

Tepeyac, in Guadalupe Hidalgo—the religious center of Mexico—is one of the lightning rods of recent religious conflicts which began four centuries ago and which entered on a new phase of bitterness on February 5 of 1926, culminating in the futile "strike" of the clergy on August first. Here, on the last week in July, 1926, all the potential religious fervor of the Mexicans of the capital was short-circuited into a blaze of fanaticism; a lifetime of emotions was crowded into the

span of seven days! The populace swarmed down the Cal-
zadas, whirled about the atrium, climbed up the zigzag lanes
and stairways to the high horseshoe-shaped facade of the
brown chapel of the age-old holy hill of Tepeyac.

The poor and the superstitious ever pay the piper. Great
mobs of them clawed their way through the holy portals.
Never since the days of the Juárez Reformation did collec-
tion-boxes clink so merrily; never were so many rosaries,
scapulars, and candles sold; never in such short space of time
were so many masses said, did so many processionals take
place, were so many sacred relics dusted and paraded. Bap-
tisms, confirmations, confessions, weddings followed one another in kaleidoscopic haste. Babies were torn from the womb
to the baptismal font, recklessly exposed to the suffocating
germ-laden air of the crowded interiors; long lines waited
interminable hours to buy their confirmation tickets; quarreling sweethearts suddenly buried their troubles and battled
through the aisles among the tatterdemalion throng to be
married; well-dressed women walked barefoot, *tápalos* tight
about their tear-stained cheeks, through the early morning
streets to mass; penitents kneeled, arms outstretched, before
the chapel altars; the confessional booths were besieged by
woe-stricken throngs of sinners; weary priests passed endlessly up and down the abject, close-packed rows with the
pyx, giving sacrament; the acolyte held up the red shield
under lifted chins, the Host was dropped on waiting tongues.

Another charged center of this furore was the great cathedral, the largest on this Continent, which rises on the main
plaza of the Mexican capital—the Zócalo. Here the mass at
the gates, buffeted by the soldiery, struggled into the atrium
in the shadow of the lofty gray and white facade and jammed
on through the high Portal of Pardon into the packed nave.
The Indians—the poor and the disinherited—were the ones
fighting for this last-minute salvation. The middle and upper
classes were not forced to this extremity. Their children had
been baptized, christened, confirmed, married at leisure. But

the masses streaming into the church had to postpone these
liturgical acts from week to week, hoping against hope that
next month or the month after a few pennies could be laid
aside for the confirmation veil, the necessary candles, the fees.
But now in this last minute scramble they cheated their stom-
achs and mortgaged their health to beg, borrow, or steal the
sums required for every holy act, every administration of
holy water, every declaration of bans. This tearful precipi-
tancy gave the cathedral an aspect festive and catastrophic.
Red Cross emergency tents and ambulances stood at the gates.
Armed soldiers battered the throngs. Yet in and out whirled
the hawkers of candies, kewpie-dolls, rattles, newspapers,
rosaries and pet dogs—all calling raucously. Women fainted
from the heat; mothers lost their babies; peregrinators pick-
nicked in the less-crowded corners of the atrium; they hung
serapes tent-fashion from the iron fence-spikes to ward off
the sun and spread out their meager lunches of tortillas, beans,
and frothing pulque.

On one of these mornings I struggled against the human
ebb and flow into a side portal beyond the Sagrario. The interior was a blast in my face: stench of unwashed bodies, sharp
sting of low-hanging clouds of incense. The far singing of
the choir was almost drowned out by the wails of the assemblage, by the bawl of a thousand babies. People hung like
monkeys from every column and grill; they eddied about
altar, choir and chapel. Colors clashed; blue and brown
rebozos, lace mantillas, embroidered blouses, scarlet sashes.
Inch by inch, almost suffocated, I wormed my way toward
the *barandales* of the Crujia. Tier after tier of men and
women pressed up coughing, crying, shouting, each carrying
a baby to be baptized or confirmed. Down the long runway
paced the soldiers of the state; among them neophytes dashing to and fro for holy water, ever more holy water, and
Red Cross aides with ice, cotton, and bandages. Hour after
hour, the confirmation process continued. First came a soldier, then a Red Cross aide, an acolyte with a candle, a huge

priest in white and gold robes—swipe of his thumb from holy oil to the forehead of each squalling infant, a swab of cotton by another acolyte—finally, the collectors, bringing up the rear, reaching out hands for the fifty-centavo pieces. Hour after hour. Waiting row gave way to waiting row, and still from the back of the cathedral came the press of babies, ever more babies. One woman had but twenty centavos. The coin is snatched by the collector with a snarl, "Confirmation's no good." On to the next and the next; more snarls for those who do not have their change ready. Here a peso is offered; the fifty centavos change is tossed back into the throng. The barefoot loser sprawls on his hands and knees, hugging his child in one arm, sticking his hand under the feet of the trampling multitude. A baby falls into the runway. A Red Cross attendant snatches it up. The mother is swept from sight. Crowded back against a pillar, she howls for her lost infant, holding her arms out helplessly toward the Virgin. Overhead the newspaper kodaks click, the flashlights boom, and white smoke eddies up into the fumes of incense. And the priest with his train struggles on, sweat pouring down his fat brown face.

One foot on a bench, the other pressed against the fluting of a column, I looked down on the multitude. The whole cathedral seemed to sway in the wavering light of thousands of candles, in the quiver of incense from the clanking censers. I have seen religious happenings at Lourdes; I witnessed the epochal procession of the new Virgin of Loreto from the patriarchal church of the Santa Maria Maggiore in Rome; I have followed a great procession up the slashed crooked streets of Toledo in Spain, and these occasions had an aspect of almost sublime solemnity or festivity. But this vast pawing scramble of the excited disinherited of Mexico, this flaunting of idolatry, superstition, rags, dirt, was a profanation of the human spirit. The Mexican-Spanish-Aztec church in its battle with the Mexican state showed a callous cruelty, reminiscent of the days of Innocent III. Here in the Zócalo, where the riveting machines on the work of enlarging the national palace of Cortez, were shattering the harmony of the great tolling bells of the Asunción de María Santísima; here where once rose the old teocalli of the Aztec god of war, Huitzilopochtli, here in the one-time capital of the native empire—here the old conflict between church and state in 1926 drew to a new poisonous head.

The position of the Church in Mexico, for all of its amassed power, and this show of fanaticism, is by no means assured. It faces problems more difficult than elsewhere. These spring in part from the Church's long insistence upon political and material power, a battle long since lost in most other countries of the world. In Mexico it preferred to repeat the dreary but disastrous struggles between Church and State which have disrupted so many countries. As a result today, not only the political and material power of the Mexican Church is on the wane but also its spiritual power. Since the days of its renegade priests, Hidalgo and Morelos—the heroes of independence, who were excommunicated—no important cleric has lifted his voice to utter a single reconstructive message for the distressed country of which he is a part. The National League of Religious Defense which in August, 1926, circulated the foreign legations appealing for outside intervention in behalf of the Church. This, in itself, is indicative of the Church's failure to found its strength on native forces. This same lack of perspective led the League, with the approbation of the Archbishop, to call a boycott to "paralyze the economic and social life of the country." Yet sooner or later, the principles —if not all the details—that have been embodied in the Mexican constitution of 1857 and 1917 must be accepted by the Church if Mexico is to form part of the modern world.

The Church—for all the furore and fanaticism it has so often aroused—has been on the defensive, ever since the fall of Emperor Iturbide. Once one of the balance-wheel institutions of the Mexican Superstate, along with the army, the colonial government, the aristocracy, the land-owning interests, it has lost not only that position of doubtful eminence, but much of its moral vitality. It has proved itself unable to adjust itself to the growing needs of the Mexican people. Today the Mexican-Spanish-Aztec Church is being ground between many forces.

The most powerful single tendency of the Mexican revolution was nationalism. The Aztec empire in the 16th century was unconsciously in the midst of a struggle to create a Mexican nation. The Spaniards came. The Conquistadores paralyzed native effort, though they provided unifying factors, force, a superstate, the Spanish language, the Church. We say Mexico became independent in 1824, but it is still in process of becoming a nation: its racial composition is still diverse and politically incoherent; the bias of its ruling institutions comes from abroad, is not Mexican. If we were to date the birth of a true spirit of national integrity as Europeans understand it, we would say it was aroused by the American war of conquest, its symbol, certainly, the noble gesture of the boy cadets of Chapultepec Castle, who held the American army at bay until all were killed but one. Alone, he wrapped himself in the Mexican flag and flung his body from the high parapets upon the jagged rocks rather than submit to the Yankee, the Gringo. The Díaz epoch saw a return of colonial psychology, and the giving away of the country to outside capital without guarantees for the Republic. The revolutionary era just closed, which began with a slogan of effective suffrage, culminated in the singularly nationalistic constitution of 1917, and a train of subsequent laws about foreign-property, the foreign-registration, the mineral and irrigation rights, and the non-foreign priest law —all indications not so much of proletarian, but purely nationalistic policy—conservation for the Mexican-born of natural resources and man-power, an effort to end the good old days when an American was above the law.

Inevitably the nationalistic tendency affected the Church. The Mexican State is not likely to tolerate any delimitation of its own sovereignty by any one institution obeying orders from an outside power. Neither the Government nor the Constitution recognizes the institutional "personality" of the Church (so insisted upon in the famous letter of the episcopate to President Calles, August 19, 1926). Both the Constitution and the Government declare that the priests must be considered as professionals subject to direct legal control.

The Mexican Labor movement can be said to turn, not against Church doctrines but against the Church authority. In some countries there has been a Christian Socialist movement; in Italy and elsewhere, strong Catholic labor unions and parties; but the desire of the present-day labor movement throughout the world to conquer a better material existence upon this earth even before reaching Heaven, causes institutionalized religion everywhere to become for the working classes a luxury at best. This is true in Mexico. The twentieth century worker, in process of gaining greater control over the material realities, discovered early that the Church not infrequently lends itself to the forces of oppression. In Mexico, I have seen *hacendados*, landed proprietors, cynically lead their peasants on their knees for fully a kilometer to the chapel door, after a day of terrible toil in the fields. Federico Gamboa begins the first act of his *Vengeance of the Soil* with the following description: "Two by two the peons pass in lamentable procession of herded humanity, bent double by the weight of the tools on their shoulders and by their misery. They uncover their unfortunate heads as they approach the chapel." They come after the day's toil, not in an effort to improve their lot but to find consolation in the church, to sing the evening *alabado*. Many a manufacturer—and among them an American representative of international notoriety— himself a Protestant—finds it advisable as a good safeguard against sabotage to have the machines blessed by the priest with holy water and prayers, before they are put into use. A prominent English mine owner once told me that, until the recent conflict, it was quite customary throughout the coun-

try for the mines to keep the priest on the pay-roll—it staved
off labor disputes. In many places the peons who toil all week
have had to spend their Sundays doing Sunday chores about
the church. The early literature of the Mexican labor movement—as might be expected—teems with complaints of ecclesiastical exploitation.

Julio Guerrero in his *Genesis of Crime in Mexico*—the
classic sociological study of Mexico (p. 289)—describes the
church as a business:

> "From the walls of the most humble chapel to the most
> sumptuous columns and altars of the cathedrals there are,
> in all the temples, collection boxes with signs begging con-
> tributions for the cult, for the candles, for the Divinísimo,
> or for the general needs of the Church. Before beginning
> the ceremonies, during them, and on their termination,
> sacristans, acolytes, and even pretty girls chosen for their
> good looks, go stepping on dresses, jumping over the
> kneeling ones, to beg—copper or silver tray in hand
> —a coin from each of the parishioners. . . . The sermons
> have as their obligatory epilogue, the begging of alms from
> the faithful. . . . There are established also brotherhoods
> and associations under the aegis of some saint; and the
> president or rector, whether a man or a woman, collects
> daily, weekly, and monthly donations from the members,
> which are afterwards turned over to the respective chap-
> lains; as it happens without accounting or receipt, in order
> that a door may be left open for the prior deduction of the
> honorarium for collecting. When the parishioners do not
> come to the temple, the brother or sister of these asso-
> ciations, wearing a blue, red, or yellow ribbon about the
> neck, with attitudes of mortification and sad words, go to
> private homes to beg for a tiny cent—or a larger amount.
> They leave, for a temporary visit, the Holy Child, the
> Santo Entierro, or some other image, also exvotos and a
> collection box in the same niche where the holy object is
> placed, in order that the person visited may collect from
> his friends, during the interval the image remains, all the

alms he can; no accounting here, either, leaving chances
for 'honorariums' for the collector."

Such is the "system."

"But the fiscal expedients of the Clergy are not limited
to this voluntary assessment; in its greed for richness, it
has succeeded in having itself paid, in accordance with an
onerous tariff, a remuneration for each of its liturgical acts,
or for the celebration of sacraments, making of these professional duties a means by which it exploits marvelously.
Thus, though baptism is necessary according to it, to blot
out the original sin . . . if the priest is not paid to apply
the holy oil and mumble his Latinisms, the child will not be
redeemed from the demon. Although wedlock is indispensable in order to sanctify love, the marriage will not
be celebrated unless the mass, chants, and the antiphonies
are paid for, even though a match be frustrated or the pair
lives in free love. In order to get souls out of Purgatory
masses must be said, but if the priest who delivers the
diploma of liberty is not paid, the soul of the relative will
remain in the flames of purification until he finishes his
sentence. Death cannot finish its labor of freeing the soul
from the body until the arrival of the sacerdote; only with
prayers can it go tranquilly on its journey beyond the
tomb; but if the prayers are not paid for, the journey will
be made—without this mystic passage-money—to Hell.
Indulgences remove the sorrow of sin, shorten the sufferings in Purgatory, and can even stave off eternal damnation when one dies in mortal sin; but if these are not paid
for by buying the nine days of mass in which these things
are conceded, or, the special bulls which are required, the
divine decision is irremissibly consummated. The efficacy of
the sacerdotal service is manifested even in the ills of this
life: it can cure sicknesses and prevent accidents; but for
this one must have a medallion, a scapular, one must put a
ribbon on the head, a ribbon which will be the measure
of the Virgin of Tepeyac, or of any other miraculous
image; one must recite the rosary; and for all this there
has been established a little shop of mystic trinkets at the
portal of every temple. But if one does not buy these

amulets with real coin, the illness or the accident will take place. Prayer is more effective accompanied by a candle; candles cost money, and as soon as those who offer them go away, the sacristan puts them out, gathers them up, and resells them to the candle-shops."

Señor Guerrero continues to describe what goes on in connection with the buying of jeweled robes and crowns for the many virgins and concludes:

"It is very difficult to encounter among the enemies of the Church, in the most virulent pages of Voltaire or in the anathemas of Luther, any accusation that has undermined the prestige of the priesthood and the Catholic religion in Mexico as this exploitation patent to every eye, systematized and cynical, a robbery of every pocket, putting into practice the tricks of the charlatan, to get money, out of advantage of every misfortune precisely in the moments of anguish resulting from the most cruel tribulations."

The burden rests upon the poor. Because of this, and the reactionary alliances of the Clergy, organized labor in Mexico definitely is set against the institutionalized aspects of the Church. In the 1925 convention of the C. R. O. M., the Regional Confederation of Labor, then Mexico's leading labor organization, President Calles openly attacked the alliance of the Church and Press. He declared the Press to be in the hands of "evil elements" devoted to "immoralities and orgies, elements which have seized the banner of religion to incite a new civil war" rather than support the Government's attempt to enforce the 1917 constitution. The convention passed a pointed resolution to the effect that "the Roman Apostolic Church" had been "the enemy of the nation" from the days of Hidalgo and Maximilian and Juárez and condemned its continuous efforts to bring about foreign intervention.

On the land question, the Church found itself on the side of the proprietors, never the peasants. Local Church authorities threatened to excommunicate local agrarian commissions (as in Chihuahua where most of the arable land of the state had been owned by the Terrazas family), and threatened non-absolution to those accepting land from such commissions. A member of the Vera Cruz commission, during the time of Carranza, detailed to me the various ways in which the Church obstructed the Government's work. In one instance two villages petitioning for more acreage preferred—because of the threat of excommunication—to rob each other by force rather than accept land which a few years before had been held illegally by the Church.

On the 27th of June 1924 the clergy held "a most solemn function in honor of the Sacred Heart of Jesus" under the direction of Father Joaquin Cardoso, editor of *"El Mensajero del Corazón de Jesús."* The call for this celebration read in part: "Already the division of land . . . better said, the iniquitous despoliation of the Mexican proprietors . . . is the death of agriculture . . . But the proprietors have organized and are studying how they ought by humane measures to stop the approaching catastrophe . . . No one so much as the proprietors should depend upon our Lord God, who is the One who gave the earth to man to be worked that he might aliment himself from its fruits; it is He who causes the sun to rise each day to fecundate the breast of this so prodigal Mother Earth; it is He who sends refreshing rains and beneficent warmth, the frosts and the winds to help the efforts of the peasant . . . Let all the agriculturists dedicate themselves in a very special manner to the Divine Heart of Jesus . . . proclaiming Him King of our fields, of our valleys, of our estates, of our forests, in a word of our national agriculture . . . If we deliver our fields to the Divine King He will defend them."

Another factor which the Church in Mexico—as elsewhere —must face is the general trend of modern philosophy, whose principles and ideas are incompatible with the platonic absolutism of the Catholic dogmas. Miracles have not yet reconciled themselves with modern science. All the anti-Catholic tendencies of modern thought have converged in the minds of the living Mexican intellectuals—Caso, Vasconcelos, Lombardo Toledano, Rivera, Reyes, Dr. Atl. Not only modern thinking but the modern system challenges the Church— all the tremendous material expansion of our day. It is with true instinct that the National League of Religious Defense in Mexico instituted an economic boycott against luxuries— autos, amusements, fine clothes, and epicurean foods—in its war with the Government. (The saving went to pay for boot-leg masses at fifty pesos a head.) The Church boycott failed, not because its members had become leisure-loving (its priests perhaps), but because the mass of people in Mexico are denied even the minimum of life's necessities.

Modern rationalism may not hold the key to all life's processes. But the Church in Mexico fears enlightenment, and wherever possible it still fights secular education. Recently in San Pablo Etla, I found that the priest was declaiming from the pulpit against the Federal school and incited some of the villagers to tear up the athletic field. In most rural localities, the priest threatens parents with dire punishment if they permit their children to attend government schools. In a small village in the Mixtecan Indian region, the people were frightened by the wailing of La Llorona, the ghost of Malinche (bed-companion of Cortes) that prowled the streets every night. The military commandant of the region, on visiting the village, heard of this nightly terror and set his soldiers to catch the spook. It proved to be the sacristan dressed up in a sheet and a frightful mask. After each visitation the people flocked to the church to pray, buy candles, and drop offerings. Business was bettered!

And the Indian renascence! The vulgar mind pictures the re-emergence of Indianism as reversion to barbarism. This is to lack historical and anthropological perspective. The great mass force of Mexico is Indian, and the future happiness and strength of the country depends not upon a Nordic over-lordship, not upon foreign capital, but the proper revaluation of the worthwhile elements of the native culture. Indianism —with its weird beauty and fantastic mysticism—is precisely one of the most powerful revitalizing currents which has swept over Mexico since the revolution—a current which Doctor Manuel Gamio, the eminent Mexican archaeologist, clearly appreciated, and to which he attempted to give intel-ligent and scientific direction in his monumental social-anthropological labors in Teotihuacán and Oaxaca.

This current the Church has failed to understand, promote, or profit by. The Church advertises twelve million Catholic Indians in Mexico. Possibly. Dr. Gamio in *"El Democrata"* describes the situation otherwise: "The old indigenous gods of war, of the harvests, of the rains, etc., were given the names of white gods, called 'saints'—Santiago, San Francisco, San Isidro, and many others, ruled in the new *teocallis* instead of Huitzilopochtli, Tláloc, Teozintle, etc. . . . The conse-quence of this pretended religious conversion was that the Indian saw his traditional picturesque religion degenerate and disappear; now he paid tenths, first, and other taxes; he lost part of his rural property to the convents. His labor was used, almost for nothing, for the construction of churches and monasteries, and such was the greed and cruelty of the friars, that incessant protests were carried to the Spanish Crown; among others, one famous in history, that of Archbishop Montúfar himself. The situation has been prolonged for four centuries doing incalculable injury to ten or twelve million indigenes and mestizos. About three million Mexicans, generally of the white race and inhabit-ants of the cities can rightly be denominated Catholics for they are relatively identified with the Roman Church and uncontaminated with the polytheistic crudities of the other group."

The idea of a cult of the Plumed Serpent, or Quetzalcóatl, as set forth by D. H. Lawrence, is an absurd farce; nevertheless Quetzalcóatl, Tepozteco, Tlaloc and the other old gods still live in legend and ceremony. Only there is no such mutually exclusive conflict as D. H. Lawrence has portrayed; there is no possibility of the return of the old gods because the old gods have never entirely departed. To the native mind Christ and Quetzalcóatl are not mutually exclusive, antagonistic—they are holy confreres in the newer pantheon. Nevertheless, the Indian renascence in Mexico—and there are two million Indians who do not even speak Spanish—has reemphasized native at the expense of European culture, at the expense of the universal characteristics of the Church. This uncertainty and confusion has also helped to slacken the old fervor. Mexico is just as religious as ever but the outward symbols are not so convincing. In Tepoztlán, where I described the pilgrimage to the temple of the old god, Tepozteco, there are seven smaller churches, besides the main church, in a village of four thousand souls. These seven churches are not only closed but are cracked, weed-riven and crumbling. In many an outlying part of the country the Indians have democratized the Catholic ceremony and carry on the rites after their own fashion, often behind closed doors. In some places old sacrifices continue and are a secret counterpoise to the openly practised religion. In many places the Church wedding is followed by the customary Indian ceremony. The greatest genius of the Church in Mexico was revealed when it grafted the European institution on to these practices. But as the Church became more and more an instrument of the Conquest, more a part of the traditional feudal and superstate machinery, it ceased to continue this work of welding the Church into integrated religious expression. Institutionalized cohesion was never really achieved. Today the Church in Mexico, in spite of the fanaticism of its following, is atomized; and it is divided

300

against itself on racial and caste lines. This is partly the result of the maintenance of so many foreign priests, partly due to its material smugness, partly due to its historical feudal rôle.

The Mexico of today has swept past the Church. Today the Church in Mexico is not the political factor it would impress itself as being. Its ruling authority is centralized, but its functioning is decentralized; the two are not one texture. Hence only the hierarchy responds to the prods of Rome; but the hierarchy does not effectively exercise a national force based on popular mass loyalty, except in a few of the larger centers. The Church exercises power—and often a dangerous power—because it is an intrenched institution representing vested interests.

As an instrument of control over the masses, the Church is as deficient as any other Mexican institution. The entire mass-soul of Mexico has rarely been stirred. Even the revolution with all its slogans and proletarian aims, and cries of "Land and Liberty" only agitated separate localities at non-simultaneous moments. The Indian renascence had a regional complexion. The mass population of Mexico flows on with immutable self-sufficient continuity, with an Oriental inscrutability. The Church, which claims so many faithful, finds itself unable to use them in any coordinated effective manner. The Indian of Chilpancingo will get excited if you touch his local saint or obstruct his local practice of religion —indeed for the protection of these he will gladly lay down his life. But tell him that the patron saint of Zacotlán has been desecrated and he will lift his eyes and say *"Que barbaridad!"* He will not be stirred to action. He may even have a latent jealousy of the patron saint of Zacotlán and say to himself, "Well, that's the time those sons of Zacotlán got what was coming to them." Doubly remote to him is a conflict between the Church and the Government. And so the Church has lost its power—if it ever had it—to arouse

301

the local communities towards a national action. It failed precisely because it has failed to create a truly national church and because it has failed to meet any of the needs of modern times.

The peasant loves his church, he loves his saints, he glories in the frequent fiestas, but he will not lend too steady an ear to the priest, and he is not convinced of persecution unless it occurs in his own village. And with this local religious autonomy the Government no way has interfered. The battle of the Government was against the central hierarchy and its foreign ramifications, not against the Church as a religion or even as a cult. And though the priests on August first 1926 folded up their tents and crept away, the churches remained open. The Indian could still light his candles before the altars; he could still kneel and pray; he could still organize his local fiestas; and the placing of the church in the hands of a local committee of ten stirred his imagination and flattered his self-importance, for this ran sympathetically with his ideas of communal activity and cooperation.

The Indian discovered that he could get married in a very simple but holy manner without payment of an exorbitant fee. The exactions of the clergy no longer laid on him a constant strain. He found his religion rather a more pleasurably spontaneous and less obligatory thing. The priests, by abandoning the churches, played directly into the hands of this newer Indian autonomy. The Government and the Revolution, not the Church, had given the Indians land, political rights, personal guarantees, a spirit of freedom not easily to be eradicated.

And thus the Church today, for better or worse, finds itself on the outer fringe of Mexican life. It had, early in its career, identified itself with the Indian consciousness, and the reformatory labor of the early fathers, Gante, Motolinía, Sahagún, Bartolomé de las Casas, Magá Catalá, Vasco de Quiroga, created a tradition of human liberty and racial pride that succeeding generations saw strangled. It is unnecessary here to recite the subsequent history of the political reaction of the Spanish-Aztec Church—its support of every public character who has been a blot upon the peace, justice and happiness of the country; its support of every leader who has fought against the liberation of the enslaved people, every leader who has sought to shut out the light of the modern world—Emperor Iturbide, Santa Anna, Felix Zuloaga, Emperor Maximilian, Huerta, De la Huerta; these are the backers of the Church or the puppets of the Church, and they, or their supporters, were ever the most sanguinary, brutal, and unprincipled elements in Mexican history. The Church soon after the Conquest reverted to its superstate tradition, and since then, though for centuries it piled up material wealth, it has spiritually declined; and for the whole period of independence it has not had a single constructive message for Mexico as Mexico. Today it fights a lost cause with the traditional weapons of fanaticism and blind servility, but that these weapons are now out of place is patent to every observer. The older Indian fanaticism has been balanced by a new and realer interest in land and liberty, by emphasis upon communal village life since the return of the *ejidos* or common lands.

Had the Church in Mexico built up a native priesthood, had it continued its efforts to synthesize in religious customs, had it—feeling the sad need of political intervention—built up a party half as enlightened as the Partito Popolare in Italy (which placed itself in the vanguard of agrarian reform), the Church need not have repeated once more the story of bitter futile struggle with the State—as in Italy, in France, in England, and in every country that has fought for civil liberty and international prestige.

The Spanish-Aztec Church has utterly lacked adaptability and originality. Instead of attempting to root itself in

303

the national needs and in the vital moral trends of modern times, it has preferred to fight every effort at progress, to bicker over petty legal restrictions. Had the Church more vitality and significance and world-fresh outlook, it could have afforded to obey these technicalities of the law with a sphinx-like smile aware of the eternally persistent power of the spirit. But the priests on August first 1926, practically said to the members of the Church, "We don't like the laws of the land. We refuse to register as professionals with the civil authorities. This attacks the sovereignty of the Church. Therefore we shall no longer give you spiritual consolation (unless you are very rich and pay for it on the sly at fantastic prices). You may go to Hell, we shall not save you. If you don't like going to Hell, if you want your original sin washed away through baptism, if you want to live in holy wedlock instead of free love, then you must overthrow the Government so that the laws will not be enforced." Perhaps the Church did not really desire such a drastic outcome, perhaps it only felt that such medieval tactics would frighten the government. The Church could not realize that this struggle between two contending sovereignties, ecclesiastical and civil, was not the usual Mexican fight between two ambitious ruling cliques, where the loser could run to the outside world to ask for traitorous assistance. The Church has failed to see that Mexico is almost a nation, its people are becoming politically and socially conscious, and a great racial and cultural ferment is abroad in the land.

As a matter of fact, the State in Mexico under Calles was fighting the Church's battle. It said, in general terms, to the Church, "You shall no longer meddle in unprofitable political affairs and menace the peace, stability and sovereignty of the country. You shall no longer intrigue for outside intervention. You shall no longer foment revolts against the established Government. You must become, once and for all, politically subordinate to the State. Your sphere is spiritual and moral. You cannot enter into Heaven with worldly goods; there is no need for you to accumulate them on this earth at the expense of the independence and prosperity of the people of the land. The days are gone when you can own half the cultivated area of the country and mortgage the rest. You represent, in your present attitude and your present form of organization, part of the Spanish conquest that enslaved a people. You are part of a cruel experiment in empire. It is not against your spiritual precepts that we are fighting, but against your traditions of feudal overlordship. We are doing nothing that has not been done in other modern nations; separating Church and State, prohibiting political meddling, secularizing education, eliminating foreign-born priests, lifting from the nation the dead hand of mortmain property."

The Mexican Government could go on to say, "You have not availed yourself of the great possibilities of educating a people; you have built gorgeous temples and left a people in hovels and rags. Many of these expensive temples you built in the past with conscript labor, not for religious advancement, but merely because the building of them, under colonial law, entitled you to immense *repartimientos* of land. We are liberating you from this incubus of your dead past. We remove from you the necessity of dissipating your energies in futile political and material struggles; we free you to devote yourself whole-heartedly and unobstructedly to a purely religious function; we give you once more the opportunity to build up a native priesthood which will be part of the life of the country and which will be able to found its spiritual aspiration on the native needs."

What will be the ultimate answer? Will the Church remain an inadequate and ineffective expression of the deep-seated needs of a people fundamentally mystical and religious? Will it falteringly continue trying to be a political and material force? Or will the Church, purified and made wiser by these troublous events, come to discover the real Mexico, help to liberate its people who have known four centuries of bitter humility and servitude?

These are the ideal and theoretical outlines of Mexico's religious problem; the actual struggle between government and church prior to Ambassador Morrow's settlement had degenerated to a thoroughly debased spectacle of brutality, greed and cynicism.

2

THE STRUGGLE

G-2 was the kitten that crawled along behind us. G-2 was a grim gray armored car hitched to the tail-end of our train. Turrets and rifle-holes bristled with guns. Out of the circular openings peered Nahuan soldiers. Long-visored caps concealed their peaked skulls; their broad faces had a lowering Mongolian cast. Up near the engine a black steel flat-car overflowed with more soldiers. The scuttle-holes were open; on the floor sprawled a reptilian machine-gun. Soldiers everywhere; in every coach, except the steel Pullman, huddling under red and yellow sarapes. Rifles, gripped between their

306

knees or cradled in their arms, poked in all directions—the heap looked like a bloated human pincushion. A few days previously (April 1927) more than a hundred and forty people had lost their lives in a terrible train attack by Catholic rebels. Some of the victims were burned alive in the coaches. We were going over the same route—from Mexico City to Guadalajara.

Night. Three of us deserted the hushed green alley of the Pullman for a second-class car to buy beer from the train-huckster. We stirred two soldiers from their sleep to drink with us. The car was a stack of squawking parrots, clucking chickens, thrumming guitars, squawling babes, whimpering curs. Aisles and seats were littered with fibre-bags of oranges and mameys, baskets of food, red pottery. Tall and broad straw and felt sombreros surmounted twitching huddles of flesh under scarlet sarapes. A tall Yaqui, head bandaged in a red bandana, lay on one of the benches, moaning with fever, bare sandal-shod feet hanging into the aisle. A man with long stringy half-moon moustaches reached up to rip off a banana from a bunch dangling from the rack. The dim lights flickered unsteadily, bundles and coats swayed violently, the car windows reflected the unsteady bizarre scene.

One of my companions, a tall Dorian Gray, surveyed the litter with aristocratic scorn; the other, an English clerk, out on a three years' contract for the Bank of Montreal, guzzled beer and gushed about the Crown Prince. Tiring of their twaddle, I talked with a brakeman.

He had been on the recently attacked train when bullets swept into just such a mass of humanity as lay before our eyes. From him and other eye-witnesses, I reconstructed the horrible event.

The rebels, it seemed, had torn up part of the track; the doomed train stopped with a terrific jolt. Simultaneously a hail of shots from the unseen enemy raked the train from end to end, reaping heavy toll, especially of the second-class passengers who rode, mixed in with the soldiers, in wooden cars, with windows, close together. During the four hours of fighting, rose shouts, curses, demands for surrender, defiance, in a manner typically Mexican:

LONG LIVE CHRIST THE KING!
LONG LIVE THE SUPREME GOVERNMENT!

Soldiers invaded the Pullman whose steel walls afforded some protection. The passengers, sprawled on the floor, heads tucked against the pipes, served as cushioned seats for the firing.

The last gasp of the fight. The attackers, their hats carrying pictures of the Virgin, leap through the cars, firing recklessly, jabbing under the seats with their bayonets. Only one soldier out of fifty escapes.

The rebels set fire to the second-class cars. The flames lick up the dry wood. Those who can, escape. The wounded, infirm, and aged are burned alive. In the pandemonium Pullman passengers rush out across the barren fields.

All the coaches except the steel Pullman are aflame. The crackling blaze lights up the harsh countryside, revealing a deep ditch massed with nopal cactus where the rebels have been intrenched. Further up the parallel road may now be seen a Ford automobile, draped with a purple banner carrying the picture of the Virgin of Guadalupe. From this three priests descend to give absolution to the dying.

The rebels with shouts of "Long Live Christ, the King" divest the remaining passengers of their valuables and clothing, slitting open bags, jabbing bayonets into seats. From the express car they are frantically carting off a hundred and fifty thousand pesos in silver.

For hours after, the survivors search among the embers for the remains of loved ones; a beautiful woman, her long hair hanging down, rushes to and fro, weeping and wailing, the body of her baby in her arms. A man staggers along, his dead wife in his arms. Two human beings raving mad.

A day or so later, I received a letter from a friend in El

Salto, up near the northeast border of the state, where the same rebels, four hundred strong, with new guns and cartridge belts, well mounted, had swept through the town. They murdered the secretary of the local labor federation, stoned the union and cooperative funds, sacked the post-office and city-hall and set fire to many homes. The new guns are said to have come from the United States via the Port of Vallarte.

For three hours before dawn, our train has been lying up in Celaya, so as to pass over the dangerous region during the daytime, not at night. The moon is a pale sickle dogged by the morning star. On a far hill a half-orange church dome gleams gold. Once more we roll west. Mile after mile of ripe wheat and barley fields, looking like muddy lakes in the uncanny light; then, endless stretches of brown desolation, cactus, *palo blanco*, sand, long gulleys, winding back into the jagged purple mountains. The peaks are now fringed with pale rose.

Irapuato. Two slim bell towers poking over dense trees. On the platform—packing cases and pacing soldiers.

Yurécuaro. A long pole, roped to a scrubby false pepper tree and carrying a white-sleeve wind-cone, marks a blazing red field where three gray aeroplanes crouch in the dust. Pacing soldiers.

La Barca. Enormous stacks of oranges glowing in the terrible sun. A zacate mill, mountains of yellow fibre being baled. Horse cars running out to distant haciendas—white specks on the parched slopes. Great lunging oxcarts. Singing beggars. Pacing soldiers. Pacing soldiers.

Kilometer 162. The place of the train hold-up. Twisted rails, iron frames, charred embers. Graves pegged with tilted crosses. A still stretch of heat and sagebrush; a buzzard gyring overhead. Soldiers.

Ocotlán. Blackened walls, filled with dumps of twisted blackened steel girders, sheet iron, and charred refuse, mark the one-time station. Pacing soldiers.

Gingerly our train creaks across the swaying half-burned bridge over the Cuitzeo River. Mounted guards.

3

Guadalajara. City of sun and palaces and shady plazas; of singing flower-smothered patios and twilight songs, of *mariachi* orchestras and open doors; and in the barred balconies women lovely as the dawn and warm as the sun. Guadalajara, the Pearl of the West, is the second largest city in the Republic, center of the wealthiest agricultural region, citadel of Catholicism, home of the landed aristocracy, seat of venerable traditions. Founded in 1530 (nearly a century before the coming of the "Mayflower") by Captain Juan de Oñate and elevated to a Bishopric as early as 1560, both as capital of the Kingdom of New Galicia, and as the outstanding city of western Mexico, it has ever worn the seal of historical dignity. Today it is the seat of an Archbishopric; and the holder of this high position, during the religious war, Orozco and Jiménez, is known as the fighting bishop. Earlier in his career he took the field of battle against enemies of the Church. He was one of the few members of the Episcopate not seized and deported during the Calles Administration. From his hiding place, he secretly directed the Catholic offensive.

Guadalajara, the capital of a rich state comprising every variety of tropical and temperate farming land and possessing a coast-line of nearly two hundred miles, in many ways has been the most provincial of the leading Mexican states, clinging to Catholicism, conserving the Colonial creole traditions of aristocracy, harboring a wealthy, conservative, but unprogressive landed class.

Here in this city of people, beautiful and disciplined, where the homes of the poorest are clean, simple, and hospitable, and the sky is almost eternally blue, bitterness cankered worst. Reprisal met reprisal; and a feud, which for all of its ghastliness cannot quite destroy the charm and grace of the people and their city, culminated in murder and battle.

The slogans, slapped on the cathedral itself in glaring black letters, shout the vendetta:

THE CATHOLIC BOYCOTT IS PAID FOR BY THE WORKERS.
WE SHALL REPAY WITH AN EYE FOR AN EYE AND A TOOTH FOR A TOOTH.

VIVA CHRIST THE KING.

THE REVOLUTION SHOULD GUILLOTINE THE PRIESTS BEFORE THE PRIESTS GUILLOTINE THE REVOLUTION.

Here in Guadalajara, at the end of July 1926, when the priests went on strike rather than register with the Municipal authorities, the irate congregation of the Sanctuary of Our Mother of Guadalupe poured down stones and defiance from the Carmelite belfries, and machine-guns reaped a harvest of forty lives. For two years, soldiers camped with their blankets and sooty braziers and played *naipes* for cartridges there between the massive buttresses of the portal.

311

During 1927, Catholic baiting became an official sport, surpassing bull-fighting—not only in Guadalajara but elsewhere in the Republic. At dawn the gleaming streets were filled with dark *rebozo*—hooded women, hurrying to or from secret masses. Raids followed. The penalty was hush money or a fine of two hundred and fifty pesos or more a head, very little of which found its way into the public treasury. Neither sincere nor nicely legal—for on one occasion the wife of one of the most prominent Government officials held an elaborate and secret mass in her home, which was not raided. It became good sport to arrest Catholics on suspicion, holding them in jail without preferring charges until they paid thousands of pesos for release and promised to keep their mouths shut. A Government edict, ordering the confiscation of the properties of rebels was extended to civilians, and their properties found their way into the hands of official favorites. A game of officialized kidnapping and ransom grabbing! Catholics were arbitrarily deported from their home towns. This happened to Marín Alonso, head of the Knights of Columbus in Guadalajara, who was seized at noon and shipped off on the afternoon train to Mexico City. This happened before Christmas 1926, and for nearly a year he did not dare return to his family.

The military committed worse excesses. More than one Catholic civilian was seized on the street, in his office, or in his home, hurried to a barracks and summarily shot. The local authorities in Guadalajara boasted to me that forty old men and women had been thus shot at night in the cemetery. The outstanding martyr in Guadalajara was the prominent and esteemed lawyer González Flores. The Government never presented documentary evidence that he was directly connected with the rebel bands operating in the state.

From fact, the tales pass to atrocity rumors favoring both sides: captives who had their tongues torn out before execution; a *barranca,* full of Federals, surrounded and over a hundred bayoneted to death; drunken soldiers who had shot up the saints in a church and desecrated the high altar, seized and converted into living petrol torches.

Other brutalities come closer to hand. The office of a dentist friend. A tall Indian client from Acutitlán way.

"They are shooting the women and children, and so my wife and I have had to come to Guadalajara. The soldiers came to my neighbor's house. The woman was in bed with a two days' child. 'Where is your husband?' the officer asked. 'I don't know,' 'Kill her,' were the orders. And so they shot her and the child, took two other children outside and cremated the two bodies by burning the house. Of course, her husband was in the hills with a rifle, but I ask you, is it right to murder women?"

4

Out in the sleepy town of Zapopan near the capital of Jalisco, on the gate of the magnificent church of Saint Paul, a poster stated that all Catholics who died "fighting against the tyrannical Jacobin Government" would become saints in heaven. Those who "fail to take up arms for the Supreme Faith" would "lose their souls in eternal damnation." Drinking a *tequila* lemonade in the corner store under the pink and white plaza arcades, I was told by the despondent mestizan proprietor—thick brown lips drooping over sparkling white teeth—that I would find it difficult to go on into the interior. All auto service had been suspended on account of the danger.

Two days previously in the rear of the University of Guadalajara, near a carved door depicting a worker and a peasant respectively carrying on their backs a cathedral and a general, a red and black official poster of the Chief of Operations had announced the bombardment, as reprisal, of the hostile countryside of all northeastern Jalisco. This vast war zone stretched from Guadalajara and Santiago River along the Rio Verde to the Zacatecas and Aguas Calientes border-lines—a district known as Los Altos, a fifth of the state. By order of the Chief of Military Operations, General Jesús M. Ferreira, the rural inhabitants of this immense region were ordered to concentrate in a dozen named *plazas* in order not to be considered rebels and to avoid the general bombardment and razing of the entire countryside scheduled to begin May fifth. Nor could inhabitants of this sector go outside of the arbitrary boundaries. And though the State Government advised local authorities to give every sort of aid to the refugees and to create emergency Public Charity Councils, this proved bitter recompense for such wholesale uprooting, breaking the old ties, the loss of years of labor and thrift. One vast concentration camp reminiscent of Weyler's Cuban bull-pens! In this way a blow was to be struck at "the *fanáticos* who had been spilling the blood of the country."

The edict represented economic disaster for one of the richest and most progressive agricultural regions of the country, with an area of about eight hundred thousand

314

square miles, with fifty thousand settled inhabitants; and crops of wheat, barley, and fruit ready to harvest, estimated at forty million pesos. Heart-broken refugees piled into Guadalajara. The larger haciendas hurriedly transported furniture, machinery, equipment, supplies to the same city. One owner made personal request to the military to be allowed ten men to gather in the crop. The reply: "If a single peon remains, he will be shot." Not even a caretaker permitted! An Acadia migration that has left bitter memories and hateful scars.

As a result new rebels soon took to the mountains further north. By desolation the region was pacified—for the time being. Unscrupulous officers harvested the crops and stole the proceeds—a haul mounting into millions—modern crop-raiding in the name of the law. The most prosperous and productive agricultural region in all Mexico, the granary of the country was set back for years.

And so, on both sides, the conflict became complicated with other issues and personal greed. Catholic lawyers, given power-of-attorney by persecuted co-religionaires, lined their pockets with as much sangfroide as the Government officials. The old plunder-bund instincts of the Army, the feudal army of the Santa Annas, the Villas, the Gonzaleses, the Aguilares, flamed up. Federal ammunition passed through mysterious hands to the Catholic rebels; property of Catholics was arbitrarily seized, crops were stolen, enormous bribes for immunity were paid—and the homes of the Generals—in the name of the Revolution—grew more opulent.

And so, in the name of Christ the King, trains were attacked and scores of passengers killed. So federal machine-guns were turned into churches and down the streets of towns suspected of sympathizing with the Catholic cause. Whole villages rose in arms—as Amatitlán—and took to the hills. So the lines were drawn in a religious war that had all the bloodiness and bigotry (on both sides) of the sixteenth century. One side carried red, green and white Mexican flags

315

with the Virgin of Guadalupe replacing the eagle on the cactus. The other side shouted "Down with the Fanatics!" Priests were found among the armed partisans of the Church. Agrarians, "red guards" and federal troops attempted to suppress revolts and enforce the religious provisions of the Constitution and the subsequent regulatory legislation.

Deeper issues were blotted out. It is difficult to see how Christ the King, the Prince of Peace was served by the slaughter of innocent men, women, and children; it is difficult to see how the principles of religious liberty and independence of the State were guaranteed by unjust persecutions; it is difficult to see how the cause of the proletariat, who in their May-day parade carried great banners reading "Down with the Catholic Reaction," was advanced by economic devastation and the robbery of old landlords by the bureaucratic nouveaux riches and the looting army officers who today shoot them down in strikes. It is difficult to see that any principle of human rights or justice was served in the Catholic War which went on in Jalisco and adjacent states in the middle months of 1927, and which continued more or less through the entire Calles régime.

5

On May 12, 1927, in San Pedro Tlaquepaque, chickens sold for five cents each. Tlaquepaque, a rambling elm-shaded town of Jalisco, Mexico, famous for centuries for its artistic pottery and figurines, became infamously overrun with refugees from the combat zone of Los Altos. Here, all in one afternoon, I sat at the round blue tables under the plaza arcades, trying out *tequila* and other native drinks, and listening to the wailing *mariachi* orchestras. A stream of homeless ones assaulted me to purchase at any price their meager salvaged belongings—chickens, jewelry, lace, clothing. And so in Tlaquepaque a chicken, carted a hundred kilometers, squawking over a poor peasant's shoulder or on the back

316

of a burro, was sacrificed for five centavos; a pig was worth a dollar. In any of the main towns it was the same: hundreds of penniless refugees, squatting in the lees of adobe walls under gunny-sack awnings, in lean-tos of flattened Standard Oil cans—in Yurécuaro, La Barca, Ocotlán, Aguas Calientes, Irapuato, Emergency charity commissions, Chambers of Commerce, welfare workers, town administrations busily distributed food, provided emergency lodgings in public patios, attempted to stem epidemics. I talked with a highland rancher, who was driving eight head of cattle through the Colonia Reforma. His skin-tight gray trousers, leather jacket and wide sombrero were dust-covered; his sinewy face was streaked with sweat and grime; his eyes were two black holes in his hollow face.

"I've come from a ranch a hundred kilometers up near Yagos on the Rio Verde. I, my wife, and two children, one only seven, all the way on foot." He pointed to his cattle. "All I have left in the world and they're as thin as shoe-leather now; my crops lost, my house burned."

He told me the story of a friend in a nearby town, owner of the local store and other properties. He had incurred the displeasure of the local federal "general." In the night his door was painted, he believed by the order of this same general, with the slogan "*Viva Cristo Rey*." In the morning a platoon of soldiers led him off to the guard-house; he was denounced as a rebel Catholic and robbed of everything in the world. "They didn't leave him a calabash seed, and he sits all day on a hot stone in Aguas Calientes with his head in his hands. His wife sells lemonade."

For this desolation and exodus the militarists and irresponsible bandits, not the Catholics, were responsible. Jalisco, the richest agricultural state in the union, was swept by a plague of rebels and militarists, the country stripped as after a swarm of locusts. As in Russia in 1919, when both Red Guards and White Guards robbed and killed the mujiks, so the Mexican peon suffered—especially in Los Altos.

Indeed principles became entirely subsidiary. A dislocated population shouted *"Viva Cristo Rey"* because it was a ready-made slogan; the militarists and so-called agrarians were busy keeping the country aflame, trafficking in arms, persecuting wealthier citizens, arresting Catholics on no evidence merely to mulct them. The century-old loot instinct of the Mexican army was revived in Jalisco and adjacent states. The new arrangements in Los Altos became, in part, a colossal steal, in which all the wealthy hacendados, in addition to maintaining the "Red Guard of Jalisco"—not quite amiably—were forced to grease the palms of generals and politicians in order to buy exemption from molestation and be allowed to harvest their crops. Those without ready cash dismantled their haciendas, bringing every moveable object into the larger centers. Their crops were harvested by the same "generals" whose motto was "heads I win, tails you lose." Such measures spelled economic ruin for this wealthy area. But it is the poor people who suffered most bitterly. They had no money to fork over and had to leave home and security. All they left behind them was at the utter mercy of roving bands and looting soldiers.

• • • • •

I am on the Ameca train—a spur that runs down into western Jalisco. On the next siding is the Southern Pacific. To the rear is hitched the private car of the presidential aspirant, General Arnulfo Gómez. (Six months later he went to his death.) The car is so full of political hangers-on it looks like a hotel. A movie man is frantically grinding away at everything and everybody. The whole menage smacks of the inflated egoism that spells a Mexican general. In the prosperous United States, what minor general would roll over the land in a private car with hundreds of attendants? In Mexico, in the name of the revolution and in behalf of the starving people up front in second class, a Mexican general may swagger up and down in a private palace in a land in which rolling stock is inadequate and the Govern-

318

ment owes hundreds of thousands on its railway debt. I recall the magnificent row of aristocratic residences in Guadalajara, owned by General Ferreira, the Commandant who created the neutral zone in Los Altos—all in the name of the revolution . . . .

In this part of the state the rains have not yet begun and the sun hangs hot and low over the parched crags. Great clouds of dust seep in through the closed car windows. After two and a half hours of choked breathing, the dilapidated hotel patio in Ameca is cool and inviting with its singing birds and climbing vines, its roses, begonias, lupines, and broad-leaved scarlet "parrot-wings." The place is full of officers and Agraristas in broad sombreros and bright sashes. They stagger in and out loaded down with cartridge belts. Aids rush to and fro, shine shoes, give hair-cuts, crack nuts fetch iced drinks for their superiors. Rifles are bundled in and out.

At the oil-cloth table under the patio arcades, I am joined by a young Indian official, who proves to be inspecting the arming of the Agrarians. He flings his sombrero on a bull-horn hat rack and chooses an *icpal*, native leather chair, at the head of the table. Two agrarian officers report, one has a gray bulging blind eye and a cream gray uniform, cartridge belt, pink shirt; about his neck, a red silk handkerchief. The other is in white linens; his wide sombrero carries a red-ribbon, insignia of the Agraristas. It seems armed Agrarians are now bivouacked in the leading towns. In the smaller places picked Agrarians to the number of eight or ten have been secretly armed for emergencies with carte blanche over the affairs of their respective communities —a sort of devolutionized martial law. Came next two members of the local Agrarian commission, a lanky Indian with a green sash, open pink shirt, and *guaraches* or sandals; the other carrying an embroidered leather coat with a red sleeveband over one shoulder.

"We've fifteen peasants in Ameca still without lands," they complained.

"Enlist them in the local guard," suggested the inspector in the *icpal*.

"No one gets arms unless he has a piece of land to fight for," declares the lanky Agrarista.

They talked about rebellion—fighting in practically every town around Ameca, clear to the coast and especially south toward Colima and in the Sierras of Velasco and Perote. In Tenamaxtlán, fifteen Agrarians drove off a hundred rebels.

"The rebels were fools to attack the Agraristas. Are any of the *hacendados* openly with the rebels?" asked the Inspector.

The one-eyed officer shrugged, "Who knows? Most of them are away—in Guadalajara, for good and sufficient reasons. The rebels have good arms, smuggled in from the coast, I guess."

"Much planting?"

"No one is planting. Señor M——, the Spaniard, is the best off. His range is covered with cattle."

"Lots of cattle?" laughed the Inspector, leaning back. "We'll soon get that. I'll have him denounced as a *mocho* (a rabid Catholic) next week. He can cool his heels in jail for a day or two, and in the interim the rest is up to you . . ."

Ameca is a picturesque town. The streets ray out from the plaza like the spirals of a pin-wheel, one to the redbrick building which in palmier days was a hospital but is now a cavalry barracks; another through green orchards to the river; a third dips down past doorways of Indian prostitutes; a fourth angles up to a Moorish-looking church where a tall palm-tree waves long fronds over a snow-white wall. Half a dozen ragged fellows with rifles constitute the police of the town. To maintain these at a peso a day, the leading merchants are ruinously assessed a hundred pesos a month —orders of General Ferreira, Military Commandant of all Jalisco.

320

Twilight. The torches of the watermelon stands glint dusky faces. In a latticed open-air ice-cream parlor, over lemon ice flavored with cinnamon served in a tall green tumbler, I talk with a salesman for a German drug company who knows the region like a book.

He pointed across the streets to a plaza bench. "Two months ago at ten o'clock in the morning two friends of mine from Arenguillo were sitting on that bench. At ten-thirty they were shot into graves in the cemetery by the Agrarian guard. One of the leading merchants of Arenguillo was Castro Uriarte, who supported the Catholic boycott. As a result an official mob attacked his store, killing him. Everything he owned was dumped into the plaza, trampled on and burned. His wife and little girl salvaged a few drugs which they have been peddling here in Ameca. The girl and mother accused my two friends with having abetted in the murder of Uriarte—probably due to a disordered fancy on seeing two familiar faces from their home town. On the strength of this denouncement, with no further evidence, the two men, who were innocent citizens of Arenguillo, were taken out and shot. It's the same everywhere. Throughout the country all civil restraints have broken down, and human life isn't worth the snap of a finger. Every petty militarist is an absolute monarch, with full power over the life and happiness of everyone else. The local political struggle has aggravated the situation; the campaign for governorship last year was bloody and has left a heritage of violence that permits murderous paying off of old scores."

We were jolting in a rattly *camión* over a dusty ox-cart road from Ameca to Cocula. I was tangled in with bales, bags and heaps of pyjama-clad Indians, several dark women in blue *rebozos*. The sun blazed over fields of sugar-cane. Teams of plough-oxen, muzzled with rope-nets, dragged over the endless acres. The chauffeur's assistant was a grimy faced Indian with uncombed hair and broken straw sombrero. Nicknamed Obregón, because of having lost his left arm, nevertheless he was adept at tying knots and quick to scramble out at every creek to refill the boiling radiator.

Two miles this side of San Martín, we were stopped by a group of soldiers led by a little toad with turned-up moustaches who dumped us out, bales, bundles, vegetables, Indians, and myself, upon the desolate roadside, here but a barren stretch of palo blanco and cactus, and commandeered the auto for transportation. The twenty-five soldiers pressed the springs flat and the *camión* disappeared down a rocky canyon road.

Perched on bags of grain in a white-hooded ox-cart, I jogged into San Martín, a miserable little pueblo where I found luke-warm beer and red hot chili con carne in a cubbyhole eating "joint." After much skirmishing around town, I secured two decrepit mares that had been too mangy and weak to attract the attention of the militarists. Half a mile out my horse ran around with blind staggers and collapsed. The Indian boy accompanying me, gave me his, and ran along beside me, holding to my stirrup, for four hours under the hammering sun to Cocula.

The following day "Obregón" straggled across the plaza, his good arm and his stump of an arm full of melons. He and the chauffeur had been dragged off fifty miles into the mountains, the tires cut to pieces and a spring broken, yet they had not received a cent even for gasoline. Once when their motor had refused to go ("fixed on purpose"), the officer had threatened to shoot them. "But you can bet," said "Obregón," "that the officer put in a big transportation expense account to the Government. This is our last trip till conditions get better."

Cocula is a town of sad song and a study in red and white; white buildings, white pyjamas of the Indians, red ponchos and the blood-red blossoms of the *tepeguaje* tree. The plaza was bursting with soldiers in various degrees of drunkenness; federals, agraristas, "Red" Stateguards, all jealous and quarreling, the rank and file as a matter of com-

pañerismo, the officers over possible graft. In the afternoon
occurred an open fight in the plaza and a federal had his
face bashed in with the butt of a revolver. As an attack
on the town was expected any day, ten o'clock curfew had
been established; after that hour the sentinels shot without
even the customary preliminary warning *"Quién vive?"*
Two days later, on the road to Santa Ana, I was turned
back because of fighting in Santa Teresa, three miles
further on.

Subsequently I made the trip in the company of an ex-
mayor of Cocula. He was fighting desperately for life and
property. The week previous he had been arrested and
forced to pay graft to get released. Now he was out on bail
as a *sedicioso,* though he claimed to be no more Catholic
than a roadside stone. "Unless I can quash the charge by
seeing Zuño, the state boss, or General Ferreira, I'm lost and
all my property. Already Señor A——, owner of the largest
store in Cocula, dare not show his face in town, and all the
rest are being systematically robbed by the authorities. We
have the saying in Jalisco now, 'Whoever visits the barracks
headquarters, comes away fleeced—if he comes away!' Law
has disappeared in Jalisco; there is only the law of force, and
the strongest grabs."

And thus *camiones* stopped running, products no longer
got to market, stores closed down, life was disrupted, banditry
increased on the highways; the rebellion in the name of
Christ the King fed on the disorder falsely created by
unprincipled military commanders. Local political discords,
personal feuds unrestrained by ordinary civil processes, in-
efficient meddling in local affairs by the Center, the arming
of new state guards, of irresponsible pseudo-agrarians, the
conflicts among the jealous corps, the clashing greed of
politicians and militarists, the plundering by the soldiers,
the razing of villages, left Jalisco, the richest agricultural
state in the republic, utterly prostrate. The seed for future
hurricanes of revolt was effectively sowed. In a vague way

the lines remained drawn between Catholics and hacendados on the one hand and the Government and the agrarians on the other, but the actual outcome was the ruination of a state and the grinding of the people of the rural districts under the heel of a military situation seventy five per cent of which was created by the very federal authorities fighting it.

The aftermath was assassination and political disintegration.

6

On Sunday, the 13th of November 1927, General Obregón, after lunch, motored through the extensive Chapultepec Park at the foot of the old Spanish castle which serves as the Mexican White House. Armed guards followed him in a second machine. Near the lake he was overtaken by four men in an Essex car, who hurled three bombs and fired. The fenders of Obregón's machine were badly twisted, shrapnel tore several holes in the coupe, a bullet passed between the heads of Obregón and his companion, perforating the rear glass.

The guards speeded up and pursued the Essex half way

into town overtaking it at a busy intersection. One of the occupants of the Essex, Nahum Lamberto Ruiz, was badly wounded, blinded and captured. Before he died, in the hospital, information was obtained from him leading to the arrest of other people, four of whom were shot within forty-eight hours without trial, on the basis of signed depositions and police investigations. These four were Luis Segura y Vilchis, Juan Tirado, Humberto Pro, and the priest Miguel Agustín Pro. I have carefully gone over the photostats of the depositions, supposedly signed by these four. Shooting without civil trial was justified, according to the authorities, because those implicated had been shipping arms and ammunition to the "Hail, Christ the King" rebels, in egg cases (heavy eggs!). The prisoners denied this.

Luis Segura y Vilchis, a topographical engineer, twenty four years of age, employed by the local light and power company, admitted that he planned the crime, prepared four bombs, took part in the attempt and threw one of the bombs. In a house on No. 38 Jesús María Street, he had concealed seven thousand Mauser cartridges, the destination of which he refused to disclose. The Essex automobile belonging to him, having just been bought from a man named José González. This man was never discovered, but Humberto Pro testified González had bought it from him some days previously. Juan Tirado, the fourth individual shot, had been in the Essex. According to Segura, Tirado had agreed that same Sunday morning to take part in the attempt and had thrown one of the bombs. Tirado declared he went in the Essex, without prior knowledge of the project, and that when handed one of the bombs he refused to throw it.

Humberto Pro had owned the Essex car up to a few days before the attempt was made. He had known Segura for about a year in the Association of Mexican Catholic Youth (A.C.J.M.); and prior to the crime he had taken food to Nahum Lamberto Ruíz and two other persons, hiding out from the police in the suburb of Tacuba, because they had distributed leaflets in favor of the economic Catholic boycott. Ruíz and these others were also members of the A.C.J.M. In addition, Humberto Pro and Segura were members of the League of Religious Defense, which devoted its energies to rebel activities and to civic religious labor. Early in November Humberto Pro received two hundred and fifty pesos from Segura to rent a house for two destitute Catholic girls. He had Señora Montes de Oca rent such a house on 44A Alzate Street in name of a fictitious person—María Pérez. Humberto Pro denied knowing that the bombs to kill Obregón were to be manufactured in this house, and said he was in Atzcapozalco when Obregón was attacked and that he had nothing to do with the affair. However, he turned over a mimeograph, ten thousand blank sheets of paper and "seditious" literature belonging to the League for the Defense of Religious Liberty, which were concealed in 377 Colima Street. The evidence against him is not conclusive.

The evidence against the priest Miguel Agustín Pro, brother of Humberto, though indicating that he was possibly engaged in the militant activities of the League, and may even have been secondarily involved in the November 13th attack, is entirely too flimsy to warrant his having been shot by the authorities.

Government by official execution of civilians, without trial, even though they be terrorists, is difficult to condone. It cannot be condoned in Mexico, in spite of the fact that the administration which practised it had scarcely emerged from a severe stuggle to maintain its stability. The firing squad may be the only argument understood by insurrectionary militarists, devoid of patriotism or humanity. Nevertheless, even rebels are customarily given a trial. But in the case of these four civilians, every constitutional and humanitarian guarantee was violated. The day prior to the execution, the Mexico City press carried, side by side, statements in which the prisoners declared their innocence and the police countercharges that the sworn *actos* and the search of the men's homes conclusively proved criminal participation. The same day that these accounts were published, the mother of the youngest of the accused brought him breakfast—at noon she brought lunch to his dead body. A court restraining order arrived fifteen minutes after the four were shot.

As a result, universal doubt was cast on their guilt, and a hundred rumors set afloat that the government hastened to assassinate them in order to conceal the real culprits. Probably local public opinion was never so shocked since the assassination of Madero and Pino Suárez by the underlings of Huerta; but all criticism was stifled by the iron-clad censorship maintained by the government over all newspapers and cable service and the fear engendered by the arbitrary deportation of prominent Mexican editorial writers. The flashlight violence must be stigmatized as a tactical stupidity and a moral blot on Calles' administration. Proper trial, if embodying proof of guilt would have caused the world to recoil from the spectacle of a Christian priest who had attempted murder. As it is, another martyr was added to the Church calendar and was buried with the Pope's blessing.

Obregón was finally assassinated on July 17, 1928. His assassin, José de León Toral, was in frequent contact with all the Catholic plotters of the day. He had studied in Catholic schools in Monterrey and in Mexico, the Federal District, and the Annex School of the Seminary of San Luis Potosí. In the Catholic school of San Borja he worked for some time as drawing teacher and later secured a position in the Department of Illustrations of the leading daily *Excelsior*, where he had to join the CROM (labor confederation) to hold his job.

He had been a member of the ACJM till it went to pieces, then of the FCM (Mexican Catholic Federation) and the religious Centro Unión. He was also affiliated in Monterrey and in Mexico with the Pious Association of the Sacred Heart.

When Toral first appeared in court he wore a check suit and green gabardine, striped on the sleeves. He was in a state of disarray, his face covered with a two weeks' beard; and he wore no collar or tie—these having been torn off in the attack on him at the time of Obregón's death. Too, his thick protruding lips were cut and still swollen, from the beating he then received and from subsequent fiendish torturing in his cell, directed by Valente Quintana.

Toral was a constant visitor at the house of Mother Conchita (a superior nun running a clandestine convent) who was the pivot of numerous Catholic plots and to whom he had been introduced by one Margarita Rubio the previous April. And he was greatly dominated by his father confessor, José A. Jiménez. He also heard Jiménez preach in the Centro Unión advocating the elimination of Obregón and Calles. A rather pale figure he seemed to all his associates, too gentle to kill a fly. He was extremely religious, constantly troubled by holy and moral doubts, so wrapped up in matters of the faith and devoted to the practices of the cult, that he neglected his wife and family. The wife and his father and mother agree that he was highly suggestionable and subject to the influence of other persons. Toral's wife testified that Mother Conchita and Father Jiménez had taken him away from her completely. Father Jiménez in June took Toral, Margarita Pacheco and Widow Altamira to the town of Tenancingo, where he said mass to the Catholic rebels. Toral introduced Jiménez to Mother Conchita.

Toral had also been a friend of the Pros and probably of Segura. He had brooded upon that earlier attempt on Obregón's life and upon the subsequent executions. Little by little he abandoned his original repugnance and began to accept the idea that the death of Obregón might prove a solution for the Church. About two months before the crime, he had had a conversation with Mother Conchita in which she said that the religious troubles could only be solved completely by the deaths of Obregón, Calles and the schismatic

Patriarch Juan Pérez. This made a deep impression on his mind. Mother Conchita admitted that she might have made these remarks, but that she had no idea any one would act upon them. About a week after one of Obregón's arrivals in the city, Toral told Mother Conchita that he had heard some one say that God had killed the aviator Emilio Carranza with a thunderbolt, and asked her why God didn't do the same to Obregón. Mother Conchita merely smiled. Toral declared Mother Conchita was his only intellectual director, but that she did not know the effect she was having on him. He declared he told no one of his intention to kill Obregón, and that Manuel Trejo, a young man to whom Conchita had introduced him and who loaned him the pistol with which Obregón was killed for target practice, may have suspected his real purpose, but if so said nothing.

From the time of the last arrival of Obregón in Mexico City, July 15 (Sunday), until the murder on the afternoon of July 17 (Tuesday), Toral trailed the President-Elect. He waited among the throng at the station, wearing an Obregón pin; a kodak concealed the bulge his pistol made in his coat. He followed the president-elect down the Paseo; he went to Obregón headquarters; and he hung around Obregón's house. During these two days he saw Trejo (and the ardent Catholic Widow Altamira, in whose house Trejo lived) with regard to retaining the pistol he had been loaned. Twice on Monday he met the priest Jiménez—in a pharmacy; and Jiménez secured him a room for the night in the house of one Señora Ascova. Late this same afternoon, Toral also called on Mother Conchita, talked with her about the disturbed state of his mind, and received counsel that fortified his soul. Tuesday morning, the day of the assassination, Toral received the sacrament in the house of Mother Conchita and assisted in the service of two masses. He remained until all had gone, then took leave of Mother Conchita. After this he went to the pharmacy to keep an appointment with

329

Father Jiménez; but the latter did not show up; and so Toral went out to the vicinity of Obregón's house.

About noon, autos came out; and Toral imagined Obregón was going with friends to some restaurant. As they took the Insurgentes Calzada, probably either of the two garden restaurants Trepieddi or La Bombilla. Toral had a beer in the first, then went on to the second. Many autos were parked; there were many people about. He went into the bar and had another beer, then went on through to the garden, where a banquet was set. In his breast he carried the gun, and in his hand a sketch pad. First he made a caricature of the orchestra leader, then a caricature of Obregón (What irony!). He showed this caricature to Ricardo Topete, who looked at him suspiciously, then to Aarón Saenz—the two men seated on either side of Obregón. He then moved to Obregón's armless right side, pulling out the pistol and holding it under the pad. Obregón half turned; Toral remembered afterwards that he had given him a kindly glance; but at that moment, when the orchestra was playing a loud piece, Toral pulled the trigger once and the pistol sprayed out nine shots into the neck and shoulder blade of Obregón. A tenth cartridge remained in reserve. Obregón gave a little moan, rose a bit in his chair and slumped. The third bullet had gone through his heart.

Toral declared that in addition to solving the religious problem, he wished to save Obregón's soul.

Toral condemned to death. Mother Conchita to twenty years. In the bitterness of this religious strife, even a trial could only be a travesty of impartiality. Perhaps even so, justice was meted out. But not through a fair and impartial trial. The verdict came as a result of the menacing attitude of the Obregón bloc in the National Chamber of Deputies. On February fifth, fifty armed deputies, supposedly elected to uphold the law of the land, led by the killer and demagogue Gonzalo Santos, leader of the National Revolutionary Party, invaded the precincts of the courtroom, announcing

to the jurors that if Toral was not condemned to death they would kill him and the jurors. The attorney for the defense was also threatened with violence, and pistols were actually levelled at the head of Toral. From then on the court-room was packed with these same armed ruffians, protected by their *fueros* as deputies from all punishment. They shouted insults at Mother Conchita of a sort which most men would hesitate to address to the lowest prostitute. So was justice vindicated! The only conclusion is that Mexico has yet to learn the most elementary lessons of fair play and legality.

So was Obregón's soul saved a second time!

XIX   BLACK GOLD

1

Except agriculture no other industry has so influenced the social and political life of Mexico during the revolutionary period as the production of petroleum. Largely in the hands of American and British capital, concentrated in the two coast states of Vera Cruz and Tamaulipas, oil has changed the habits and means of livelihood of most of the people of the region, and deeply affected the destiny of the whole nation. The acquisition of the oil fields complicated the entire system of land-tenure. During the 1910-17 revolution, the rush for black gold created conflicts not yet entirely ironed out. Petroleum certainly has been a major source of disorder south of the Río Grande. The large petroleum revenues made control of the government a growing prize; bandits, official and otherwise, found the oil companies good prey; the companies on occasion openly took sides during armed conflicts, both for and against *de facto* governments. On two occasions, petroleum has led Mexico and the United States to the brink of war; it was one of the chief considerations in the recognition of Obregón government, growing out of the 1923 Bucareli agreements engineered by Warren and Payne. The World War, the cutting off of Russian oil, the rapid increase in demand for petroleum, all made the Mexican supply of exaggerated importance during much of this period. After 1926, overproduction in the United States, the rapid development of new fields, as in Venezuela, Rumania, Baku, the renewed accessibility of Russian oil, made the Mexican output, momentarily of less importance. As a result of the Mexican Revolution, of restrictive and regulatory legislation, decreased demand, general reorganization of the industry, Mexican production declined, reaching its lowest level in 1930. Mexico dropped from second place, the United States being first, was surpassed by Russia, and Venezuela, and shunted to seventh place.

In a time when Mexico was passing through a violent transition period, the world-wide petroleum industry, quite apart from local, national, and international complications, on its side, also passed through a special crisis. The industry is unlikely ever again to hold such an abnormal preponderance in the national affairs or to contribute so large a proportion of the national revenues, or to cause such diplomatic indigestion. International conflict seems more or less settled. Mexico as a nation, and oil as an industry, are both entering upon a new era.

The matter may be summarized thus: 1901 to 1922 was a period of wild-cat oil. Part of this era coincided with the worst Mexican political disorder. For a time the petroleum companies carried on their production in armed camps; and their relative importance was greatly increased by the fact that, while other industries in Mexico were shattered, petroleum alone strode ahead to maximum production. Oil holdings were the greatest single aggregate of wealth in Mexico, and the resultant conflicts with revolutionary chiefs, hard-pressed for funds, gave rise to innumerable altercations. And the nationalistic and socialistic doctrines involved in the prolonged upheaval, doctrines which resulted in the Querétaro Constitution of 1917, with the moot Article 27 establishing *dominio directo* of the nation in the subsoil, bred constant dissension.

The period from 1922-1928 found the major known fields

staked out, the first rush for black gold over. It was marked by a serious, less hectic attempt to achieve legal equilibrium between various interests, private, governmental, international. It opened with the Supreme Court decisions of 1922-23 in the Texas Company cases notably, declaring Article 27 non-retroactive, and with the Bucareli agreements of 1923, further guaranteeing non-retroactivity. The 1925 oil law attempted a new modification of the meaning of retroactivity. The period draws to a close with the reiteration by the Supreme Court in November, 1927, of the inviolability of certain rights acquired prior to 1917.

Without doubt the period from 1928 on saw the emergence of a more orderly industry, more in accord with national policy, compromising at least with revolutionary juridical precepts. The industry has passed, violently to be sure, from a wild-cat era to one of regulation, a course not unlike that of more than one industry in the United States from the Civil War down to the Sherman anti-trust law. Mexico's whole destiny and stability in 1922 depended upon a single resource supplying thirty percent of its revenues. In the year 1927, petroleum contributed only about 7 percent of the total revenue. With the passing of revolutionary warfare, mining revived; new undertakings sprouted, commerce expanded.

The significant features of today's Mexican petroleum industry are about as follows: Overproduction in the United States and the development of profitable fields in other parts of the world, caused the dizzy decline in production from 194,755,710 barrels in 1921 to less than 45,000,000 barrels in 1929; the successful enforcement of the main features of the 1917 constitution with regard to the nationalization of the subsoil, but guaranteeing to the owner of the surface of his subsoil rights on lands acquired before 1917, definitely "tagged" for oil purposes; the reorganization of the industry itself, a change featured by the passing of Doheny, who typifies the wild-cat era, and the concentration of production in the hands of the Standard Oil Companies of New Jersey, Indiana, and California (producing nearly 60% of Mexico's oil); the emergence of the Mexican Government as a producer (El Control de Administración del Petroleo Nacional in 1928 supplied nearly 5 percent of the total national output); and the passing of the smaller independent companies. By 1928 there remained but five minor concerns of any importance (since Sinclair may be considered as controlled by the Standard): the Mellon interests (Mexican Gulf, 5.6%); the Marland Oil Company (Morgan), producing through its various subsidiaries, chiefly the Cía. Petrolera Franco Española S. A., 1.2%; and the Texas Company (0.7%). The latter has had bad luck with recent drilling and will probably leave the field. These facts represent a definite realignment in the industry.

The old wild-cat period was movie stuff. There were gold-rush scenes; claims, so to speak, were staked out, violence was rampant; options on new property changed hands from hour to hour at ever steeper prices, six figures being made over night. From the time Doheny secured the Hacienda del Tulillo (280,000 acres purchased at $325,000) in 1900, and the first well was shot at Ebano on May 14, 1901, the industry gathered headway. In 1904, the first official records showed 220,650 barrels; by 1912, during the administration of the revolutionary president Francisco I. Madero, production had reached 16,558,217 barrels. The ordinary California well, above the average for the United States, yielded from 100 to 200 barrels per day, and 600 barrels has been considered big. In Mexico, Casiano No. 7 started with a flow of 70,000 barrels daily (September 10, 1910). In less than a decade it had produced over 100 million barrels. Cerro Azul, the greatest oil-well in the world, ran 1,400,000 barrels before it could be capped, then under a back pressure of about 900 pounds produced about 50,000 barrels per day. There are wells drilled fifteen years ago which still produce 800 barrels a day. And while in the United States most wells have to be pumped, in Mexico many wells flow under their own pressure. Of course the sky is not entirely without dark clouds. The average Mexican well must be drilled not into oil-bearing sands as in the United States (with the exception of the Isthmus of Tehuantepec and one other small area), but into basalt folds, so that the perforation cost is usually treble. The exploitable zone in each field is extremely narrow. Near the coast there is the constant danger, not of one well, but the whole field turning to salt water. In the initial development period and down through the administration of Carranza, the scramble for oil lands by individuals and companies continued frantically. Doheny, in on the ground floor, already producing and on the upgrade, was able to expand consistently and ruthlessly; so that his companies, which he disposed of in 1925 to a holding company of the Standard Oil Company of Indiana, were still in 1929 the heaviest producers in the field—36 percent of Mexico's entire output.

Picturesque buccaneers emerged: the president of one of the largest companies in the field today landed on the Tampico swamps as a beachcomber, secured a job as a mechanic, and by daring and unscrupulous tactics, shot to the top; a local representative of another large concern, cleaned his company of several million dollars and started out independently, by playing in with Mexican officials. As president of an independent company, he became one of the most active concession-hunters on the Mexican scene.

The wild-cat period saw the rise of the port of Tampico from a dozen miserable mud huts to a city of paved streets and American homes and the semblance of sanitation. Its heyday was in '21-22. A wide-open town, with one of the largest red-light districts in the history of the world. Money did not flow but gushed like oil. In the jazz-hammering cabarets, the man who did not spend his thousand a night was a piker. And though the prostitutes who flocked from all corners of the globe, did not carry stilettos in their stockings as Hergesheimer would have us believe in his *Tampico*, more than one American, whose death worked diplomatic apoplexy in Washington, passed out at the hands of Tampico Delilas. Poker by the week and month, and sumptuous roulette wheels made Monte Carlo look shabby. The bodegas of Europe were ransacked for wine and champagne; whiskey, aged with fake labels. The port of Tampico in more days harbored one of the most elegant opium dens on the continent. And mechanics, adding-machine slaves, rod and chain men, camp-carpenters, and other menials, hired at managerial salaries, because of the terrible climate and the reckless expansion of the industry, learned to leave their tobacco plugs at home and sport dress-suits at the local American Club.

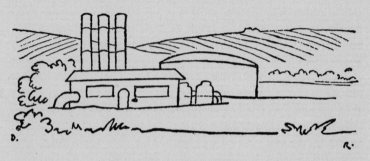

2

THE SCRAMBLE FOR LANDS

This rush of frontiersmen was dumped upon an unsuspecting countryside, where Indians and ranchers lived a simple bucolic existence, and passed the time leisurely, singing *corridos*, strumming guitars. The system of land tenure was effective, though complicated. No particular land-hunger made disputes pressing. The system was a tangle of many systems of jurisprudence and an outgrowth of ancient social customs, dating from pre-Conquest days, altered a little from colonial days and from independence days. There was communal holding of *ejidos*, there were enclosures, never properly legalized, there were Crown grants for irrigation, for pasturage, surface-cultivation, sub-soil exploitation—sometimes four separate grants for the same piece of property. Crown titles for pasturage, strictly limited to grazing purposes were sold for about $100 per *sitio*; i.e., for about 2¼ cents per acre. The mining unit was the *pertinencia* of about two and one-tenth acres. There were "federal zones" and remnants of Church holding in the name of the Indian. The public records were thoroughly faulty. Many lands had their titles registered, not with the legal authorities as required by the law of 1884, but on the parochial records. Many lands were held without recorded title, but had been handed down from generation to generation, the ownership recognized by the community. Titles, kept by village elders, were even drawn in the form of pictographs with quaint foot-prints, and cactus plants, and strings of beads, indicating prices paid. Some deeds recorded the boundaries in this fashion: "From the Cacalayo falls southwest two hours on horseback to a pile of stones (which pile had long since disappeared, probably to build an Indian *jacal*), thence west one hour . . ."

In the mad skurry for oil lands, there was no time to examine the validity of all of these titles. The main thing was to grab a piece of land before someone else did, hold it against all comers, at the point of the gun, if necessary, and sink your shaft as quickly as possible. Any title would do. To this day one of the richest little corners of the land in the whole area is being drilled on a pasturage title, and other belated claimants have been held off by compromise, legal and illegal proceedings. Many an owner of property woke up, rubbed his eyes, and discovered oil flowing from wells, to be informed that he no longer owned it. If he had money he fought for a share of the spoils, and the outcome usually depended on who paid the biggest graft to the officials. To get lands often you had to deal with a hundred, three, four hundred owners, or an entire community. If a blanket title could not be obtained from the community as a whole, you simply bought up a few rights from two or three local citizens and slammed in a well. In any case, you were never sure of an iron-clad deed. Other properties, originally bought by a group for so many *pesos primitivos*, had through the years seen the moities endlessly subdivided. The Hacienda Aguada had close to four hundred owners. The parochial records of many such properties read that Juan Pedro sold two hectares to Isidro—no surnames; there are about a million Juan Pedros in Mexico, each of which, taken in tow by a clever shyster, may become a potential claimant. One widow, needing money, decided to sell her ranch. She sent her profligate son to talk it over with the oil companies. With no right of attorney, he sold the land for a few thousand pesos, and blew it all in a night's debauch. One bright morning the widow discovered that a company had sunk wells upon her property. To this day she has never been able to get redress. In such a mix-up, with unscrupulous adventurers on every hand, revolution convulsing the land, and all law a farce, no limit stopped individuals or companies. Men were murdered; legitimate children were made bastards; bastards were made legitimate; minors were kidnapped and sent to the states. The sane were declared insane. Married couples suddenly found themselves divorced. Dusky Indian maidens without shoes on their unwashed feet, but with moities in property under which ran the black and golden stream, found their persons most desirable in legal wedlock to southern gentlemen of otherwise violent color prejudices. Pages were torn out of public records; false pages were inserted in public records; dates changed; names changed. Came upon the scene the venders of faked titles, some of which the oil companies brought in quite good faith. Came upon the scene every type of shyster lawyer, snooting around for ignorant Indians with claims fancied or real to oil-bearing properties, and the companies were made to pay the piper for earlier indiscretions. Oftentimes companies were forced to buy the title to the same piece of land half a dozen times. Corruption stalked. Scarcely a judge who did not have his price. Scarcely an inspector who could not be purchased. Revolution continued to rage up and down the land; money had to be paid to officials and money had to be paid to bandits, like Pelaez.

And yet, with it all, the companies made fortunes.

Production proceeded apace. There was scarcely any charge the industry could not bear; and the wells ran to fabulous production.

But as taxes increased, came subterfuges, false bottom tankers, secret pipe-lines, palm-crossed inspectors. Private armed guards even drove Government officials off properties at the point of the gun. It is doubtful if either the Mexican government, the companies, or the American State Department could stand thorough investigation of their several parts in the wild-cat drama. But gradually, order of a kind succeeded chaos. The smaller fry were gobbled up, or pushed off the stage; a dozen outstanding companies survived, above all, Doheny. All were faced with the urgent necessity of straightening out their titles, half of which were perfectly imperfect.

A gentleman's agreement was made to respect each other's claims. But outside poachers had to be driven off. All the leading oil people faced interminable suits; for years one company paid a single lawyer $100,000 a year merely to keep busy on the question of clearing up the titles. Many of the suits brought against the companies made demands for a share of the profits taken out of the soil over a period of ten or twenty years, claims frequently running into millions of dollars. Thus one Carmen Dominguez was not represented in the purchase division of the money received of the Cocadilao estate; and her heirs attached the company's property and persons for immense sums. During the De la Huerta revolt in 1923-24, Doheny, whose titles on the Juan Felipe property were under dispute, made one of his brilliant master strokes by advancing the Government 10,000,000 pesos in taxes in return for an agreement that the Government would recognize the right to drill in cases where titles representing 35% of the property were held.

Also titles became a bone of international contention. Since 1884 Mexico has had a law which requires that land-titles must be filed with the proper authorities. This was also one of the requirements laid down by President Carranza. Oil titles then and since could not, in many cases, stand filing. The oil companies publicly stated that they would be willing to submit their titles to the State Department but not to the Mexican Government.

3

SETTLING THE QUESTION

The Querétaro Constitution of 1917, with its Article 27 establishing national "dominion" over the sub-soil, marked the first serious indication of governmental intention to regulate the petroleum industry. The American State Department, promptly grasping the implications of the new document, hurried to obtain assurances from Carranza— whose memory still bled with the Pershing Expedition and the Vera Cruz occupation—that the constitutional provisions would not be applied retroactively. For this contention there was also Article 14 providing "No law will be given retroactive effect to the injury of any person." It was obvious, however, that while the industry was rampantly expanding, the country still unpacified, and the United States involved in the European war, that neither imposition of conditions upon the industry by the Mexican Government nor serious effort at securing a determinative definition of the Constitutional provisions would be successful. The serious period of negotiations really opens after the petroleum companies' drive in 1920-21 to get back their super-legal status and to precipitate interventions, had proved a complete failure. The Revindicating Régime founded by Obregón and Calles showed definite intention and capacity to pacify and govern the country in 1922-23, after the Texas Company and other decisions had been handed down by the Supreme Court and after the Bucareli agreements signed by Warren and Payne laid the basis for the recognition of Obregón's Administration.

To understand the negotiations from 1922-28, it is necessary to start with the earlier legal provisions governing ownership and exploitation of sub-soil products, especially petroleum.

The Colonial Crown grants separated surface uses and mining rights; the ultimate title of all lands and their products was vested in the emperor, a dominion which passed into the hands of the Mexican Republic at the declaration of independence. The whole legal concept of property holding in Mexico is fundamentally different from our own. Nor were such grants as these unconditional. They were revocable at any time. The Laws of the Indies in 1523 definitely stipulated conditions for use: "Lands must be properly marked out, and the house must be lived in . . . the lands must be cultivated, planted with trees and cattle placed thereon . . . under pain of forfeiture of the grant . . . plus a certain return in money." These various laws, particularly those vesting mineral rights (including those bituminous, or "juices" of the earth) which thus guarded all property as royal patrimony, were reaffirmed in the famous laws of Carlos III in 1783. The various legal documents of the independence period held to the same concept. The constitution of 1857 distinctly stated that "in the nation is vested direct ownership (dominio directo) of all minerals, solid, liquid, or gaseous. However, the Díaz mining law of 1884 (Article 10) provided: "Salts found on the surface, fresh and salt water, whether surface or subterranean, petroleum and gaseous springs, or the springs of warm medicinal waters" were the "exclusive property of the owner of the land" who was given the right "to develop and enjoy them, without formality of claim or formal adjudication." The expression "petroleum and gaseous springs" was sufficiently ambiguous, but the subsequent law of 1892 definitely gave to the owner of the surface perpetual subsoil rights in petroleum, rights reiterated in even more specific terms in the law of 1909.

The Constitution of 1917 reverted to the principle that the subsoil was the property of the nation and could only be worked by concession. Pending proper legislation the Constitution was to be put into effect by Presidential decree. The first inroads by the Government upon the independent position of the petroleum companies, came in the form of abrupt increases in taxes (Executive Decree, February 19, 1928): five percent tax on production, five pesos per square kilometer tax on all oil-bearing lands, and a graduated tax up to fifty percent upon the output of wells on rented property. This and other rapid increases in taxes drew forth the note to the Mexican Government by the United States that these taxes "savoured of confiscation." This is debatable. Mr. W. E. Black, at that time vice-president of the Tampico Petroleum Pipe Line and Refining Company, issued a press statement early in 1920:

"Obeying the law in Mexico is no more onerous than obeying the law in the United States, and the Mexican tax on oil cannot even touch the tax on the business in this country when you consider the state taxes and the income tax assessed by the Federal Government . . .

"The Government of Mexico is getting far less from Mexican oil than Uncle Sam. In a recent report of the Mexican Petroleum Company, Ltd., it is shown that the Carranza Government received from the company $1,-917,541, while the American taxes on the company's *Mexican output* were $5,000,000. The report shows a gross income of $26,320,545, and in spite of the Mexican tax and the excess profit tax in this country, the profits of the company were $6,699,644, or more than 100 percent greater than for any previous year."

Carranza also required that all owners and lessors make a declaration within three months that they intended to drill on their property, or else permit the Government to grant concessions to other parties, regardless of the surface ownership. The protests of the oil companies and the American State Department prevented application. In November, 1918, Carranza presented a bill (which was never passed) to Congress embodying most of the provisions of the 1925 law put through by Calles. The United States Government sent a note that it could not accept the constitutional principle of governmental ownership of the sub-soil whether enforced by "decrees or by law."

Carranza's efforts led to the intervention drive by the oil people during the last days of his administration. A ramified plot was under way to set up a new government, a plot nipped in the bud, by the prior revolt of Obregón. The anti-Mexican propaganda in the United States continued during Obregón's period—a concerted campaign to convince the American public of disorder south of the Río Grande, to spread news of Americans killed, and of other irregularities. Notes from the State Department showered thick and fast upon Mexico. The Fall investigating committee carried on its sessions along the border in order to "unmask" Mexico.

This intervention propaganda failed because of three forces. In spite of all difficulties, Mexico was gradually growing more stable, and as a result ordinary trade and commerce was improving. Chambers of Commerce, municipal Administrations and some fifteen state legislatures petitioned Congress to establish normal relations. The Obregón Government in its turn maintained professional lobbyists to secure the passage of many of these resolutions. The second force that broke the intervention drive was the reemergence of active independent companies, not enrolled with the Ameri-

can Association of Petroleum Producers. Small Texas companies entered the Mexican field. They were discovering that
if money could be made by bucking the Mexican Government, money could also be made by playing in with it.
Naturally these independent companies had the right of way,
and new concessions, even on lands previously bought by the
older companies, proved a new thorn for the established oil
people; the uncertainty over titles and the fact that these
newer companies were not included in the gentlemen's agreement to protect each other's rights, opened the way for every
sort of encroachment. The English oil people, "El Aguila,"
were the first to see which way the wind was blowing and
jumped out of the Association, with the announcement that
El Aguila would obey all laws. This was the occasion of the
memorable letter from Mr. Fall, read by Senator Lodge upon
the floor of the Senate charging that the British oil corpora-
tions in Mexico had betrayed the Association "by accepting
the Mexican Government's demands with reference to oil-
drilling permits," and abiding by its laws. Perfidious Albion!
This led to factor three in the breaking of the intervention
drive. Five of the leading oil men, Teagle, Doheny, Sinclair,
Van Dyke, and Beatty, alarmed at the change of front, made
a special trip to Mexico to arrange for the payment of taxes
and discuss other disputed matters. It was agreed that part
of the payment of taxes should be made in Mexican bonds
and other paper, resulting in a great reduction. Enter the
New York bankers, who saw in this arrangement too good a
bargain. The result was the Lamont-De la Huerta debt settlement, a settlement which threw the weight of the House of
Morgan on the side of non-intervention.

Still another development relieved the tension between the
two countries. The Carranza decrees were finally tested in the
United States Supreme Court, in a series of decisions handed
down in favor of the Texas Company, the International
Petroleum Company, etc., in 1922-23.

The case of the Texas Company was this: The Mexican

Department of Industry, Commerce and Labor, in conformity with the Carranza decrees of July 31, August 8 and 12, 1918, had granted on December 10, 1920, a concession to Rafael Cortina to explore and exploit the petroleum contained in Lot Number 36 of Zacamixtle, Municipality of Tancoco, Canton of Tuxpán, in the State of Vera Cruz, which superseded the rights acquired by the Texas Company in conformity with the laws of 1884, 1892, and 1909. The Supreme Court, holding that the decree regulating Article 27 could not be applied retroactively, proceeded to ascertain whether the specific Cortina concession, injured acquired sub-soil rights. The decision pointed out that the property under dispute had been acquired from the previous owners by the Texas Company at a price sufficiently above the normal to indicate that it was proposed to utilize it for exploiting petroleum; and that therefore to grant a concession for the sub-soil rights to a third person was a retroactive violation. (Semanario Judicial de la Federación, Tomo IX, Núm. 7, July 22, 1922, pp. 432 ff.)

With the Supreme Court decisions as a basis, the controversy soon found led directly to the negotiations preliminary to the recognition of Obregón. The American delegates (nominated April 25, 1923) were Charles B. Warren, subsequently ambassador to Mexico, and John Barton Payne, President of the American Red Cross and former head of the United States Shipping Board; the Mexican delegates, Señores Ramón Ross, General Director of Public Benevolence, and Fernando González Roa, former Secretary of the Interior. In these negotiations, the Mexican Government was forced to recede from its position of attempting to bring the pre-1917 petroleum property under the general decrees and regulations affecting all sub-soil and to guarantee pre-1917 rights. The American Government by this time had been obliged to withdraw from its position that national dominion over the sub-soil would not be tolerated, and even to recede from its position that all lands owned by Americans prior to 1917 were entitled to possess the sub-soil. It now restricted its demands to those lands definitely "tagged" as petroleum prior to that date.

Nevertheless, the controversy again surged to the front under Calles, with the passing of the new petroleum law of 1925—actually the thirty-sixth oil bill to be discussed by Congress. Once more—in contravention of the Bucareli agreements—the new law delimited the pre-1917 rights. It declared that such rights would be "confirmed by fifty year concessions." Undoubtedly this petroleum legislation was in accordance with the general program of President Calles to press through the Chamber and the Senate the essential fundamental laws necessary to put into operation the leading provisions of the 1917 Constitution, among which were such nationally and internationally significant laws as those dealing with Family Patrimony, Foreign Holdings in Frontier areas, Religious acts, forestry conservation, labor rights, and various tax and irrigation laws.

The 1925 petroleum law protects rights derived in accordance with the various presidential decrees of 1918 (July 30, August 8 and 12) even where the title was not finally expedited. Also petroleum rights and titles are confirmed without further cost to all those who obtained them in accordance with previous laws, viz: to the holders of surface lands who commenced their petroleum work before May 1, 1917, when the present constitution was adopted, and to their successors; to the holders of surface-lands who manifested to the Government before this date that they had lands destined for petroleum production; to all pipe-line operators and refiners who at present are operating with the actual authorization of the Department of Industry Commerce and Labor. Confirmation of previous rights had to be obtained within one year if they were to continue in effect.

Simultaneous with the discussion of this law, the President announced his intention to create extensive petroleum reserves, to promote Government drilling, and establish Gov-

ernment oil-tanks capable of holding enormous federal
reserves of oil.

The passing of the new law immediately precipitated
strained relations between the two Governments. A series of
protests were sent by Mr. Kellogg pointing out that a concession was not a confirmation of existing rights, and insisting
upon no retroactive applications of the law to the detriment
of American property. The Mexican Government took the
position that the fifty year concession and the thirty year
renewal features of the law amply guaranteed the companies'
rights, since no well had been known to last that length of
time. The Americans maintained that the companies were
not bound to exploit their sub-soil rights until such time as
they saw fit, and that if the companies were obliged to exchange titles (which according to the prior Díaz laws under
which they were acquired included free right to exploit the
sub-soil without prior denouncement), for limited concessions, then a future government could reduce the concession
from fifty to ten years if it saw fit. The Mexican Government
replied that the American Government should wait until a
specific act of confiscation had been committed; that the law
in itself was not such an act; that not until the concessions
had expired and confiscation then resulted could such an act
be said to have been committed; that in any case no act of
confiscation could become subject to diplomatic protest until
it had been fully passed upon by the Mexican legal machinery.
In addition, the Mexican Government set up its own definition of retroactivity, and declared categorically that the law
was not retroactive. Here both sides rested their cases. The
American Government was obliged to wait for what it might
consider a direct act of confiscation and the decision of the
Supreme Court of Mexico upon such a step.

As the time for signing up under the new law and taking
out concessions approached the tension grew greater. Undoubtedly if the companies could have been assured of a carte
blanche recognition of their titles, they would have been only

too willing to accept the concession feature. Even without this absolute guarantee, but with such a tacit understanding, they were willing to sign up, had it not been for the eleventh hour intimation of the State Department that they should not do so.

A deadlock resulted. According to the law, the companies were required to apply for concessions by December 31, 1926. No provision provided for the steps to be taken against non-complying companies. And so the matter dragged along until the arrival of Ambassador Dwight W. Morrow, who at once instigated secret negotiations.

Largely because of his intervention, on November 17, the Supreme Court of Mexico rendered a decision in favor of the Mexican Petroleum Company of California (the Doheny Company which some time ago passed into the hands of the Standard Oil Company of Indiana), regarding the revocation of drilling permits by the Department of Industry Commerce and Labor. This was the first decision rendered by the Supreme Court since the 1925 law went into effect.

The present decision, though in favor of the company, in no way set the petroleum law aside as unconstitutional. It was, therefore, a minor decision, but important in that it indicated the probable trend of future decisions. The Government obviously selected, for tactical reasons, a case which could be decided in favor of the recalcitrant companies, on which to render its first decision.

The Supreme Court, in its decision, maintained that so long as there existed a conflict between the Government and the company as regards what constitutes "confirmation," those rights have not been forfeited. The Department declared that the granting of fifty-year concessions constituted such confirmation. The company declared that a concession for a limited period of time is not a confirmation of previous rights. In this contention the Court upheld the company, and added that until this contention be satisfactorily settled, the company cannot be considered to have forfeited its rights, and is therefore privileged to continue in status quo.

By February 18, Congress, at the suggestion of Calles, amended the law to put it into line with the Court's decision. After a series of conferences between Morrow and the oil companies on the one hand and Morrow and Luis N. Morones, Secretary of Industry on the other, a new set of working regulations were drawn up. These for all practical purposes returned to the Warren and Payne agreements, the oil companies were forced to swallow the word "concession" though concessions on "tagged" pre-1917 property were to be given for perpetuity. The Mexican Government also established its right to revise all titles.

Thus, with the settlement by Morrow, the general legal basis of the petroleum industry has been established and removed from the sphere of international controversy. A balance between the Díaz system and the revolutionary system has been established. Pre-1917 rights are confirmed and follow more or less the older principle of identifying sub-soil rights with surface tenure in fee simple. All other rights fall under the revolutionary prescription of the nationalization of the sub-soil, making exploitation a concession right.

It now becomes possible for the industry to develop along more sound, orderly and regulated lines.

XX   MEXICO AND THE
                    MACHINE AGE

Wʜᴀᴛ will happen to Mexico
when the expansive tendencies of the American industrial
system really make headway? What will happen to the native
Indian population when the economic forces of the modern
world finally sweep across the Mexican land; when the iron
knuckles of the machine age batter at the feudal façade?

The barriers are frail. Protective laws, race pride, Boxerism, even disorder cannot keep Mexico isolated from the
twentieth-century system of world economy, rapidly inter-
locking the peoples of the world. Water inevitably flows
into a lower level; in this case no dams can hold it out.
All through the revolutionary period American capital has
seeped into Mexico. Disorder, the un-capitalist legal system,
antagonism to white foreigners, diplomatic resistance—none
of these have dissuaded American financial and industrial
penetration.

During the Díaz period the American invasion banged

352

with trumpets through the land. The recent revolutionary period, in Mexico as in China, has been in large part a brutal reaction to that invasion. But it has also been an adaptation to it. Opposition invariably drags compromise in its train.

Thus, proletarian slogans in a semi-colonial country signify something different than they do in an industrialized country. They are tinged with the democratic implications of the French furor. Labor freedom—as opposed to feudal serfdom—is the *sine qua non* of factory slavery. Labor mobility ever precedes commodity mobility. Labor is the initial commodity. Modern industry cannot be run with peonage; feudal contracts cannot cope with the forces of the machine age; only a free labor supply can make possible the emergence of Mexico into a modern independent producing nation, or even into a producing nation dominated by foreign capital. The revolutionary freeing of labor heralds the coming of the machine; Mexican labor shouts against the foreigner, but the very fact that it has grown and organized itself sufficiently to shout indicates that it has been prepared. It will adopt the factory system. That system is inevitable. But it is a system which can only be successfully implanted by foreigners wielding foreign capital.

The attempts of Calles to create a national economy failed. His period was too short. He himself hauled down the flag. His relations with Ambassador Morrow told the tale. Mexico had no time to work out its own economic salvation. Technical knowledge was lacking; capital was lacking; industrialized habits among the people was lacking; political security was lacking; racial homogeneity was lacking. And so American capital inevitably, it seems, will overrun Mexico. What will happen to Mexico as the process is accelerated? What will happen to indigenous Tepoztlán, to Tlaxcala, to the native culture?

Two possibilities present themselves. First: military and

political conquest, either as a prelude or an epilogue to economic penetration. At present no such war seems imminent; but always it remains a possibility: intervention, partial annexation (of the oil regions); imposition of a president through a militarily supervised plebiscite. The impossibility of any such president sustaining himself would necessitate permanent intervention. Military governorships would result. A carpet-bag era would follow, then a gradual extension of political security. Mexico being territorially contiguous to the United States, it would not under these conditions seem too much to prophesy ultimate gradual absorption into our own federal system.

Consider the possible effect of this both on the United States and on the Mexican people. To the voting population of the United States would be added fifteen million dark-skinned people. Fifteen million added to the existing thirteen million negroes, and the three million Spanish-speaking peoples already residing in the United States would be an alien race bloc of over thirty million people. We would be adding fifteen million Catholics. In other words many of the racial and religious problems now acute in Mexico would become acute in the United States as a whole and would perpetuate and intensify foci of disintegration which would profoundly alter the character of American institutions, lower living standards, and probably ultimately lead to the downfall of American democratic practices. In addition, the United States, though made territorially more extensive by such a move would be weaker internally and at the same time more isolated internationally. The hostility of South America and the world would be definitely mobilized against us.

The effect on Mexico. Such a change would, of course, accelerate sanitation, the building of roads, railways, factories, and the rapid development of tropical agriculture. Sanitation and industry would soon cause a quickening of

the native birth-rate, as in South Africa. Many of the regions being inhospitable to white colonization, there would result no intimate fusion of the race-stocks over a region extending from the Great Lakes to the Isthmus of Tehuantepec. We would crush many vital and beautiful things in the Mexican cultures; at the same time, the people would organize against us, and in the end Mexico would carve out its independence anew. Mexico, though racially, economically and politically still far from being a unified nation, nevertheless ideologically is definitely a nation. The various nation groups of Europe have hewn their way to independence against great odds during the past few centuries. Ireland has accomplished it—with a scant population of four million—in the face of the power of the British Empire.

Economic penetration coupled with steady diplomatic pressure would probably prove less disastrous for both the United States and Mexico. Much of the Mexican culture would be preserved though Americanization would go on apace. Roads are inevitable, and in their wake automobiles, gasolene stations, tourist inns, orange-crush stands, jazz dance halls—all of these things will probably, within the next quarter of a century, descend upon Tepoztlán, and Taxco, and Chilpancingo. Much that is lovely in the native handicraft will go by the boards. Kewpie dolls will probably crowd out the delightful terra cotta figurines and straw-woven horsemen. Five gallon oil cans, rather than beautifully molded native jars, in many places, already grace the swaying shoulders of the local Rebeccas. Gresham's law. Cheap art drives out good art.

Will Indian and mestizo adapt themselves to the factory system? Up till now they have shown themselves less adaptable in this direction than the negroes. Still, in the United States, the Mexican is being increasingly used. The negro has not yet shown whether he is amenable to the factory system in Africa nor anywhere else. The only feudal country which has accepted modernism has been Japan; which has managed to reconcile its ancient customs with the needs of the modern world. But Japan has a closely knit social structure; it was a compact country. Something quite different has happened to China. Something quite different has happened to Mexico. Mexico is not closely knit; it is not compact. It still has grave racial and cultural problems to solve. And even in Japan the entire story may not yet have been told. Technical efficiency, knowledge, modern habits of work, are things not developed in a day. Formulae are not enough. We seized the German dye patents; but we were not able to equal the quality of German dyes. German recipes for making beer do not result in a product equally refined in other countries.

What will all this modern influx mean to the native life? No man can foresee. Probably some sort of a new amalgam and the gradual evolution of new norms. But the mould, in spite of the poor organization of Mexico, will probably remain Spanish-Indian, mestizan, with the upthrust of the native Indian elements continuing, perhaps retarded, but ever gathering force. England was a disorganized country when the Normans descended upon it in 1066. English was a proscribed language for two hundred years. Any one who spoke it was liable to punishment. But English is the language today. Today in English "sheep" is a good Anglo-Saxon word. By the time the animal arrives at the table it becomes French, "mutton." "Cow" becomes "beef." "Pig" becomes "pork." "Calf" becomes "veal." The homely words are Anglo-Saxon; the texture of the language is Anglo-Saxon. Something similar is happening in Mexico. The Indian will probably yet modify the Spanish considerably, both in vocabulary and morphologically. English cannot conquer Mexico. History teaches that unless a people is exterminated the conquered always conquers the conqueror. The subjected race remains closer to the soil; its values are more

enduring. The patience of the Mexican Indian is eternal.
His very lack of aggressiveness will save him. The humble
conquer the earth—for only the strong can be humble.

And the Mexican indigenous population cannot be exterminated. Nor can it be herded into reservations. The population of Mexico, in the beginning, was denser, more
compact than that of the native population in the United
States. It had reached a degree of culture, even of civilization, which prevented any chaff-like scattering such as occurred north of the Río Grande. The Mexican population
and much of its culture will survive whatever form our invasion takes. In two, three, four centuries even the possession
of our southwest may again be contested by this same despised race. This irredenta region is one with the Mexican
domain—geographically and climatically. The foothold of
man on the earth is precarious, never assured—even by all
the devices of science and industry. The white man's portion
can be conserved in part or entirety but perhaps not in-
definitely extended. Yesterday the energy of the world was
coal; today it is petroleum; and the political axis of the
world has changed. Tomorrow it may be electricity, and the
axis may change again. Italy may have its day once more;
and Mexico and the Andes region of South America. Man's
energies continually alter the map of the world. The flame
passes from people to people. Even despised Mexico may be
great at some future era, when we have sunk into materialistic lethargy, or have split into various nations.

Here and there, somewhat at random, I have given intimate vital pictures of the human spirit and the human association in Mexico; things humble that have seemed to me
beautiful and enduring and proud. Strangely enough, these
things have given me faith in this land so prone to murder
and cruelty. Violence is sometimes a sign of deep vitality,
not of death. This was true of the Italian City States. Violence may be a sign of energies not properly directed and

organized; its very vitality ultimately imposes order, reconciles conflicting forces, welds cultures, integrates societies.

Underneath the surge of Mexican political life is the surge of Indian culture struggling toward the light. The American industrial invasion will once more obstruct that surge and thwart it, but I doubt if it ultimately can destroy this emergence of racial helots.

The economic forces of the United States, expansive in tendency, are perhaps equally immutable, but they can be partially directed. Our industrial system demands raw products in uninterrupted quantities. This has led, inevitably, to the industrialization of the tropics. The rapid industrialization of the tropics necessitates a mobile labor supply, industrious habits, and political stability. And so we have attempted to enforce, in certain parts of Latin America, the norm of stability. We have, because of the exigencies of our factory system, been obliged to enforce this stability by the quickest and most ruthless means. We have, therefore, allied ourselves inevitably with the reactionary rather than the liberal forces of the countries to the south of us. We have maintained the feudal régimes wherever possible, brutally insisted upon the status quo, for a social system once rent takes long to mend. Force is a quick means of achieving stability. It may seem to promote the ends of rapid large scale production which stability postulates. But international oppression is equivalent to knocking off the safety valve and blindly hoping you are not piling on too much fuel to cause an explosion. In the long run, it works against our own interests. The industrialization of the tropics cannot continue to go on in alliance with the feudal system. It cannot march hand in hand with the ideas of the Spanish conquest, nor continue to ignore the racial conflicts.

These forces must be given an outlet. The South American republics, and Mexico, must be permitted to set their houses in order, even at the cost of violence and disorder.

To prevent this is ultimately to create greater disorder. This was the lesson of Porfirio Díaz in Mexico. It has been the lesson of Nicaragua in Central America. The greatest disorder has ever occurred where we have meddled the most. All our good intentions cannot settle problems which only the people of the nation involved can solve. There is always something obtuse in foreign administration and too great foreign control. Measures, seemingly wise and logical, do not somehow spring from the soil; they are alien to the psychology and aspirations of the local peoples. Mechanistic expedients but not vital currents. These expedients are ever fundamentally false, ill timed. Hard-headed American proconsuls, in foreign lands, become queer idealists; systematics; dogmatists. Such people serve in pointing new roads, but not for administration. Poor native administration always benefits more than enlightened foreign administration of a land and its peoples. Enlightenment may be according to a world norm, but it is usually ignorant of native norms. If Mexico is to catch up with the modern world, it must be permitted to experiment with liberal tendencies; it must try out its own radical slogans, it must test its own sinews.

The contentment, peace and happiness of Mexico and the United States depends, by and large, upon Mexico maintaining its political independence and as rapidly as possible achieving its economic independence. It is to our advantage to accelerate this, by insisting that American capital in Mexico conform to certain regulations, just as it must do at home. It is to our interest that Mexico become a purchaser of finished products, enjoys independent life, happiness, and prosperity.

All this is particularly true, because Mexico and the United States can never be, except to a limited degree, industrial competitors. They are complimentary. The development of tropical agriculture and native resources on a proper scale, but without breaking the native mould, would provide

360

many things which cannot be produced in the United States; and Mexico would at the same time become a greater purchaser of American goods.

This is all utilitarian doctrine. Over and beyond it are the happiness and peace of two peoples. Over and beyond it are the aspirations of a people enslaved for four centuries, now attempting to liberate themselves from economic, religious, and political oppression. Mexico is, in spite of all its crass violence, an inspiring picture of the eternal struggle of the human spirit to liberate itself. We can be parties to that liberation, or we can frustrate it for many years to come. We can strangle a nation and a people. But nations are reborn phoenix-like from their ashes.

England and Spain, the two great conquerors and colonizers of Renaissance Europe, stood on the Atlantic outposts, as the two poles of the European spirit—Latin and Gothic; Latin and Teutonic. Today the American and Latin-American cultures also represent two poles of the human spirit. Neither is complete in itself. In general our genius is practical, Roman, legal, mechanistic, materialistic. Theirs is romantic, spiritual, song-making, beauty-loving, idealistic, adventurous.

Any aggression against Latin America is a profanation of the human spirit of which we are but a part. My admiration goes to the United States, for its many notable achievements; its conquest over nature rather than over man. But much of my love and hope goes out to the Latin World. We in the United States are powerful. Why now should we desert our traditions and use our power for purposes of aggression and subjugation? So is our ruin spelt, if not today, tomorrow, in the next century. For we cannot do without Latin America nearly as well as she can do without us. Our pride has blinded us to this elemental truth. Let both worlds, both expressions of human destiny, our own and that of the southern races, shine out, undefiled, to make a joint future. Not conquest but mutual tolerance; not strife but cooperation; not blind egoism but even-handed participation in the benefits of both cultures; not slavery but common freedom. The New World may then become an ampler experiment in human achievement than history has yet witnessed.

INDEX

Index

A

Acevedo, 45
Actopan, 20
Ahuizotl, 154
Alameda, 158, 160
Altamirano, 54, 102
Alvarez, Elena, 264
Amecameca, 94, 97, 98, 104
Amecamécans, 102
Americanization, 352, 354, 356, 359
Anáhuac Valley, 63
Apizaco, 56
Arce, Maples, 266
Army, the, 43, 44
Arzubide, List, 264, 266
Atl, 45
Atlocoalco, month of, 61
Atzcapotzalco, 152
Avellaneda, Don José, 214-231
　early life, 218-220
　death, 230-231
　famous address, 224-225
　political success, 223-224
　unscrupulousness, 224-226
Axayacatl, 81, 82
Ayacataíh, 83
Aztec Empire, 80, 83
Aztecs, 35, 62, 81, 82, 98, 125, 152-154
　chief temple of, 156
　faiths, 35
Azuela, Mariano, 264, 267-271

B

Basques, origin of, 161
Bishop Zumárraga, 63, 64
Bolsheviks, 128

Bolshevism, 53
Boxerism, 187
　tendency towards, 187
Bucareli, 155
Bucareli agreement, 333, 343

C

Caborca, 166
Cabral, García, 243
Cajeme, 178, 182, 186
Calles, 44, 47, 53, 54, 158, 176, 177, 304
Camargo, Muñoz, 82
Camaxtli, 74-76, 79, 80, 84
Campo Santo, 130
Cañada, 140
Capital, 46, 47, 53
Caricature, 232-247
　native art, 234
Carranza, 42, 44, 126, 177, 219, 345, 346
Carrillo, 54
Caso, 45
Catholic baiting, 312
Cempoalla, 80
Chalcas, 81, 97
Chalma, 171
Chalqueses, 73
Chapingo, 48
Chapultépec, 153, 262
Chapultépec Castle, 156
Chapultépec Park, 158
Charles V, 154
Chichén Itzá, 11, 12
Chichimecas, 67
Chilar, 139
Chimalhuacán, 74
Cholula, 100, 172

Church, the, 27, 52, 53, 159
Church and State, 284, 296, 301, 302
   and Indians, 298-302
   and Labor, 292, 293, 295
   and land question, 295-296
   and modern philosophy, 296
   and Press, 295
   and secular education, 297
Cohuatichán, 74
Cohuazacoalco, 80
Colhuas, 73
Colima, 21
Collonia Vallejo, 152
Conquistadores, 154
Córdoba, 215
Cortés, Erasto, 243, 244
Cortez, 67, 70, 73, 81-83, 92, 108, 136, 153, 156-158, 180
Covarrubias, Miguel, 243
Creole rule, 36
Cristobal de Aguirre, 62
Cruz, Gutiérrez, 264
Cuatla, 22
Cuauhtémoc, 54
Cuautla, 122, 126, 134, 136
Cuernavaca, 23, 126
Cuicatlán, 140, 144, 148
Curiacán, 182

D

Darío, Ruben, 120
Del Bajío, 174
Díaz, Porfirio, 38, 43, 63, 128, 145, 155, 176, 177, 180, 183, 196
Diego, Juan, 55, 57, 63, 64
Doheny, 335, 336, 337, 341
Dominguilla, 139, 144
Don Romueldo, 72, 89, 91, 92
Don Vicente, 128, 131
Durango, bank in, 198
Durango sierras, 16

E

El Cerro, 122, 123, 130, 131, 132, 134, 135, 138
Emperor Iturbibe, 155
Emperor Maximilian, 155
Enciso, Jorge, 278
Esperanza, 111-116
Estridentismo, 264
Estridentista, 264, 266
Expressionism, 264

F

Factory system, 353, 356
Flores, Angel, 176
Frías, Heriberto, 276
Fujiyama, 95

G

Gallardo, Salvador, 264
Gamio, Dr. Manuel, 34, 188, 298
   restorations, 188
Gigedo, Revilla, 154
Giovanni della Croce, 58
Gómez, Arnulfo, 176
Góngora y Argote, Luis de, 237,
Guadalajara, 19, 20, 21, 278, 310, 311
Guadalupe Hidalgo, 55, 60, 61, 66-69, 88, 101, 102, 156, 172
Guanajuato, bank in, 198
Guerrero, 68, 121
Guerrero, Xavier, 278
Gutierrez, Rodrigo, 82
Guzmán, Martín Luis, 271-274
Guzmán, Nuñoz de, 180, 183

H

Hacienda Guendulain, 144, 146, 147

INDEX

Hidalgo, 66
bank in, 198
Hidalgo, Luis, 243, 244
Hippodrome subdivision, 152
Huejotzincas, 78, 99
Huerta, Adolfo de la, 176, 177, 219
Huitzilopochtli, 32, 36, 49, 53, 54,
74, 153

I

Icaza, Xavier, 264
Inclán, Luis G., 276
Indian renascence, 297, 298, 300
Indian, the New, 190-204
educational problem, 198-204
Ixtaccíhuatl, 63, 94, 95, 120

J

Jalisco, 19, 176
Juárez, Bénito, 37, 54, 67, 120, 155,
176, 196
Junkers, 43

L

Labor leaders, 47
Labor movement, 45
Labor Party, 41
Lake Texcoco, 63, 152
Lamont–De la Huerta agreement,
348
Land scramble, 338
La Rueda, 142
Laws of Reform, 155
"Literature of the revolution," 264-
277
Lizardi, Joaquin Fernández de, 275
Los Altas, 19
Luis Díaz, Don, 83

M

Machine Age, 352
American influence, 352, 353
Madero, 177, 219
revolution of, 40, 41
Magdalena, 166
Malinche, 70, 74, 92, 93
Manzo, 186
María Guadalupe, 88
Matlacueze, 74
Maya, 10
chiefs, 11
peoples, 10, 11
speech, 10
stone carvings, 10
Mayas, 35
Melchor, Don, 209-213
Mendoza, 183
Mérida, Carlos, 278
Mexico City, 21, 24, 146, 151, 159,
160, 161
architecture, 152
bull fights in, 161-163
Mexitli, 152, 153
Michoacán, 121
bank in, 198
Mictlantécutli, 111
Milpa Alta, 107, 108-113, 116-118,
120
Mírida, 11
Mixtecs, 35
Mizquitl, 76
Moctezuma, 61, 156, 158, 183
Moctezumas, 32
Monastery of St. Francis, 84
Morelas, 121
Morrow, 351
Motolinía, 102
Muleteers, 164-175
centers for, 174
objects transported, 174-175

367

Municipal Palace, 158
Muñoz, Rafael, 271
Musio Nacional, 157

N

Nahuas, 35
Nahuatl, 97, 108, 125
National League of Religious Defense, 297
National Palace, 156
Nayarit, 68, 176
Nervo, Amado, 264
Nicaragua, 70

O

Oaxaca, 120, 150, 197
Oaxaca Sierras, 139, 176
Obregón, Alvara, 42, 43, 44, 176-178, 184, 186, 214, 215, 220, 221, 324-332
Oil industry, 334-351
    and American interests, 344, 345, 349
Olmecas, 74
Ortíz, Rubio, 52, 53
Otomies, 81, 82
Orozco, Carlos, 244
Orozco, José Clemente, 54, 245, 246, 278, 279

P

Palace of Moctezuma, 153
Palacio Legislativo, 63
Panchito Chapopote, 264
Panotla, 89, 90
Pantheon of Tepeyac, 63
Paracho, 205, 206, 207, 208
Paseo de la reforma, 155, 176
Political democracy, 41

"Popo," the Smoke Mountain, 95, 96, 98
Popocatépetl, 63, 71, 94, 95, 100
Portes Gil, 48, 52, 54
Posada, Guadalupe, 241-243
Principales, 13
Puebla, 72, 88, 90
Puerto, Felipe Carrillo, 11

Q

Querétaro constitution, 342
Quetzalcóatl, 36, 60, 61, 100, 130
"Quiahuztlán," 76
Quinantzín, 73

R

Republic, the, 82
Republicanism, 37
Revolutionary methods, 306
Reyes, 45, 264, 297
Rivera, Diego, 34, 54, 245, 277, 279-283, 297

S

Sacremonte Hill, 172
    shrine on, 172
Sacro Monte, 94, 95, 100, 101, 105, 106
San Juan de las Lagos, 172
San Pedro Chicozapote, 139
Sanctuary of Ocatlán, 61, 71, 86
Sandoval, 67
Santa Anna, 70
Santa Teresa, 58-61, 68, 156
Santoyo, Matías, 243, 244
Serrano, Francisco, 176
Sierra, Justo, 264
Sierra Madre, 166, 182

Sonora, 176, 177, 219
Sor Juana Inez de la Cruz, 237
Spaniards, 11, 36, 67, 76, 82, 92, 154, 171, 222
Spanish-Aztec Church, 303
Spanish rule, 36
Street Theatres, 248-258

T

Tabasca, 80
Tacuba, 157
Tamazula river, 166
Taniya, Kin, 264, 266
Tarascans, 35
Tegotepíc, 139
Tehuantepec, 13, 14, 15, 68
Tenochtitlan, 61, 67, 73, 75, 153, 156, 157
Teochichimecas, 74
Teotihuacán, 277
Tepanecas, 73
Tepeticpac, 74
Tepeyac, 55, 62-64, 68
Tepolohuatécutli, 76
Tepozteco, 122-124, 130, 131, 134-136, 138
Tepoztlan, 27, 108, 121-126, 129, 130, 137
    churches in, 125, 126
Terranzas, José Joaquín, 101
Teteoinán, 103
Tezcatlipoca, 36, 110
Texcocans, 35
Texcoco, 152
Thin river, 144
Tlaloc, 98, 111, 152, 153
Tlalocs, 36
Tlaloques, 62
Tlaxcala, 61, 70-75, 90, 91, 172
    churches in, 84, 88
Tlaxcalan Senate, 75, 82

Tlaxcalans, 67, 72-77, 80-90
    independence of, 85
Toledano, Lombardo, 297
Toltecs, 67, 97
Tomellín, 140
Tonatiu, 36
Tonantzín, 31, 62, 63, 65
    temple of, 62
Totonoqui Indians, 31
Totuta, 9
Tuxtla, 80

U

United States, 70
Uruápam, 18
Uxmal, 11

V

Vacconcelas, 45, 291
Valbuena, 152, 157
Valencia, Fray Martín de, 100, 102
Valerio Trujano, 139, 140, 144, 145, 149
Vela, Arequelas, 266
Vera Cruz, 67, 266
Villa, 42, 44, 54, 220
Virgen de los Remedios, 66
Virgin of Guadalupe, 66, 67, 101, 256, 285
Virgin of Ocotlán, 88

W

Wenceslao, 128, 132, 133, 134
Wild-cat period, 337
Wilson, Henry Lane, 41

X

Xicalancas, 74
Xicontencátl, 76, 83

INDEX

Xiuhtlehuitécutli, 76
Xochimilcans, 73
Xochimilco, 107, 152, 157
Xochiquetzal, 98
Xoltocamecas, 81

Y

Yaqui river, 178, 179, 183
Yaquis, 176, 177, 182-186, 187, 196
  attack by, 179, 180
Yautépec, 23, 129
Yautépec river, 121, 126
Yoaltecat Hill, 61

Yucatán, 11, 196
Yucatán peninsula, 9

Z

Zandunga, 14
Zapata, Emeliano, 22, 23, 42, 44,
  54, 108, 197
Zapatistas, 126
Zapotecs, 35
Zócalo, 158
Zodiaco Mariano, 172
  miracles described in, 172, 173
Zuno, J. Guadalupe, 278